COMPUTER VISION IN VEHICLE TECHNOLOGY

COMPUTER VISION IN VEHICLE TECHNOLOGY

LAND, SEA, AND AIR

Edited by

Antonio M. López

Computer Vision Center (CVC) and
Universitat Autònoma de Barcelona, Spain

Atsushi Imiya

Chiba University, Japan

Tomas Pajdla

Czech Technical University, Czech Republic

Jose M. Álvarez

National Information Communications Technology Australia (NICTA),
Canberra Research Laboratory, Australia

Library of Congress Cataloging-in-Publication Data

Names: López, Antonio M., 1969- editor. | Imiya, Atsushi, editor. | Pajdla,
  Tomas, editor. | Álvarez, J. M. (Jose M.), editor.
Title: Computer vision in vehicle technology : land, sea and air / Editors Antonio M.
  López, Atsushi Imiya, Tomas Pajdla, Jose M. Álvarez.
Description: Chichester, West Sussex, United Kingdom : John Wiley & Sons,
  Inc., [2017] | Includes bibliographical references and index.
Identifiers: LCCN 2016022206 (print) | LCCN 2016035367 (ebook) | ISBN
  9781118868072 (cloth) | ISBN 9781118868041 (pdf) | ISBN 9781118868058
  (epub)
Subjects: LCSH: Computer vision. | Automotive telematics. | Autonomous
  vehicles–Equipment and supplies. | Drone aircraft–Equipment and
  supplies. | Nautical instruments.
Classification: LCC TL272.53 .L67 2017 (print) | LCC TL272.53 (ebook) | DDC
  629.040285/637–dc23
LC record available at https://lccn.loc.gov/2016022206

A catalogue record for this book is available from the British Library.

Cover image: jamesbenet/gettyimages; groveb/gettyimages; robertmandel/gettyimages

ISBN: 9781118868072

Set in 11/13pt, TimesLTStd by SPi Global, Chennai, India

Printed in the UK

Contents

List of Contributors

Ricard Campos, Computer Vision and Robotics Institute, University of Girona, Spain

Arturo de la Escalera, Laboratorio de Sistemas Inteligentes, Universidad Carlos III de Madrid, Spain

Armagan Elibol, Department of Mathematical Engineering, Yildiz Technical University, Istanbul, Turkey

Javier Escartin, Institute of Physics of Paris Globe, The National Centre for Scientific Research, Paris, France

Uwe Franke, Image Understanding Group, Daimler AG, Sindelfingen, Germany

Friedrich Fraundorfer, Institute for Computer Graphics and Vision, Graz University of Technology, Austria

Rafael Garcia, Computer Vision and Robotics Institute, University of Girona, Spain

David Gerónimo, ADAS Group, Computer Vision Center, Universitat Autònoma de Barcelona, Spain

Nuno Gracias, Computer Vision and Robotics Institute, University of Girona, Spain

Ramon Hegedus, Max Planck Institute for Informatics, Saarbruecken, Germany

Natalia Hurtos, Computer Vision and Robotics Institute, University of Girona, Spain

Reinhard Klette, School of Engineering, Computer and Mathematical Sciences, Auckland University of Technology, New Zealand

Antonio M. López, ADAS Group, Computer Vision Center (CVC) and Computer Science Department, Universitat Autònoma de Barcelona (UAB), Spain

Laszlo Neumann, Computer Vision and Robotics Institute, University of Girona, Spain

Tudor Nicosevici, Computer Vision and Robotics Institute, University of Girona, Spain

Ricard Prados, Computer Vision and Robotics Institute, University of Girona, Spain

Davide Scaramuzza, Robotics and Perception Group, University of Zurich, Switzerland

ASM Shihavuddin, École Normale Supérieure, Paris, France

David Vázquez, ADAS Group, Computer Vision Center, Universitat Autònoma de Barcelona, Spain

Preface

This book was born following the spirit of the *Computer Vision in Vehicular Technology* (*CVVT*) Workshop. At the moment of finishing this book, the 7th CVVT Workshop CVPR'2016 is being held in Las Vegas. Previous CVVT Workshops include the CVPR'2015 in Boston (http://adas.cvc.uab.es/CVVT2015/), ECCV'2014 in Zurich (http://adas.cvc.uab.es/CVVT2014/), ICCV'2013 in Sydney (http://adas.cvc .uab.es/CVVT2013/), ECCV'2012 in Firenze (http://adas.cvc.uab.es/CVVT2012/), ICCV'2011 in Barcelona (http://adas.cvc.uab.es/CVVT2011/), and ACCV'2010 in Queenstown (http://www.media.imit.chiba-u.jp/CVVT2010/). This implies throughout these years, many invited speakers, co-organizers, contributing authors, and sponsors have helped to keep CVVT alive and exciting. We are enormously grateful to all of them! Of course, we also want to give special thanks to the authors of this book, who kindly accepted the challenge of writing their respective chapters.

He would also like to thank the past and current members of the Advanced Driver Assistance Systems (ADAS) group of the Computer Vision Center at the Universitat Autònoma de Barcelona. He also would like to thank his current public funding, in particular, Spanish MEC project TRA2014-57088-C2-1-R, Spanish DGT project SPIP2014-01352, and the Generalitat de Catalunya project 2014-SGR-1506. Finally, he would like to thank NVIDIA Corporation for the generous donations of different graphical processing hardware units, and especially for their kind support regarding the ADAS group activities.

Tomas Pajdla has been supported by EU H2020 Grant No. 688652 UP-Drive and Institutional Resources for Research of the Czech Technical University in Prague.

Atsushi Imiya was supported by IMIT Project *Pattern Recognition for Large Data Sets* from 2010 to 2015 at Chiba University, Japan.

Jose M. Álvarez was supported by the Australian Research Council through its Special Research Initiative in Bionic Vision Science and Technology grant to Bionic Vision Australia. The National Information Communications Technology Australia was founded by the Australian Government through the Department of Communications and the Australian Research Council through the ICT Center of Excellence Program.

The book is organized into seven self-contained chapters related to CVVT topics, and a final short chapter with the overall final remarks. Briefly, in Chapter 1, there is a quick overview of the main ideas that link computer vision with vehicles. Chapters 2–7 are more specialized and divided into two blocks. Chapters 2–4 focus on the use of computer vision for the self-navigation of the vehicles. In particular, Chapter 2 focuses on land (autonomous cars), Chapter 3 focuses on air (micro aerial vehicles), and Chapter 4 focuses on sea (underwater robotics). Analogously, Chapters 5–7 focus on the use of computer vision as a technology to solve specific applications beyond self-navigation. In particular, Chapter 5 focuses on land (ADAS), and Chapters 6 and 7 on air and sea, respectively. Finally, Chapter 8 concludes and points out new research trends.

Antonio M. López

Computer Vision Center (CVC) and
Universitat Autònoma de Barcelona, Spain

Abbreviations and Acronyms

ACC	adaptive cruise control
ADAS	advanced driver assistance system
AUV	autonomous underwater vehicle
BA	bundle adjustment
BCM	brightness constancy model
BoW	bag of words
CAN	controller area network
CLAHE	contrast limited adaptive histogram equalization
COTS	crown of thorns starfish
DCT	discrete cosine transforms
DOF	degree of freedom
DVL	Doppler velocity log
EKF	extended Kalman filter
ESC	electronic stability control
FCA	forward collision avoidance
FEM	finite element method
FFT	fast Fourier transform
FIR	far infrared
FLS	forward-looking sonar
GA	global alignment
GDIM	generalized dynamic image model
GLCM	gray level co-occurrence matrix
GPS	global positioning system
GPU	graphical processing unit
HDR	high dynamic range
HOG	histogram of gradients
HOV	human operated vehicle
HSV	hue saturation value
IR	infrared
KPCA	kernel principal component analysis
LBL	long baseline

LBP	local binary patterns
LCA	lane change assistance
LDA	linear discriminant analysis
LDW	lane departure warning
LHC	local homogeneity coefficient
LKS	lane keeping system
LMedS	least median of squares
MEX	MATLAB executable
MLS	moving least squares
MR	maximum response
MST	minimum spanning tree
NCC	normalized chromaticity coordinates
NDT	normal distribution transform
NIR	near infrared
OVV	online visual vocabularies
PCA	principal component analysis
PDWMD	probability density weighted mean distance
PNN	probabilistic neural network
RANSAC	random sample consensus
RBF	radial basis function
ROD	region of difference
ROI	region of interest
ROV	remotely operated vehicle
SDF	signed distance function
SEF	seam-eliminating function
SIFT	scale invariant feature transform
SLAM	simultaneous localization and mapping
SNR	signal-to-noise ratio
SSD	sum of squared differences
SURF	speeded up robust features
SVM	support vector machine
TJA	traffic jam assist
TSR	traffic sign recognition
TV	total variation
UDF	unsigned distance function
USBL	ultra short base line
UUV	unmanned underwater vehicle
UV	underwater vehicle

1

Computer Vision in Vehicles

Reinhard Klette

School of Engineering, Computer and Mathematical Sciences, Auckland University of Technology, Auckland, New Zealand

This chapter is a brief introduction to academic aspects of computer vision in vehicles. It briefly summarizes basic notation and definitions used in computer vision. The chapter discusses a few visual tasks as of relevance for vehicle control and environment understanding.

1.1 Adaptive Computer Vision for Vehicles

Computer vision designs solutions for understanding the real world by using cameras. See Rosenfeld (1969), Horn (1986), Hartley and Zisserman (2003), or Klette (2014) for examples of monographs or textbooks on computer vision.

Computer vision operates today in *vehicles* including cars, trucks, airplanes, unmanned aerial vehicles (UAVs) such as multi-copters (see Figure 1.1 for a quadcopter), satellites, or even autonomous driving rovers on the Moon or Mars.

In our context, the *ego-vehicle* is that vehicle where the computer vision system operates in; *ego-motion* describes the ego-vehicle's motion in the real world.

1.1.1 Applications

Computer vision solutions are today in use in manned vehicles for improved safety or comfort, in autonomous vehicles (e.g., robots) for supporting motion or action control, and also for misusing UAVs for killing people remotely. The UAV technology has also good potentials for helping to save lives, to create three-dimensional (3D) models of

Computer Vision in Vehicle Technology: Land, Sea, and Air, First Edition.
Edited by Antonio M. López, Atsushi Imiya, Tomas Pajdla and Jose M. Álvarez.
© 2017 John Wiley & Sons Ltd. Published 2017 by John Wiley & Sons Ltd.

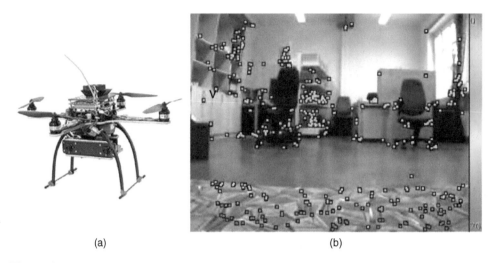

(a)   (b)

Figure 1.1   (a) Quadcopter. (b) Corners detected from a flying quadcopter using a modified FAST feature detector. Courtesy of Konstantin Schauwecker

the environment, and so forth. Underwater robots and unmanned sea-surface vehicles are further important applications of vision-augmented vehicles.

1.1.2   Traffic Safety and Comfort

Traffic safety is a dominant application area for computer vision in vehicles. Currently, about 1.24 million people die annually worldwide due to traffic accidents (WHO 2013), this is, on average, 2.4 people die *per minute* in traffic accidents. How does this compare to the numbers Western politicians are using for obtaining support for their "war on terrorism?" Computer vision can play a major role in solving the true real-world problems (see Figure 1.2). Traffic-accident fatalities can be reduced by controlling traffic flow (e.g., by triggering automated warning signals at pedestrian crossings or intersections with bicycle lanes) using stationary cameras, or by having cameras installed in vehicles (e.g., for detecting safe distances and adjusting speed accordingly, or by detecting obstacles and constraining trajectories).

Computer vision is also introduced into modern cars for improving driving comfort. Surveillance of blind spots, automated distance control, or compensation of unevenness of the road are just three examples for a wide spectrum of opportunities provided by computer vision for enhancing driving comfort.

1.1.3   Strengths of (Computer) Vision

Computer vision is an important component of intelligent systems for vehicle control (e.g., in modern cars, or in robots). The Mars rovers "Curiosity" and "Opportunity" operate based on computer vision; "Opportunity" has already operated on Mars for

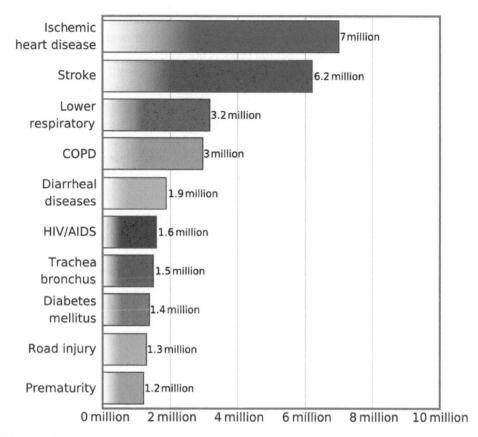

Figure 1.2   The 10 leading causes of death in the world. Chart provided online by the World Health Organization (WHO). Road injury ranked number 9 in 2011

more than ten years. The visual system of human beings provides a proof of existence that vision alone can deliver nearly all of the information required for steering a vehicle. Computer vision aims at creating comparable automated solutions for vehicles, enabling them to navigate safely in the real world. Additionally, computer vision can also work constantly "at the same level of attention," applying the same rules or programs; a human is not able to do so due to becoming tired or distracted.

A human applies accumulated knowledge and experience (e.g., supporting intuition), and it is a challenging task to embed a computer vision solution into a system able to have, for example, intuition. Computer vision offers many more opportunities for future developments in a vehicle context.

1.1.4   Generic and Specific Tasks

There are *generic visual tasks* such as calculating distance or motion, measuring brightness, or detecting corners in an image (see Figure 1.1b). In contrast, there are *specific visual tasks* such as detecting a pedestrian, understanding ego-motion, or calculating the *free space* a vehicle may move in safely in the next few seconds. The borderline between generic and specific tasks is not well defined.

Solutions for generic tasks typically aim at creating one self-contained *module* for potential integration into a complex computer vision system. But there is no general-purpose corner detector and also no general-purpose stereo matcher. *Adaptation* to given circumstances appears to be the general way for an optimized use of given modules for generic tasks.

Solutions for specific tasks are typically structured into multiple modules that interact in a complex system.

Example 1.1.1 Specific Tasks in the Context of Visual Lane Analysis *Shin et al. (2014) review visual lane analysis for driver-assistance systems or autonomous driving. In this context, the authors discuss specific tasks such as "the combination of visual lane analysis with driver monitoring..., with ego-motion analysis..., with location analysis..., with vehicle detection..., or with navigation...." They illustrate the latter example by an application shown in Figure 1.3: lane detection and road sign reading, the analysis of GPS data and electronic maps (e-maps), and two-dimensional (2D) visualization are combined into a real-view navigation system (Choi et al. 2010).*

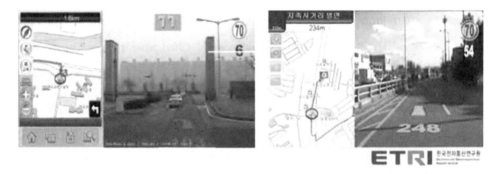

Figure 1.3   Two screenshots for real-view navigation. Courtesy of the authors of Choi et al. (2010)

1.1.5   Multi-module Solutions

Designing a multi-module solution for a given task does not need to be more difficult than designing a single-module solution. In fact, finding solutions for some single modules (e.g., for motion analysis) can be very challenging. Designing a multi-module solution requires:

1. that modular solutions are available and known,
2. tools for evaluating those solutions in dependency of a given situation (or *scenario*; see Klette et al. (2011) for a discussion of scenarios) for being able to select (or adapt) solutions,
3. conceptual thinking for designing and controlling an appropriate multi-module system,
4. a system optimization including a more extensive testing on various scenarios than for a single module (due to the increase in combinatorial complexity of multi-module interactions), and
5. multiple modules require control (e.g., when many designers separately insert processors for controlling various operations in a vehicle, no control engineer should be surprised if the vehicle becomes unstable).

1.1.6 Accuracy, Precision, and Robustness

Solutions can be characterized as being *accurate*, *precise*, or *robust*. *Accuracy* means a systematic closeness to the true values for a given scenario. *Precision* also considers the occurrence of random errors; a precise solution should lead to about the same results under comparable conditions. *Robustness* means approximate correctness for a set of scenarios that includes particularly challenging ones: in such cases, it would be appropriate to specify the defining scenarios accurately, for example, by using video descriptors (Briassouli and Kompatsiaris 2010) or data measures (Suaste et al. 2013). Ideally, robustness should address *any* possible scenario in the real world for a given task.

1.1.7 Comparative Performance Evaluation

An efficient way for a comparative performance analysis of solutions for one task is by having different authors testing their own programs on identical benchmark data. But we not only need to evaluate the programs, we also need to evaluate the benchmark data used (Haeusler and Klette 2010, 2012) for identifying their challenges or relevance.

Benchmarks need to come with *measures* for quantifying performance such that we can compare accuracy on individual data or robustness across a diversity of different input data.

Figure 1.4 illustrates two possible ways for generating benchmarks, one by using computer graphics for rendering sequences with accurately known ground truth,[1] and the other one by using high-end sensors (in the illustrated case, ground truth is provided by the use of a laser range-finder).[2]

---

[1] For EISATS benchmark data, see www.mi.auckland.ac.nz/EISATS.
[2] For KITTI benchmark data, see www.cvlibs.net/datasets/kitti/.

(a)   (b)

Figure 1.4   Examples of benchmark data available for a comparative analysis of computer vision algorithms for motion and distance calculations. (a) Image from a synthetic sequence provided on EISATS with accurate ground truth. (b) Image of a real-world sequence provided on KITTI with approximate ground truth

But those evaluations need to be considered with care since everything is not comparable. Evaluations depend on the benchmark data used; having a few summarizing numbers may not be really of relevance for particular scenarios possibly occurring in the real world. For some input data we simply can not answer how a solution performs; for example, in the middle of a large road intersection, we cannot answer which lane border detection algorithm performs best for this scenario.

1.1.8   There Are Many Winners

We are not so naive to expect an all-time "winner" when comparatively evaluating computer vision solutions. Vehicles operate in the real world (whether on Earth, the Moon, or on Mars), which is so diverse that not all of the possible event occurrences can be modeled in underlying constraints for a designed program. Particular solutions perform differently for different scenarios, and a winning program for one scenario may fail for another. We can only evaluate how particular solutions perform for particular scenarios. At the end, this might support an optimization strategy by adaptation to a current scenario that a vehicle experiences at a time.

1.2   Notation and Basic Definitions

The following basic notations and definitions (Klette 2014) are provided.

1.2.1   Images and Videos

An *image I* is defined on a set

$$\Omega = \{(x, y) : \; 1 \leq x \leq N_{\text{cols}} \wedge 1 \leq y \leq N_{\text{rows}}\} \subset \mathbb{Z}^2 \qquad (1.1)$$

of pairs of integers (*pixel locations*), called the image *carrier*, where N_{cols} and N_{rows} define the number of columns and rows, respectively. We assume a left-hand coordinate system with the coordinate origin in the upper-left corner of the image, the *x*-axis to the right, and the *y*-axis downward. A *pixel* of an image *I* combines a location $p = (x, y)$ in the carrier Ω with the value $I(p)$ of *I* at this location.

A *scalar image I* takes values in a set $\{0, 1, \ldots, 2^a - 1\}$, typically with $a = 8$, $a = 12$, or $a = 16$. A *vector-valued image I* has scalar values in a finite number of channels or bands. A video or image sequence consists of *frames* $I(.,.,t)$, for $t = 1, 2, \ldots, T$, all being images on the same carrier Ω.

Example 1.2.1 Three Examples *In case of an RGB color image $I = (R, G, B)$, we have pixels $(p, I(p)) = (p, R(p), G(p), B(p))$.*

A geometrically rectified gray-level stereo image or frame $I = (L, R)$ consists of two channels L and R, usually called left *and* right *images; this is implemented in the multi-picture object (mpo) format for images (CIPA 2009).*

For a sequence of gray-level stereo images, we have pixel $(p, t, L(p, t), R(p, t))$ in frame t, which is the combined representation of pixels $(p, t, L(p, t))$ and $(p, t, R(p, t))$ in $L(.,.,t)$ and $R(.,.,t)$, respectively, at pixel location p and time t.

1.2.1.1 Gauss Function

The zero-mean *Gauss function* is defined as follows:

$$G_\sigma(x, y) = \frac{1}{2\pi\sigma^2} \exp\left(-\frac{x^2 + y^2}{2\sigma^2}\right) \tag{1.2}$$

A convolution of an image *I* with the Gauss function produces smoothed images

$$L(p, \sigma) = [I \star G_\sigma](p) \tag{1.3}$$

also known as *Gaussians*, for $\sigma > 0$. (We stay with symbol *L* here as introduced by Lindeberg (1994) for "layer"; a given context will prevent confusion with the left image *L* of a stereo pair.)

1.2.1.2 Edges

Step-edges in images are detected based on first- or second-order derivatives, such as values of the *gradient* ∇I or the *Laplacian* ΔI given by

$$\nabla I = \mathbf{grad}\, I = \left[\frac{\partial I}{\partial x}, \frac{\partial I}{\partial y}\right]^\top \quad \text{or} \quad \Delta I = \nabla^2 I = \frac{\partial^2 I}{\partial x^2} + \frac{\partial^2 I}{\partial y^2} \tag{1.4}$$

Local maxima of L_1- or L_2-magnitudes $\|\nabla I\|_1$ or $\|\nabla I\|_2$, or zero-crossings of values ΔI are taken as an indication for a step-edge. The gradient or Laplacian is commonly preceded by smoothing, using a convolution with the zero-mean Gauss function.

Alternatively, *Phase-congruency edges* in images are detected based on local frequency-space representations (Kovesi 1993).

1.2.1.3   Corners

Let I_{xx}, I_{xy}, I_{yx}, and I_{yy} denote the second-order derivatives of image I. *Corners* in images are localized based on high curvature of intensity values, to be identified by two large eigenvalues of the *Hessian matrix*

$$\mathbf{H}(p) = \begin{bmatrix} I_{xx}(p) & I_{xy}(p) \\ I_{xy}(p) & I_{yy}(p) \end{bmatrix} \tag{1.5}$$

at a pixel location p in a scalar image I (see Harris and Stephens (1988)). Figure 1.1 shows the corners detected by FAST. Corner detection is often preceded by smoothing using a convolution with the zero-mean Gauss function.

1.2.1.4   Scale Space and Key Points

Key points or *interest points* are commonly detected as maxima or minima in a $3 \times 3 \times 3$ subset of the *scale space* of a given image (Crowley and Sanderson 1987; Lindeberg 1994). A finite set of differences of Gaussians

$$D_{\sigma,a}(p) = L(p, \sigma) - L(p, a\sigma) \tag{1.6}$$

produces a *DoG scale space*. These differences are approximations to Laplacians of increasingly smoothed versions of an image (see Figure 1.5 for an example of such Laplacians forming an *LoG scale space*).

1.2.1.5   Features

An *image feature* is finally a *location* (an *interest point*), defined by a key point, edge, corner, and so on, together with a *descriptor*, usually given as a data vector (e.g., in case of scale-invariant feature transform (SIFT) of length 128 representing local gradients), but possibly also in other formats such as a graph. For example, the descriptor of a step-edge can be mean and variance of gradient values along the edge, and the descriptor of a corner can be defined by the eigenvalues of the Hessian matrix.

1.2.2   Cameras

We have an $X_w Y_w Z_w$ *world coordinate system*, which is not defined by a particular camera or other sensor, and a *camera coordinate system* $X_s Y_s Z_s$ (index "s" for "sensor"), which is described with respect to the chosen world coordinates by means of an affine transform, defined by a rotation matrix $\mathbf{R}$ and a translation vector $\mathbf{t}$.

Figure 1.5 Laplacians of smoothed copies of the same image using `cv::GaussianBlur` and `cv::Laplacian` in OpenCV, with values 0.5, 1, 2, and 4, for parameter σ for smoothing. Linear scaling is used for better visibility of the resulting *Laplacians*. Courtesy of Sandino Morales

A point in 3D space is given as $P_w = (X_w, Y_w, Z_w)$ in world coordinates or as $P_s = (X_s, Y_s, Z_s)$ in camera coordinates. In addition to the *coordinate notation* for points, we also use *vector notation*, such as $P_w = [X_w, Y_w, Z_w]^T$ for point P_w.

1.2.2.1 Pinhole-type Camera

The Z_s-axis models the *optical axis*. Assuming an ideal pinhole-type camera, we can ignore radial distortion and can have *undistorted projected points* in the image plane with coordinates x_u and y_u. The distance f between the $x_u y_u$ image plane and the projection center is the *focal length*.

A visible point $P = (X_s, Y_s, Z_s)$ in the world is mapped by *central projection* into pixel location $p = (x_u, y_u)$ in the undistorted image plane:

$$x_u = \frac{fX_s}{Z_s} \quad \text{and} \quad y_u = \frac{fY_s}{Z_s} \tag{1.7}$$

with the origin of $x_u y_u$ image coordinates at the intersection point of the Z_s-axis with the image plane.

The intersection point (c_x, c_y) of the optical axis with the image plane in xy coordinates is called the *principal point*. It follows that $(x, y) = (x_u + c_x, y_u + c_y)$. A pixel location (x, y) in the 2D xy image coordinate system has 3D coordinates $(x - c_x, y - c_y, f)$ in the $X_s Y_s Z_s$ camera coordinate system.

1.2.2.2   Intrinsic and Extrinsic Parameters

Assuming multiple cameras C_i, for some indices i (e.g., just C_L and C_R for binocular stereo), camera calibration specifies intrinsic parameters such as edge lengths e_x^i and e_y^i of camera sensor cells (defining the aspect ratio), a skew parameter s^i, coordinates of the principal point $\mathbf{c}^i = (c_x^i, c_y^i)$ where optic axis of camera i and image plane intersect, the focal length f^i, possibly refined as f_x^i and f_y^i, and lens distortion parameters starting with κ_1^i and κ_2^i. In general, it can be assumed that lens distortion has been calibrated before and does not need to be included anymore in the set of intrinsic parameters. Extrinsic parameters are defined by rotation matrices and translation vectors, for example, matrix $\mathbf{R}^{ij}$ and vector $\mathbf{t}^{ij}$ for the affine transform between camera coordinate systems $X_s^i Y_s^i Z_s^i$ and $X_s^j Y_s^j Z_s^j$, or matrix $\mathbf{R}^i$ and vector $\mathbf{t}^i$ for the affine transform between camera coordinate system $X_s^i Y_s^i Z_s^i$ and $X_w Y_w Z_w$.

1.2.2.3   Single-Camera Projection Equation

The camera projection equation in homogeneous coordinates, mapping a 3D point $P = (X_w, Y_w, Z_w)$ into image coordinates $p^i = (x^i, y^i)$ of the ith camera, is as follows:

$$k \begin{bmatrix} x^i \\ y^i \\ 1 \end{bmatrix} = \begin{bmatrix} f^i/e_x^i & s^i & c_x^i & 0 \\ 0 & f^i/e_y^i & c_y^i & 0 \\ 0 & 0 & 1 & 0 \end{bmatrix} \begin{bmatrix} \mathbf{R}^i & -[\mathbf{R}^i]^\top \mathbf{t}^i \\ \mathbf{0}^T & 1 \end{bmatrix} \begin{bmatrix} X_w \\ Y_w \\ Z_w \\ 1 \end{bmatrix} \tag{1.8}$$

$$= [\mathbf{K}^i | \mathbf{0}] \cdot \mathbf{A}^i \cdot [X_w, Y_w, Z_w, 1]^\top \tag{1.9}$$

where $k \neq 0$ is a scaling factor. This defines a 3×3 matrix $\mathbf{K}^i$ of intrinsic camera parameters and a 4×4 matrix $\mathbf{A}^i$ of extrinsic parameters (of the affine transform) of camera i. The 3×4 *camera matrix* $\mathbf{C}^i = [\mathbf{K}^i | \mathbf{0}] \cdot \mathbf{A}^i$ is defined by 11 parameters if we allow for an arbitrary scaling of parameters; otherwise it is 12.

1.2.3   Optimization

We specify one popular optimization strategy that has various applications in computer vision. In an abstract sense, we assign to each pixel a *label l* (e.g., an optical flow vector $\mathbf{u}$, a disparity d, a segment identifier, or a surface gradient) out of a set L of possible labels (e.g., all vectors pointing from a pixel p to points in a Euclidean distance to p of less than a given threshold). Labels $(u, v) \in \mathbb{R}^2$ are thus in the 2D continuous plane.

1.2.3.1   Optimizing a Labeling Function

Labels are assigned to all the pixels in the carrier Ω by a *labeling function* $f : \Omega \to L$. Solving a labeling problem means to identify a labeling f that approximates somehow an optimum of a defined *error* or *energy*

$$E_{\text{total}}(f) = E_{\text{data}}(f) + \lambda \cdot E_{\text{smooth}}(f) \tag{1.10}$$

where $\lambda > 0$ is a weight. Here, $E_{data}(f)$ is the *data-cost term* and $E_{smooth}(f)$ is the *smoothness-cost term*. A decrease in λ works toward reduced smoothing of calculated labels. Ideally, we search for an optimal (i.e., of minimal total error) f in the set of all possible labelings, which defines a *total variation* (TV).

We detail Eq. (1.10) by adding costs at pixels. In a current image, label $f_p = f(p)$ is assigned by the value of labeling function f at pixel position p. Then we have that

$$E_{total}(f) = \sum_{p \in \Omega} E_{data}(p, f_p) + \lambda \cdot \sum_{p \in \Omega} \sum_{q \in A(p)} E_{smooth}(f_p, f_q) \qquad (1.11)$$

where A is an adjacency relation between pixel locations.

In optical flow or stereo vision, label f_p (i.e., optical flow vector or disparity) defines a pixel q in another image (i.e., in the following image, or in the left or right image of a stereo pair); in this case, we can also write $E_{data}(p, q)$ instead of $E_{data}(p, f_p)$.

1.2.3.2 Invalidity of the Intensity Constancy Assumption

Data-cost terms are defined for windows that are centered at the considered pixel locations. The data in both windows, around the start pixel location p, and around the pixel location q in the other image, are compared for understanding "data similarity."

For example, in the case of stereo matching, we have $p = (x, y)$ in the right image R and $q = (x + d, y)$ in the left image L, for disparity $d \geq 0$, and the data in both $(2k + 1) \times (2k + 1)$ windows are identical if and only if the data-cost measure

$$E_{SSD}(p, d) = \sum_{i=-l}^{l} \sum_{j=-k}^{k} [R(x + i, y + j) - L(x + d + i, y + j)]^2 \qquad (1.12)$$

results in value 0, where SSD stands for *sum of squared differences*.

The use of such a data-cost term would be based on the *intensity constancy assumption* (ICA), that is, intensity values around corresponding pixel locations p and q are (basically) identical within a window of specified size. However, the ICA is invalid for real-world recording. Intensity values at corresponding pixels and in their neighborhoods are typically impacted by lighting variations, or just by image noise. There are also impacts of differences in local surface reflectance, differences in cameras when comparing images recorded by different cameras, or effects of perspective distortion (the local neighborhood around a surface point is differently projected into different cameras). Thus, energy optimization needs to apply better data measures compared to SSD, or other measures are also defined based on the ICA.

1.2.3.3 Census Data-Cost Term

The census-cost function has been identified as being able to compensate successfully bright variations in input images of a recorded video (Hermann and Klette 2009;

Hirschmüller and Scharstein 2009). The *mean-normalized census-cost function* is defined by comparing a $(2l + 1) \times (2k + 1)$ window centered at pixel location p in frame I_1 with a window of the same size centered at a pixel location q in frame I_2. Let $\bar{I}_i(p)$ be the mean of the window around p for $i = 1$ or $i = 2$. Then we have that

$$E_{\text{MCEN}}(p, q) = \sum_{i=-l}^{l} \sum_{j=-k}^{k} \rho_{ij} \qquad (1.13)$$

with

$$\rho_{ij} = \begin{cases} 0 & I_1(p + (i,j)) < \bar{I}_1(p) \text{ and } I_2(q + (i,j)) < \bar{I}_2(q) \\ & \text{or } \quad I_1(p + (i,j)) > \bar{I}_1(p) \text{ and } I_2(q + (i,j)) > \bar{I}_2(q) \\ 1 & \text{otherwise} \end{cases} \qquad (1.14)$$

Note that value 0 corresponds to consistency in both comparisons. If the comparisons are performed with respect to values $I_1(p)$ and $I_2(q)$, rather than the means $\bar{I}_1(p)$ and $\bar{I}_2(q)$, then we have the *census-cost function* $E_{\text{CEN}}(p, q)$ as a candidate for a data-cost term.

Let $\mathbf{a}_p$ be the vector listing results $\text{sgn}(I_1(p + (i,j)) - \bar{I}_1(p))$ in a left-to-right, top-to-bottom order (with respect to the applied $(2l + 1) \times (2k + 1)$ window), where sgn is the signum function; $\mathbf{b}_q$ lists values $\text{sgn}(I_2(q + (i,j)) - \bar{I}_2(q))$. The mean-normalized census data-cost $E_{\text{MCEN}}(p, q)$ equals the Hamming distance between vectors $\mathbf{a}_p$ and $\mathbf{b}_q$.

1.3   Visual Tasks

This section briefly outlines some of the visual tasks that need to be solved by computer vision in vehicles.

1.3.1   *Distance*

Laser range-finders are increasingly used for estimating distance mainly based on the time-of-flight principle. Assuming sensor arrays of larger density in the near future, laser range-finders will become a standard option for cost-efficient accurate distance calculations. Combining stereo vision with distance data provided by laser range-finders is a promising multi-module approach toward distance calculations.

Stereo vision is the dominant approach in computer vision for calculating distances. *Corresponding pixels* are here defined by projections of the same surface point in the scene into the left and right images of a stereo pair. After having recorded stereo pairs rectified into canonical stereo geometry, one-dimensional (1D) correspondence search can be limited to identical image rows.

Figure 1.6 (a) Image of a stereo pair (from a test sequence available on EISATS). (b) Visualization of a depth map using the color key shown at the top for assigning distances in meters to particular colors. A pixel is shown in gray if there was low confidence for the calculated disparity value at this pixel. Courtesy of Simon Hermann

1.3.1.1 Stereo Vision

We address the detection of corresponding points in a stereo image $I = (L, R)$, a basic task for distance calculation in vehicles using binocular stereo.

Corresponding pixels define a *disparity*, which is mapped based on camera parameters into *distance* or *depth*. There are already very accurate solutions for stereo matching, but challenging input data (rain, snow, dust, sunstroke, running wipers, and so forth) still pose unsolved problems (see Figure 1.6 for an example of a depth map).

1.3.1.2 Binocular Stereo Vision

After camera calibration, we have two virtually identical cameras C^L and C^R, which are perfectly aligned defining *canonical stereo geometry*. In this geometry, we have an identical copy of the camera on the left translated by *base distance b* along the X_s-axis of the $X_s Y_s Z_s$ camera coordinate system of the left camera. The projection center of the left camera is at $(0, 0, 0)$ and the projection center of the cloned right camera is at $(b, 0, 0)$. A 3D point $P = (X_s, Y_s, Z_s)$ is mapped into undistorted image points

$$p_u^L = (x_u^L, y_u^L) = \left(\frac{f \cdot X_s}{Z_s}, \frac{f \cdot Y_s}{Z_s} \right) \tag{1.15}$$

$$p_u^R = (x_u^R, y_u^R) = \left(\frac{f \cdot (X_s - b)}{Z_s}, \frac{f \cdot Y_s}{Z_s} \right) \tag{1.16}$$

in the left and right image planes, respectively. Considering p_u^L and p_u^R in homogeneous coordinates, we have that

$$[p_u^R]^\top \cdot \mathbf{F} \cdot p_u^L = 0 \qquad (1.17)$$

for the 3×3 *bifocal tensor* $\mathbf{F}$, defined by the configuration of the two cameras. The dot product $\mathbf{F} \cdot p_u^L$ defines an *epipolar line* in the image plane of the right camera; any stereo point corresponding to p_u^L needs to be on that line.

1.3.1.3   Binocular Stereo Matching

Let B be the *base image* and M be the *match image*. We calculate corresponding pixels p^B and q^M in the *xy* image coordinates of carrier Ω following the optimization approach as expressed by Eq. (1.11). A labeling function f assigns a disparity f_p to pixel location p, which specifies a corresponding pixel $q = p^f$.

For example, we can use the census data-cost term $E_{\mathrm{MCEN}}(p, p^f)$ as defined in Eq. (1.13), and for the smoothness-cost term, either the Potts model, linear truncated cost, or quadratic truncated costs is used (see Chapter 5 in Klette (2014)). Chapter 6 of Klette (2014) discusses also different algorithms for stereo matching, including *belief-propagation matching* (BPM) (Sun et al. 2003) and *dynamic-programming stereo matching* (DPSM). DPSM can be based on scanning along the epipolar line only using either an ordering or a smoothness constraint, or it can be based (for symmetry?) on scanning along multiple scanlines using a smoothness constraint along those lines; the latter case is known as *semi-global matching* (SGM) if multiple scanlines are used for error minimization (Hirschmüller, 2005). A variant of SGM is used in Daimler's stereo vision system, available since March 2013 in their Mercedes cars (see also Chapter 2 by U. Franke in this book).

Iterative SGM (iSGM) is an example for a modification of baseline SGM; for example, error minimization along the horizontal scanline should in general contribute more to the final result than optimization along other scanlines (Hermann and Klette, 2012). Figure 1.7 also addresses confidence measurement; for a comparative discussion of confidence measures, see Haeusler and Klette (2012). *Linear BPM* (linBPM) applies the MCEN data-cost term and the linear truncated smoothness-cost term (Khan et al. 2013).

1.3.1.4   Performance Evaluation of Stereo Vision Solutions

Figure 1.8 provides a comparison of iSGM to linBPM on four frame sequences each of 400 frames length. It illustrates that iSGM performs better (with respect to the used measure, see the following section for its definition) on the `bridge` sequence that is characterized by many structural details in the scene, but not as good as linBPM on the other three sequences. For sequences `dusk` and `midday`, both performances are highly correlated, but not for the other two sequences. Of course, evaluating on only

Figure 1.7   Resulting disparity maps for stereo data when using only *one* scanline for DPSM with the SGM smoothness constraint and a 3 × 9 MCEN data-cost function. *From top to bottom and left to right*: Left-to-right horizontal scanline, and lower-left to upper-right diagonal scanline, top-to-bottom vertical scanline, and upper-left to lower-right diagonal scanline. Pink pixels are for low-confidence locations (here identified by inhomogeneous disparity locations). Courtesy of Simon Hermann; the input data have been provided by Daimler A.G.

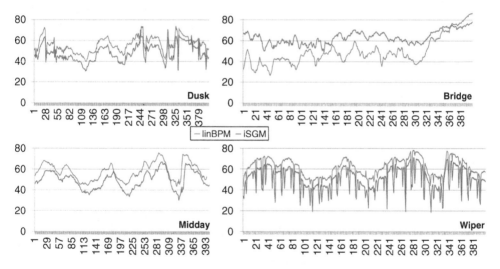

Figure 1.8   Normalized cross-correlation results when applying the third-eye technology for stereo matchers iSGM and linBPM for four real-world trinocular sequences of Set 9 of EISATS. Courtesy of Waqar Khan, Veronica Suaste, and Diego Caudillo

a few sequences of 400 frames each is insufficient for making substantial evaluations, but it does illustrate performance.

The diagrams in Figure 1.8 are defined by the *normalized cross-correlation* (NCC) between a recorded third-frame sequence and a virtual sequence calculated based on the stereo matching results of two other frame sequences. This *third-eye technology* (Morales and R 2009) also uses masks such that only image values are compared which are close to step-edges (e.g., see Figure 1.5 for detected edges at bright pixels in LoG scale space) in the third frame. It enables us to evaluate performance on any calibrated trinocular frame sequence recorded in the real world.

Example 1.3.1 Environment Reconstruction *3D road-side visualization or 3D environment modeling is the application where a 3D reconstruction from a moving platform can be used (Xiao et al. 2009), possibly in combination with 3D reconstructions from a flying platform such as a multi-copter.*

There are unresolved issues in the required very high accuracy of ego-motion analysis for mapping 3D results obtained at time t in a uniform world coordinate system. This is in particular apparent when trying to unify results from different runs through the same street (Zeng and Klette 2013). Figure 1.9 shows the 3D results from a single run (for a site at Tamaki campus, Auckland).

Figure 1.9   (a) Reconstructed cloud of points. (b) Reconstructed surface based on a single run of the ego-vehicle. Courtesy of Yi Zeng

1.3.2   Motion

A sequence of video frames $I(.,.,t)$, all defined on the same carrier Ω, is recorded with a time difference δt between two subsequent frames; frame t is recorded at time $t \cdot \delta t$ counted from the start of the recording.

The projection of a static or moving surface point into pixel $p_t = (x_t, y_t)$ in frame t and into pixel $p_{t+1} = (x_{t+1}, y_{t+1})$ in frame $t + 1$ defines a pair of *corresponding pixels* represented by a *motion vector* $[x_{t+1} - x_t, y_{t+1} - y_t]^\top$ from p_t to p_{t+1} in Ω.

1.3.2.1   Dense or Sparse Motion Analysis

Dense motion analysis aims at calculating approximately correct motion vectors for "basically" every pixel location $p = (x, y)$ in frame t (see Figure 1.10 for an example).

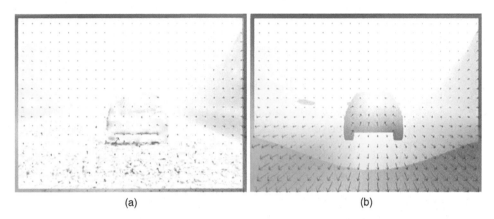

(a)   (b)

Figure 1.10 Visualization of optical flow using the color key shown around the border of the image for assigning a direction to particular colors; the length of the flow vector is represented by saturation, where value "white" (i.e., undefined saturation) corresponds to "no motion." (a) Calculated optical flow using the original Horn–Schunck algorithm. (b) Ground truth for the image shown in Figure 1.4a. Courtesy of Tobi Vaudrey

Sparse motion analysis is designed for having accurate motion vectors at a few selected pixel locations.

Motion analysis is a difficult 2D correspondence problem, and it might become easier by having recorded high-resolution images at a higher frame rate in future. For example, motion analysis is approached by a single-module solution by *optical flow* calculation, or as a multi-module solution when combining image segmentation with subsequent estimations of motion vectors for image segments.

1.3.2.2 Optical Flow

Optical flow $\mathbf{u}(p, t) = [u(p, t), v(p, t)]^{\top}$ is the result of dense motion analysis. It represents motion vectors between corresponding pixels $p = (x, y)$ in frames $I(.,.,t)$ and $I(.,.,t + 1)$. Figure 1.10 shows the visualization of an optical flow map.

1.3.2.3 Optical Flow Equation and Image Constancy Assumption

The derivation of the *optical flow equation* (Horn and Schunck 1981)

$$0 = u(p, t) \cdot I_x(p, t) + v(p, t) \cdot I_y(p, t) + I_t(p, t) \tag{1.18}$$

for $p \in \Omega$ and first-order derivatives I_x, I_y, and I_t follows from the ICA, that is, by assuming that corresponding 3D world points are represented in frame t and $t + 1$ by the same intensity. This is actually not true for computer vision in vehicles. Light intensities change frequently due to lighting artifacts (e.g., driving below trees), changing angles to the Sun, or simply due to sensor noise. However, the optical flow equation is often used as a *data-cost term* in an optimization approach (minimizing energy as defined in Eq. (1.10)) for solving the optical flow problem.

1.3.2.4   Examples of Data and Smoothness Costs

If we accept Eq. (1.18) due to Horn and Schunck (and thus the validity of the ICA) as data constraint, then we derive

$$E_{\mathrm{HS}}(f) = \sum_{p \in \Omega} [\, u(p,t) \cdot I_x(p,t) + v(p,t) \cdot I_y(p,t) + I_t(p,t) \,]^2 \qquad (1.19)$$

as a possible data-cost term for any given time t.

We introduced above the zero-mean-normalized census-cost function E_{MCEN}. The sum $E_{\mathrm{MCEN}}(f) = \sum_{p \in \Omega} E_{\mathrm{MCEN}}(p, p + f(p))$ can replace $E_{\mathrm{HS}}(p,q)$ in an optimization approach as defined by Eq. (1.10) (see Hermann and Werner (2013)). This corresponds to the invalidity of the ICA for video data recorded in the real world.

For the smoothness-error term, we may use

$$E_{\mathrm{FO\_}L_2}(f) = \sum_{p \in \Omega} \left[\frac{\partial u(p,t)}{\partial x}\right]^2 + \left[\frac{\partial u(p,t)}{\partial y}\right]^2 + \left[\frac{\partial v(p,t)}{\partial x}\right]^2 + \left[\frac{\partial v(p,t)}{\partial y}\right]^2 \qquad (1.20)$$

This smoothness-error term applies squared penalties to first-order derivatives in the L_2 sense. Applying a smoothness term in an approximate L_1 sense reduces the impact of outliers (Brox et al. 2004).

Terms E_{HS} and $E_{\mathrm{FO\_}L_2}$ define the TVL_2 optimization problem as originally considered by Horn and Schunck (1981).

1.3.2.5   Performance Evaluation of Optical Flow Solutions

Apart from using data with provided ground truth (see EISATS and KITTI and Figure 1.4), there is also a way for evaluating calculated flow vectors on recorded real-world video assuming that the recording speed is sufficiently large; for calculated flow vectors for frames $I(.,.,t)$ and $I(.,.,t + 2)$, we calculate an image "half-way" using the mean of image values at corresponding pixels and we compare this calculated image with frame $I(.,.,t + 1)$ (see Szeliski (1999)). Limitations for recording frequencies of current cameras make this technique not yet practically appropriate, but it is certainly appropriate for fundamental research.

1.3.3   Object Detection and Tracking

In general, an *object detector* is defined by applying a classifier for an object detection problem. We assume that any decision made can be evaluated as being either correct or false.

1.3.3.1   Measures for Object Detection

Let tp or fp denote the numbers of true-positives or false-positives, respectively. Analogously we define tn and fn for the negatives; tn is not a common entry for performance measures.

   Precision (PR) is the ratio of true-positives compared to all detections. *Recall* (RC) (or *sensitivity*) is the ratio of true-positives compared to all potentially possible detections (i.e., to the number of all visible objects):

$$PR = \frac{tp}{tp + fp} \quad \text{and} \quad RC = \frac{tp}{tp + fn} \tag{1.21}$$

The *miss rate* (MR) is the ratio of false-negatives compared to all objects in an image. *False-positives per image* (FPPI) is the ratio of false-positives compared to all detected objects in an image:

$$MR = \frac{fn}{tp + fn} \quad \text{and} \quad FPPI = \frac{fp}{tp + fp} \tag{1.22}$$

   In case of multiple images, the mean of measures can be used (i.e., averaged over all the processed images).

   How to decide whether a detected object is true-positive? Assume that objects in images have been locally identified manually by bounding boxes, serving as the ground truth. All detected objects are matched with these *ground-truth boxes* by calculating ratios of areas of overlapping regions

$$a_o = \frac{\mathcal{A}(D \cap T)}{\mathcal{A}(D \cup T)} \tag{1.23}$$

where $\mathcal{A}$ denotes the area of a region in an image, D is the detected bounding box of the object, and T is the area of the bounding box of the matched ground-truth box. If a_o is larger than a threshold T, say $T = 0.5$, then the detected object is taken as a true-positive.

Example 1.3.2 Driver Monitoring *Besides measurements for understanding the steadiness of driver's movement of the steering wheel, cameras are also an appropriate tool for understanding the state of the driver (e.g., drowsiness detection, or eye gaze).*

   Face and eye detection (Viola and Jones 2001b) or head pose analysis (Murphy-Chutorian and Trivedi 2009) are basic tasks in this area (Figure 1.11). Challenging lighting conditions still define unsatisfactorily solved scenarios (e.g., see Rezaei and Klette (2012) for such scenarios).

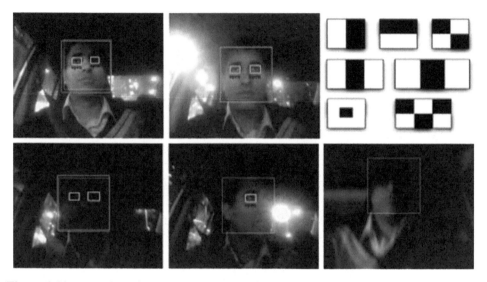

Figure 1.11 Face detection, eye detection, and face tracking results under challenging lighting conditions. Typical Haar-like features, as introduced in Viola and Jones (2001b), are shown in the upper right. The illustrated results for challenging lighting conditions require additional efforts. Courtesy of Mahdi Rezaei

Driver awareness *can be defined by relating driver monitoring results to environment analysis for the given traffic scenario. The driver not only needs to pay attention to driving, eye gaze or head pose (Rezaei and Klette 2011) should also correspond (for some time) to those outside regions where safety-related events occur.*

1.3.3.2   Object Tracking

Object tracking is an important task for understanding the motion of a mobile platform or of other objects in a dynamic environment. The mobile platform with the installed system is also called the *ego-vehicle* whose *ego-motion* needs to be calculated for understanding the movement of the installed sensors in the three-dimensional (3D) world.

Calculated features in subsequent frames $I(.,.,t)$ can be tracked (e.g., by using RANSAC for identifying an affine transform between feature points) and then used for estimating ego-motion based on bundle adjustment. This can also be combined with another module using nonvisual sensor data such as GPS or of an inertial measurement unit (IMU). For example, see Geng et al. (2015) for an integration of GPS data.

Other moving objects in the scene can be tracked using repeated detections or by following a detected object in frame $I(.,.,t)$ to frame $I(.,.,t + 1)$. A *Kalman filter* (e.g., linear, general, or unscented) can be used for building a model for the motion as well as for involved noise. A *particle filter* can also be used based on extracted weights for potential moves of a particle in particle space. Kalman and particle filters are introduced, with references to related original sources, in Klette (2014).

1.3.4   Semantic Segmentation

When segmenting a scene, ideally obtained segments should correspond to defined objects in the scene, such as a house, a person, or a car in a road scene. These segments define *semantic segmentation*. Segmentation for vehicle technology aims at semantic segmentation (Floros and Leibe 2012; Ohlich et al. 2012) with temporal consistency along a recorded video sequence. Appearance is an important concept for semantic segmentation (Mohan 2014). The concept of super pixels (see, e.g., Liu et al. (2012)) might be useful for achieving semantic segmentation. Temporal consistency requires tracking of segments and similarity calculations between tracked segments.

1.3.4.1   Environment Analysis

There are *static* (i.e., fixed with respect to the Earth) or *dynamic* objects in a scenario which need to be detected, understood, and possibly further analyzed.

A flying helicopter (or just multi-copter) should be able to detect power lines or other potential objects defining a hazard. Detecting traffic signs or traffic lights, or understanding lane borders of highways or suburban roads are examples for driving vehicles. Boats need to detect buoys and beacons.

Pedestrian detection became a common subject for road-analysis projects. After detecting a pedestrian on a pathway next to an inner-city road, it would be helpful to understand whether this pedestrian intends to step onto the road in the next few seconds.

After detecting more and more objects, we may have the opportunity to model and understand a given environment.

Example 1.3.3 Use of Stereo Analysis and Optical Flow Calculations *Modules for solving stereo matching and optical flow calculation can be used for designing a system for video segmentation. For example, following Hermann et al. (2011), stereo matching for images L(.,.,t) and R(.,.,t) of frame t results in a depth map that is segmented by*

1. *preprocessing for removing noisy (i.e., isolated) depth values and irrelevant depth values (e.g., in the sky region),*
2. *estimating a ground manifold using v-disparities—depth values identified as being in the ground manifold are also removed—and*
3. *performing a segmentation procedure (e.g., simple region growing) on the remaining depth values.*

Resulting segments are likely to be of similar shape and location as those obtained for stereo frame t + 1 by the same procedure. For each segment obtained for frame t, the mean optical flow vector for pixels in this segment defines the expected move of this segment into a new position in frame t + 1. Those expected segments (of frame t after expected moves into frame t + 1) are compared with the actual segments of frame t + 1 for identifying correspondences, for example, by applying a set-theoretical metric, which represents the ratio between overlap and total area of both segments.

1.3.4.2   Performance Evaluation of Semantic Segmentation

There is a lack of provided ground truth for semantic segmentations in traffic sequences. Work reported in current publications on semantic segmentation, such as Floros and Leibe (2012) and Ohlich et al. (2012), can be used for creating test databases. There is also current progress in available online data; see www.cvlibs .net/datasets/kitti/eval_road.php, www.cityscapes-dataset.net, and (Ros et al. 2015) for a study for such data.

Barth et al. (2010) proposed a method for segmentation, which is based on evaluating pixel probabilities of whether they are in motion in the real world or not (using scene flow and ego-motion). Barth et al. (2010) also provides ground truth for image segmentation in Set 7 of EISATS, illustrated by Figure 1.12. Figure 1.12 also shows resulting SGM stereo maps and segments obtained when following the multi-module approach briefly sketched earlier.

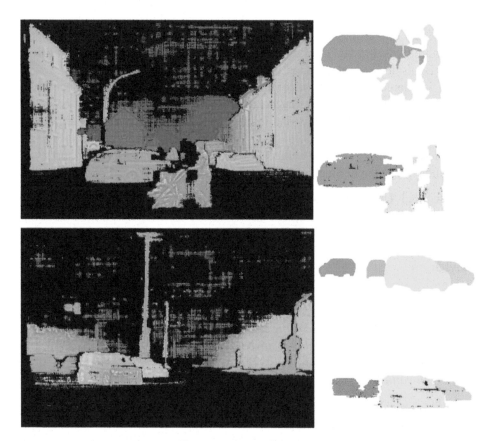

Figure 1.12   Two examples for Set 7 of EISATS illustrated by preprocessed depth maps following the described method (Steps 1 and 2). Ground truth for segments is provided by Barth et al. (2010) and shown on top in both cases. Resulting segments using the described method are shown below in both cases; courtesy of Simon Hermann

Modifications in the involved modules for stereo matching and optical flow calculation influence the final result. There might be dependencies between performances of contributing programs.

1.4 Concluding Remarks

The vehicle industry worldwide has assigned major research and development resources for offering competitive solutions for vision-based components for vehicles. Research at academic institutions needs to address future or fundamental tasks, challenges that are not of immediate interest for the vehicle industry, for being able to continue to contribute to this area.

The chapter introduced basic notation and selected visual tasks. It reviewed work in the field of computer vision in vehicles. There are countless open questions in this area, often related to

1. adding further alternatives to only a few existing robust solutions for one generic or specific task,
2. a comparative evaluation of such solutions,
3. ways of analyzing benchmarks for their particular challenges,
4. the design of more complex systems, and
5. ways to test such complex systems.

Specifying and solving a specific task might be a good strategy to define fundamental research, ahead of currently extremely intense industrial research and development within the area of computer vision for vehicles. Aiming at robustness including challenging scenarios and understanding interactions in dynamic scenes between multiple moving objects are certainly examples where further research is required.

Computer vision can help to solve true problems in society or industry, thus contributing to the prevention of social harms or atrocities; it is a fundamental ethical obligation of researchers in this field not to contribute to those, for example, by designing computer vision solutions for the use in UAVs for killing people. Academics identify *ethics in research* often with subjects such as plagiarism, competence, or objectivity, and a main principle is also social responsibility. Computer vision in road vehicles can play, for example, a major role in reducing casualties in traffic accidents, which are counted by hundreds of thousands of people worldwide each year; it is a very satisfying task for a researcher to contribute to improved road safety.

Acknowledgments

The author thanks Simon Hermann, Mahdi Rezaei, Konstantin Schauwecker, Junli Tao, and Garry Tee for comments on drafts of this chapter.

2

Autonomous Driving

Uwe Franke
Image Understanding Group, Daimler AG, Sindelfingen, Germany

During the last two decades, unprecedented progress has been achieved in computer vision research. At the same time, the quality of images delivered by modern CMOS imagers in outdoor scenarios has improved significantly and the available computational power constantly doubled in less than 2 years. As a consequence, computer vision for cars has evolved from simple lane keeping to powerful driver assistance systems, as described in Chapter 7. The most ambitious and highly attractive research goal is Autonomous Driving, especially through busy urban traffic.

This chapter is organized as follows: first, we give some general remarks on Autonomous Driving and the environment perception for autonomous vehicles. Subsequently, we concentrate on image understanding for complex urban traffic scenes. Finally, ongoing research topics are outlined.

2.1 Introduction

2.1.1 The Dream

The dream of Autonomous Driving is nearly as old as the car itself. As early as 1925, Francis P. Houdina publicly demonstrated his radio-controlled driverless car "Linrrican Wonder" on the streets of New York City, traveling up Broadway and down Fifth Avenue, through the thick of the traffic. Some years later at the 1939 New York's World Fair, Norman Bel Geddes designed the Futurama exhibition that presented a possible model of future traffic including automated highways where cars would drive on inductive cables while being controlled by radio from a base station.

Computer Vision in Vehicle Technology: Land, Sea, and Air, First Edition.
Edited by Antonio M. López, Atsushi Imiya, Tomas Pajdla and Jose M. Álvarez.
© 2017 John Wiley & Sons Ltd. Published 2017 by John Wiley & Sons Ltd.

Figure 2.1   The way people think of usage and design of Autonomous Cars has not changed much over the last 60 years: (a) the well-known advert from the 1950s, (b) a design study published in 2014

Throughout 1956 and 1957, the electric utility company *Central Power and Light Company* launched an advertisement that was posted in many leading newspapers, predicting Autonomous Cars. The famous picture from their advert is shown in Figure 2.1. Their slogan was: "Electricity may be the driver. One day your car may speed along an electric super-highway, its speed and steering automatically controlled by electronic devices embedded in the road. Highways will be made safe - by electricity! No traffic jams … no collisions … no driver fatigue."

Also during the 1950s and 1960s, General Motors showcased their Firebirds, a series of experimental cars that were described to have an "electronic guide system that can rush it over an automatic highway while the driver relaxes."

Today, 60 years later, the dream is more alive than ever and the motivations are the same as in the 1950s:

Safety: We hope for fewer accidents due to an autonomous system's increased reliability and shorter reaction time compared to human drivers. Taking into account that human errors count for about 95% of all traffic accidents, which kill 1.24 million people per year worldwide, this is worth major efforts.

Comfort: If Autonomous Driving relieves the driver of the responsibility to control the car or to supervise the system, they will be able to read and write emails, surf on the Internet, watch videos, or relax.

Increased Road Capacity: Optimizing the throughput of existing highways might be achievable since vehicle-to-vehicle communication allows for smaller gaps. This was the basic motivation for the US Automated Highway Project (1995–1997).

2.1.2   Applications

Autonomous Driving on highways is probably the most popular, but by far not the only application of automation in traffic. Above all, autonomous parking at home or in the form of valet parking attracts many people. The latter would allow for a reduction of space required for vehicle parking and an alleviation of parking scarcity, as cars could drop off passengers, park further away where space is less scarce, and return as needed to pick up passengers.

Another motivation is the elimination of redundant human trips. Humans are not required to take the car anywhere, as the robotic car can drive independently to wherever it is required, such as to pick up passengers or to go in for maintenance. This would be especially relevant for trucks, taxis, and car-sharing services.

In certain specialized areas, Autonomous Vehicles are already in operation. The Dover-Calais tunnel runs about 20 vehicles conducted by inductive cables for maintenance and rescue. In Australia, Rio Tinto, a leading mining company runs automated haul trucks in their (above ground) mines using GPS for navigation and guidance. Automated Guided Vehicles have also been used in Rotterdam harbor for years. However, none of these systems use computer vision so far.

2.1.3   Level of Automation

In the United States, the National Highway Traffic Safety Administration (NHTSA) has established an official classification system consisting of five levels. German authorities ("Bundesanstalt für Straßenwesen" BAST) distinguish between four levels:

- Level 0 (No automation): The driver completely controls the vehicle at all times.
- Level 1 (Function-specific automation): Individual vehicle controls are automated, such as electronic stability control or braking assist.
- Level 2 (Combined function automation/BAST: partly automated): More than one control function is automated. The driver is expected to be available for control at all times and on short notice.
- Level 3 (Limited self-driving automation/BAST: highly automated): The vehicle takes control most of the time. The driver is expected to be available for occasional control with a comfortable transition time.
- Level 4 (Full self-driving automation/BAST: fully automated): The vehicle takes control all the time from the beginning to the end of the journey. The driver is not expected to be available for control at any time.

Level 2 systems are already commercially available. For example, Mercedes-Benz offers its "Intelligent Drive" concept for upper and middle class cars. It combines ACC (automatic cruise control), lane keeping, and autonomous emergency braking capabilities. A hands-on recognition together with limited actuator performance forces the driver to be ready to take over control all times. In particular, the moment that the systems adds to the steering rod is limited such that the car cannot go through narrow highway curves by itself but needs the assistance of the driver.

The step toward level 3 systems seems to be small from a technical point of view. However, the fact that the driver is not available in emergency situations renders this mode to be highly challenging. If we expect a highly automated car to drive as safely as a human driver, the probability of a minor accident on a highway should be lower than about 10^{-5} per hour and the chance of a serious accident with fatalities should not exceed 10^{-7} per hour, based on German accident statistics. It is obvious that this requires redundancy for lane recognition as well as for obstacle detection. Since roads are built for human perception, vision will be an essential part of the sensing system.

2.1.4 Important Research Projects

Research on Autonomous Driving using vision goes back to the 1980s, when the CMU vehicle Navlab 1 drove slowly across the Pittsburgh campus using cameras. The introduction of Kalman filtering for image sequence analysis by Dickmanns was a milestone allowing real-time performance on restricted hardware. As early as in 1987, his 4D approach allowed him to demonstrate vision-based lane keeping on a German highway with speeds up to 100 km/h (see Dickmanns (1988)). With his seminal work, he laid the foundations for nearly all commercially available lane keeping systems on the market today. The pioneer cars of the 1980s were huge since much space and energy were needed for the ambitious computation. Figure 2.2 shows the

(a)   (b)

Figure 2.2 (a) CMU's first demonstrator vehicle Navlab 1. The van had five racks of computer hardware, including three Sun workstations, video hardware and GPS receiver, and a Warp supercomputer. The vehicle achieved a top speed of 32 km/h in the late 1980s. (b) Mercedes-Benz's demonstrator vehicle VITA built in cooperation with Dickmanns from the university of armed forces in Munich. Equipped with a bifocal vision system and a small transputer system with 10 processors, it was used for Autonomous Driving on highways around Stuttgart in the early 1990s, reaching speeds up to 100 km/h

first Navlab vehicle on (a) and the famous demonstrator vehicle "VITA" operated by the Mercedes-Benz and Dickmanns' group on (b).

At the final presentation of the European PROMETHEUS project in Paris in 1994, vision-based Autonomous Driving on public highways was demonstrated, including lane change maneuvers. In July 1995, Pomerleau (CMU) drove with the Navlab 5 vehicle from Washington DC to San Diego using vision-based lateral guidance and radar-based ACC at an autonomy rate of 98.2% (see *No Hands Across America Webpage*, 1995). In the same year, Dickmanns' team drove approximately 1750 km from Munich, Germany, to Odense, Denmark, and back at a maximum speed of 175 km/h. The longest distance traveled without manual intervention by the driver was 158 km. On average, manual intervention was necessary once every 9 km. In the 1990s, the author himself drove more than 10,000 km "autonomously" in daily commute traffic as well as on long-distance trips.

All these approaches had two things in common. Firstly, they performed autonomy on level 2 with a safety driver behind the steering wheel. Secondly, they were focused on well-structured highway scenarios, where the Autonomous Driving task is much easier than in complex and chaotic urban traffic. Sparked by the increased methodical and technical availability of better algorithms and sensors, initial steps toward taking Autonomous Driving into urban scenarios were made in Franke et al. (1995).

One notable and highly important event was the DARPA Urban Challenge in 2007, which was won by CMU's car "Junior." The teams had to solve several driving tasks in minimum time and in full autonomy. All six finalists based their work on high-end laser scanners coupled with radars for long-range sensing. The impressive work by Google in the field of Autonomous Driving is based on the experience gained in the Urban Challenge. As a result, they also adopted high-end laser scanners and long-range radars as the main sensing platform in their system, augmented by a high-resolution color camera for traffic light recognition. Figure 2.3 shows "Junior"

(a)   (b)

Figure 2.3   (a) Junior by CMU's Robotics Lab, winner of the Urban Challenge 2007. (b) A Google car prototype presented in 2014 that neither features a steering wheel nor gas or braking pedals. Both cars base their environment perception on a high-end laser scanner

(a)   (b)

Figure 2.4 (a) Experimental car BRAiVE built by Broggi's team at University of Parma. Equipped with only stereo cameras, this car drove 17 km along roads around Parma in 2013. (b) Mercedes S500 Intelligent Drive demonstrator named "Bertha." In August 2013, it drove autonomously about 100 km from Mannheim to Pforzheim, following the historic route driven by Bertha Benz 125 years earlier. Close-to-market radar sensors and cameras were used for environment perception

and a prototype of an autonomous vehicle presented by Google in spring 2014. This Google taxi neither has a steering wheel nor pedals.

On July 12, 2013, Broggi and his team performed an impressive Autonomous Driving experiment in Parma, Italy (see *VisLab PROUD-Car Test* (2013)). Their vehicle, shown in Figure 2.4, moved autonomously through public traffic. The 13 km long route included rural roads, two freeways with junctions, and urban areas with pedestrian crossings, a tunnel, artificial bumps, tight roundabouts, and traffic lights.

In August 2013, a Mercedes-Benz S-class vehicle (see Figure 2.4) equipped with close-to-market stereo cameras and radar sensors drove autonomously from Mannheim to Pforzheim, Germany, following the 100 km long historical route Bertha Benz took 125 years before. This route includes busy cities such as Heidelberg and also narrow villages in the Black Forest. The experiment showed that Autonomous Driving is not limited to highways and similar well-structured environments anymore.

Further interesting work that also aims for Autonomous Driving with close to production vehicles was presented by a CMU group (see Wei et al. (2013)).

Another project worth mentioning is the European vCharge project (see Furgale et al. (2013), *vCharge Project* (n.d.)). The objective of this project is to develop a smart car system that allows for Autonomous Driving in designated areas, for example, valet parking, park and ride, and offers advanced driver support in urban environments. A stereo camera system and four fish-eye cameras are used to localize the vehicle relative to a precomputed map, to park the car in the assigned parking lot, and to avoid obstacles. A comprehensive summary of activities in the quickly developing field of Autonomous Driving can be found in Wikipedia (n.d.).

2.1.5   Outdoor Vision Challenges

Although cameras are becoming part of our daily lives and common in modern driver assistance systems, too, vision for Autonomous Driving is still a challenge, as many requirements must be fulfilled at the same time:

1. **Robustness:** In contrast to the large number of applications in industrial inspection, indoor robotics, and medicine, the vision system has to operate under difficult illumination conditions (low sun, night, glare) and adverse weather conditions such as snow, rain, fog, and any combination thereof. The quest for an all-weather system has several consequences: firstly, the most attractive algorithms will always be a compromise between performance and robustness. Secondly, the cameras have to be mounted such that they can be cleaned by wipers or air flow. Therefore, forward-facing cameras are usually located in front of the rear-view mirror. In this case, reflections on the windshield caused by objects on the dashboard have to be avoided by sun shields or polarizing filters. In addition, robustness requires a reliable self-diagnosis that generates a valuable confidence measure for the subsequent sensor fusion step.
2. **Precision:** Since cameras have a significantly higher resolution than radars and lidars, they can best determine the geometry of obstacles. Stereo cameras used for measuring the distance and motion state of other objects have to strive for maximum accuracy. Precise sub-pixel interpolation is required since the stereo baseline is constrained by design and packaging issues. Unfortunately, camera resolution and imager size are limited due to costs and nighttime performance requirements. Since the cameras are being exposed to strong temperature changes and vibrations, a powerful online calibration becomes necessary in order to guarantee precise calibration of the stereo system throughout the whole life cycle.
3. **Real time:** Standard automotive cameras deliver 25–40 frames per second. It is evident that these images have to be processed online. High image rates are necessary to reliably estimate the motion state of other traffic participants. Furthermore, the latency between the first detection of a potential obstacle and the notification to the subsequent processing stage has to be as short as possible to avoid losing valuable time.
4. **Power Consumption and Price:** There is no lack of energy in the car. However, if the processing is to be done in the camera box for cost reasons, power dissipation turns out to be a serious problem, as it heats the imagers. Cooling is not permitted and, if the camera is mounted behind the windshield, heating by sunshine is maximal. In addition, the total price has to be within the range of a few hundred dollars only, otherwise customers will not buy the offered driver assistance system.

2.2 Autonomous Driving in Cities

Since both autonomous parking and Autonomous Driving on highways have entered the pre-development phase, we will concentrate on computer vision for Autonomous Driving in cities in this chapter. In view of the complexity of the topic, we abstain from mathematical details but refer to the cited literature.

The main statements of this chapter are based on the experience gained in the "Bertha" project mentioned earlier (see Ziegler et al. (2014a)). The selected route comprises overland passages, urban areas (e.g., Mannheim and downtown Heidelberg), and 23 small villages, partly with narrow streets (see Figure 2.5). In that sense, the route is representative at least for European countries. The autonomous vehicle

Figure 2.5 The Bertha Benz Memorial Route from Mannheim to Pforzheim (103 km). The route comprises rural roads, urban areas (e.g., downtown Heidelberg), and small villages and contains a large variety of different traffic situations such as intersections with and without traffic lights, roundabouts, narrow passages with oncoming vehicles, pedestrian crossings, cars parked on the road, and so on

named "Bertha" had to handle traffic lights, pedestrian crossings, intersections, and roundabouts in real traffic. It had to react to a variety of objects including parked cars, preceding and oncoming vehicles, bicycles, pedestrians, and trams.

Its system architecture is outlined in Figure 2.6. The main sensing components are as follows:

Cameras: A forward-facing stereo camera system, a wide-angled high-resolution camera for traffic light recognition and a second wide-angled camera for localization.

Radars: Four long-range radars facing ahead, behind, and toward both sides of the car, accompanied by wide-angled short-range radars for a 360° view around the car.

Maps: Another important source of information is a detailed digital map. This map contains the position of lanes, and the topology between them, as well as

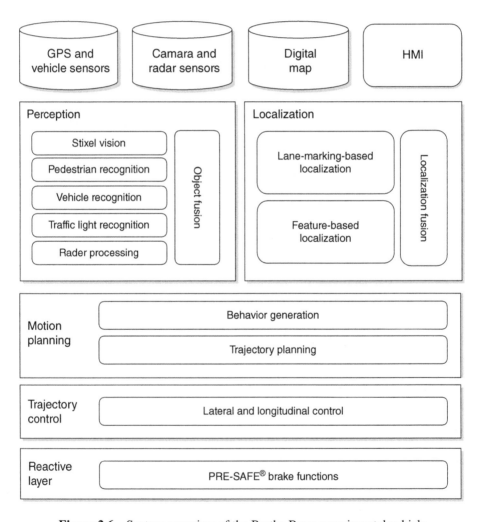

Figure 2.6 System overview of the Bertha Benz experimental vehicle

attributes and relations defining traffic regulations (e.g., right of way, relevant traffic lights, and speed limits). An important prerequisite for using such digital maps is a precise self-localization on the map. Bertha employed two complementary vision algorithms—point feature based localization and lane marking based localization—to accomplish this task.

The fusion module is of central importance, as none of the sensors shows the recognition performance necessary for Autonomous Driving solely.

The objective of the motion planning modules is to derive an optimal trajectory, that is, the path of the vehicle as a function of time, from the given sensor and map information. This trajectory is transformed into actuator commands by respective lateral and longitudinal controllers. The reactive layer consists of all standard safety systems, so that emergency braking does not need to be considered in the trajectory planning and control modules.

Precise and comprehensive environment perception is the basis for safe and comfortable Autonomous Driving in complex traffic situations occurring in cities. The questions to be answered by the vision sensors are as follows:

1. Localization: *Where is the car in relation to the map?*
2. Free-space analysis and obstacle detection: *Can the car drive safely along the planned path or is it blocked by obstacles? Are they stationary or moving? What size are they? How do they move?*
3. Object classification: *What type are detected obstacles, for example, pedestrians, bicyclists, or vehicles? Is the relevant traffic light green?*

The reminder of this section is organized as follows: first, we describe the principles used for vision-based localization. Then, we present a stereo vision pipeline for 3D image analysis. The third section focuses on object recognition. Each section is completed by a discussion on lessons learned, remaining problems, and possible future work.

2.2.1 Localization

A detailed map significantly simplifies the driving task compared to a situation where the planning has to be performed without this additional knowledge. Since such high-quality maps are commercially not available yet, they were generated in a semi-automatic manner. Infrastructural elements that are relevant to our application, for example, speed limits, pedestrian crossings, or stop lines, have also been included into the digital map. Similar to successful Urban Challenge approaches, optimal driving paths have been calculated in an off-line step. Given a precise ego-localization relative to the map in online mode, an autonomous vehicle can easily follow the preplanned path as long as the traffic situation permits. This planning and decision module has to continuously analyze the scene content delivered by the environment perception and to react by replanning whenever driving paths are currently blocked or will be obstructed by other traffic participants in the near future.

It has become a well-known fact that GPS accuracy is often not sufficient in cities and villages to achieve the self-localization precision required for Autonomous Driving. Hence, vision-based localization is essential and has attracted much research in recent years.

2.2.1.1 Feature-Based Localization

A commonly used approach is feature-based localization, as illustrated in Figure 2.7. Figure 2.7a shows one frame of an image sequence recorded in a mapping run. Figure 2.7b has been acquired during an autonomous test drive from a rear-facing camera. Clearly, both images have been obtained from approximately the same position and angle, yet at a different time of year. The two images are registered spatially by means of a descriptor-based point feature association: salient features of the map sequence (so-called *landmarks* shown in blue in Figure 2.7) are associated with detected features (red) in the current image of the vehicle's rear-facing camera. Given that the 3D positions of these landmarks have been computed beforehand, for example, by bundle adjustment, it is possible to compute a 6D rigid-body transformation between both camera poses that would bring associated features in agreement. By fusing this transformation with the global reference pose of the

Figure 2.7 Landmarks that are successfully associated between the mapping image (a) and online image (b) are shown.

map image and the motion information from wheel encoders and yaw rate sensors available in the vehicle, an accurate global position estimate can be recovered. More details on this feature-based localization can be found in Ziegler et al. (2014b).

2.2.1.2 Marking-Based Localization

In feature-rich environments such as urban areas, the feature-based localization method yields excellent map-relative localization results, achieving centimeter accuracy in many cases. However, this approach has two main problems: first, in suburban and rural areas, the required landmark density may drop below a required reliability level. Secondly, there is currently no feature descriptor that is robust with respect to illumination and time of year (see Valgren and Lilienthal (2010)). This is still an open problem.

Using lane markings for localization is a natural alternative. Figure 2.8 illustrates the principle presented in Schreiber et al. (2013).

Let us assume that a precise map containing all visible markings, stop lines, and curbs is available. If one projects these features onto the image, it is easy to estimate

Figure 2.8   Given a precise map (shown later), the expected markings (blue), stop lines (red), and curbs (yellow) are projected onto the current image. Local correspondence analysis yields the residuals that are fed to a Kalman filter in order to estimate the vehicle's pose relative to the map.

the vehicle's pose relative to the map. In practice, the matching can be done with a nearest neighbor search on the sampled map and the resulting residuals can be used to drive a Kalman filter. In suburban areas, the boundary lines of the road are often substituted with curbs. In this case, it is beneficial to support the measurements with a curb classifier. Such a system is described in Enzweiler et al. (2013) for example.

2.2.1.3 Discussion

Precise digital maps have to be gathered, processed, stored, and continuously updated. All these steps can be managed within an experiment like the Bertha drive, but cause problems for a commercial system. According to official statistics, the total length of the street network in Germany is about 650 000 km and 6.5 Mio km in the United States.

Lategahn (2013) points out that the feature-based localization scheme sketched earlier leads to an average storage size of almost 1 GB/km. This still ignores the mentioned sensitivity of descriptors to changing illumination and time of the year. Even if this amount of data could be significantly reduced by optimization, storing the 3D map for an entire country would still be a challenge. This problem does not exist if only small areas need to be mapped, for example, for autonomous parking.

A second challenge is keeping the up-to-date maps. This requires the online detection of changes and a continuous update of the maps by the provider. Such a tool chain does not exist and requires further research.

The mentioned problems raise the question whether the approach of (extremely) precise maps used by numerous teams today scales to larger areas. Since humans are able to find their way safely using only simple and geometrically inaccurate maps, one might argue for more sophisticated solutions for Autonomous Driving with less precise maps and no need for a precise localization. Obviously, this would require a more powerful environment perception. For example, Zhang et al. (2013) show that the outline of an intersection can be determined from various vision cues only. The future will reveal the best compromise between map quality and image analysis effort.

2.2.2 Stereo Vision-Based Perception in 3D

Path planning and behavior control require a precise perception of the three-dimensional environment and a fast detection of moving traffic participants. As described earlier, many research projects were or are still using the expensive Velodyne HD 64 laser scanner that delivers 64 scans with a horizontal resolution of $1/10°$ at a rate of 10 Hz. Its accuracy is within 10 cm, and its measurement ranges around 80 m. A much cheaper alternative is Stereo Vision, which allows depth estimation at 25 Hz at high spatial resolution, and the computation of object motion is within a few frames only. However, due to the triangulation principle of stereo cameras, the precision decreases quadratically with distance. Thus, a powerful

Figure 2.9   Visual outline of a modern stereo processing pipeline. Dense disparity images are computed from sequences of stereo image pairs. Red pixels are measured close to the ego-vehicle (i.e. dist $\leq$ 10 m), while green pixels are far away (i.e., dist $\geq$ 75 m). From these data, the Stixel World is computed. This medium-level representation achieves a reduction of the input data from hundreds of thousands of single depth measurements to a few hundred Stixels only. Stixels are tracked over time in order to estimate the motion of other objects. The arrows show the motion vectors of the tracked objects, pointing 0.5 seconds in advance. This information is used to extract both static infrastructure and moving objects for subsequent processing tasks. The free space is shown in gray

vision architecture is required to compensate this deficiency by exploiting the high resolution and the information contained within the images.

The stereo processing pipeline successfully used in the Bertha experiment consists of four main steps: the dense stereo reconstruction itself, the compact representation of the depth data by means of Stixels to facilitate further processing steps, a motion estimation of the Stixels, and finally the object segmentation. The different processing steps are briefly illustrated in Figure 2.9 and summarized in the following.

2.2.2.1   Depth Estimation

The stereo camera systems used in Mercedes-Benz serial cars today have two 1280×960 px high dynamic range color imagers with 53° field-of-view lenses and a baseline of 22 cm. The depth information is computed for a field of 1024×440 px. Color is necessary for various tasks such as adaptive high beam (intelligent headlight control), traffic sign recognition, and construction site recognition.

Since we decided not to change the standard safety systems of our test vehicle, we were free to add and optimize a second stereo camera system just for the Autonomous Driving task. In order to get the best stereo performance possible with available FPGA hardware and imagers, we abstained from using color (no de-Bayering necessary) and enlarged the baseline to 35 cm.

On the delivered images, dense disparity images are reconstructed using semi-global matching (SGM) (see Hirschmüller (2005)). The Census metric is used because it yields better results than classical scores such as the correlation coefficient, especially under adverse weather conditions and in the presence of calibration deficiencies. Due to its robustness and efficiency, SGM has been commercially used in Mercedes-Benz cars since 2013. Gehrig et al. (2009) show how to run this powerful scheme on energy-efficient, cheap FPGA hardware, allowing to compute dense high-quality depth maps in real time.

As stated in Chapter 1, SGM outperforms all known local disparity estimation schemes. A current ranking of stereo algorithms on the Middlebury data set can be consulted at Scharstein and Szeliski (2002). The KITTI Benchmark, published in 2012, contains data from real traffic scenes and has triggered new research on disparity estimation for this specific field (see Geiger (n.d.) and Geiger et al. (2012)).

The large measurement range and the high measurement accuracy necessary for DAS make sub-pixel estimation indispensable. For the used Census metric, the so-called equiangular fit has proven to be superior to the classical polynomial fit. Unfortunately, the achievable precision is limited by its preference of integer disparities (see Shimizu and Okutomi (2001)). This "pixel-locking effect" can lead to deviations of up to 0.3 px in global stereo methods. Although solutions have been proposed, this problem has not yet been resolved. As sub-pixel accuracy is not demanded in current stereo benchmarks, only little attention is devoted to this problem by academia.

As previously mentioned in Section 2.1, precise depth estimation requires a careful camera calibration. In practice, an online calibration is indispensable. While the change of internal parameters may be neglected, the external parameters need to be estimated continuously. For example, in the area of horizontal structures, uncorrected pitch errors of 0.2 px only can result in completely wrong estimates. If the relative speed of two approaching vehicles is determined from subsequent disparity measurements, squint angle errors are critical, especially if the object distance is equivalent to only a few disparities. Driving at urban speeds, a calibration error of just 1 px is sufficient to observe trucks approaching with 130 km/h. Therefore, special care needs to be put on the online estimation of the squint angle. Best results are achieved when objects whose depth is known from other sensors, for example, leading vehicles tracked by an active sensor, are used for this task.

2.2.2.2 The Stixel World

In order to cope with the large amount of data (the FPGA delivers roughly 400,000 points in 3D at 25 Hz) and reduce the computational burden of subsequent vision tasks (Badino et al. 2009) introduced the Stixel representation. Related to modern super-pixels, the so-called Stixel World is a versatile and extremely compact 3D medium-level representation. As shown in Figure 2.9, the complete 3D information is represented by only a few hundreds of small rectangular sticks of certain width, height, and position in the world. All areas of the image that are not covered with Stixels are implicitly understood as free, and thus, in intersection with the map of the route, as potentially drivable space.

The Stixel approximation exploits the fact that cities like all man-made environments are dominated by either horizontal or vertical planar surfaces. Horizontal surfaces typically correspond to the ground and exhibit a linearly decreasing disparity from the bottom of the image to the horizon. The vertical parts relate to objects, such as solid infrastructure, pedestrians, or cars and show (nearly) constant disparities. In the sense of a super-pixel, each Stixel approximates a certain part of an upright oriented object together with its distance and height.

Pfeiffer and Franke (2011) have presented a probabilistic approach to compute the Stixel World for a stereo image pair in a global optimization scheme. They treat the problem of Stixel extraction as a classical maximum a-posteriori (MAP) estimation problem, this way ensuring to obtain the best segmentation result for the current stereo disparity input.

Hence, it allows the support of the segmentation with a certain set of physically motivated world assumptions such as the following:

- Bayesian information criterion: The number of objects captured along every column is small. Dispensable cuts should be avoided.
- Gravity constraint: Flying objects are unlikely. The ground-adjacent object segment usually stands on the ground surface.
- Ordering constraint: The upper of two adjacent object segments has a greater depth. Reconstructing otherwise (e.g., for traffic lights, signs, or trees) is still possible if sufficiently supported by the input data.

Dynamic programming is used to infer the optimal solution in real time (see Bellman (1957)).

2.2.2.3   Stixel Tracking

In a static world, the Stixel representation is sufficient to compute a safe trajectory. In real traffic, moving objects have to be detected and their motion state must be determined.

A unique feature of images is that pixels with sufficient contrast can easily be tracked from frame to frame. If the camera is static, moving objects can be directly detected in the optical flow field. However, if the observer is also moving, things are more complicated, since the apparent flow depends on the observer's motion as well as on the depth of the considered pixel. In practice, neither the motion nor the depth is known exactly. Especially at larger distances when disparity uncertainties may not be ignored, a naive motion estimation will give unreliable and highly noisy results.

(a)   (b)

Figure 2.10   A cyclist taking a left turn in front of our vehicle: (a) shows the result when using 6D-Vision point features and (b) shows the corresponding Stixel result

Much better results can be achieved by an optimal fusion of depth and optical flow measurements, as proposed in Franke et al. (2005). In their scheme, pixels are tracked over time and image positions as well as disparities are measured at each time step. Assuming a constant motion of the tracked features and a known motion of the observer, a Kalman filter uses the measured pixel positions and disparities together with the measurement covariances to simultaneously estimate 3D-position and 3D-motion for each tracked feature. Thus, the approach has become known as "6D-Vision". Figure 2.10 shows on the left side the obtained result applying this algorithm to a sequence of a turning bicyclist. The arrows point to the expected positions 0.5 seconds ahead.

The motion of the observer comes as a by-product. As the complete motion is determined for thousands of points, it is straightforward to select good static features and use those for ego-motion calculation following the approach of Badino (2004).

This "6D-Vision" principle can also be applied to Stixels in order to precisely estimate their motion states. Given that objects of interest are expected to move earthbound, the estimated state vector can be reduced to 4D, which represents the position and velocity of the Stixel. The dynamic Stixel results for the cyclist scenario are illustrated in Figure 2.10b. As a by-product of this simplification, the estimation puts fewer requirements on the ego-motion estimation. In practice, the vehicle's inertial sensors are sufficient to compensate for its own motion state. Thanks to the temporal integration, the motion vectors are highly parallel although the estimation is done independently.

2.2.2.4   Stixel Grouping

So far, Stixels are a compact representation of the local three-dimensional environment, but they do not provide any explicit knowledge about which Stixels belong together and which do not. This is achieved in the last step of the processing pipeline, when tracked Stixels are grouped into the motion classes "right headed," "left headed," "with us," and "oncoming" as well as "static background." The result of the

Figure 2.11 Results of the Stixel computation, the Kalman filter-based motion estimation, and the motion segmentation step. The left side shows the arrows on the base points of the Stixels denoting the estimated motion state. The right side shows the corresponding labeling result obtained by graph-cut optimization. Furthermore, the color scheme encodes the different motion classes (right headed, left headed, with us, and oncoming). Uncolored regions are classified as static background

scheme published in Erbs and Franke (2012) is illustrated in Figure 2.9 showing the motion segmentation result for the considered scenario. Further results are shown in Figure 2.11.

The authors approach this task as a MAP estimation problem as well. Given the dynamic Stixel World, the goal is to label each Stixel with one of the previously mentioned motion classes, depending on which class conforms best with the prior knowledge about the current local 3D environment.

Apart from assuming rigid motion and striving for spatial smoothness of the segmentation, they use statistics obtained from annotated training data to express where in the scene which type of motion is likely to appear. For this purpose, Erbs and Franke (2012) model this problem using a conditional Markov random field, thus considering direct neighbor relationships (see Boykov et al. (1999)). The best labeling is extracted using the popular α-expansion graph cut (see Kolmogorov and Rother (2007)). Since the image is represented by a few hundreds of Stixels only, the optimal solution can be computed in less than a millisecond on a single I7 core.

Each resulting cluster is represented by its geometric form and a weighted average motion vector. If the object has been classified as vehicle (see Chapter 3), a special tracker is applied that exploits the kinematic limitations of cars. The vehicle tracker proposed in Barth et al. (2009) implements a bicycle model and thus allows the observation of the complete motion state including the yaw rate of oncoming vehicles, which is important for intention recognition at intersections.

2.2.2.5 Discussion

The sketched vision architecture has been systematically optimized within the Bertha project and has proven its reliability in daily traffic. Each step from pixels via Stixels to objects is based on (semi-)global optimization in order to achieve both best performance and robustness. In particular, real-time SGM is used to compute dense stereo depth maps from rectified image pairs. The Stixel World is computed from stereo also in a semi-global optimal manner, just ignoring the lateral dependencies of Stixel columns in order to achieve a real-time implementation. The motion estimation is based on the 6D-Vision principle, taking into account the temporal history of the tracked Stixel. Finally, graph-cut-based optimization is used to find the optimum segmentation of the dynamic Stixel World.

Global optimization has become the key for high-performance vision algorithms as it forces us to clearly define what we expect from the "best" solution. If we are not happy with what we get from optimization, we have to reformulate our goal function.

Disparity estimation is a good example. SGM puts a small penalty on disparity changes of one pixel and a higher penalty on large chances. This regularization leads to a robust scheme, but one can do better. The currently best performing algorithms for road scenes (according to the KITTI benchmark) assume that the world is composed of small planes with constant surface normals and restricted border conditions (see Yamaguchi et al. (2014)). This regularization is much stronger and leads to significantly better results. Unfortunately, these algorithms are computationally expensive and not (yet) suited for real-time applications.

Alternatively, one can search for stronger data terms, which means that we incorporate more information in the optimization. For example, Sanberg et al. (2014) use color to improve the Stixel estimation. Attempts to improve the disparity estimation by color have not been proven useful when contrasted with the additional computation effort. On the contrary, using color information leads to worse results when color constancy is not perfectly fulfilled (see Bleyer and Chambon (2010)).

Another cue that has been successfully used is motion, as we expect the world to consist of a limited number of moving objects. Early Scene Flow estimation schemes that just enforce local smoothness of the 3D flow field deliver noisy results compared to 6D-Vision (as shown in Rabe et al. (2010)), while powerful approaches that simultaneously generate a super-pixel representation, where each patch has a constant surface normal and 3D motion vector, deliver excellent results but are out of reach for commercial applications (see Vogel et al. (2013)).

Nevertheless, the latter scheme clearly indicates the way we will go in future. The optimization takes into account spatial and temporal information and has a strong regularization. Furthermore, it performs disparity estimation and super-pixel computation jointly. As there is no interface between these two major building blocks any longer, there is no risk that relevant information is suppressed by the disparity estimation module that usually generates just one disparity estimate per pixel.

Future vision systems will also benefit from better imagers. In the past, the step from 8-bit images to 12-bit images with increased dynamics significantly improved the performance. Next, higher resolution will help to push the limits of stereo vision and allow detection of objects at larger distances, as it increases the depth sensitivity and the size of the observed objects at the same time. However, this does not come for free.

First, the computational load for disparity estimation increases. Secondly, and even more importantly, the sensor sensitivity decreases if the imager size is kept fixed for cost reasons. This results in more noise, stronger motion blur, and a reduced night performance. In addition, an improvement by a certain factor does not necessarily lead to an increase in the measurement range by the same factor. The reason is that one has to decide whether points with noisy depth are more likely to belong to the ground surface or an obstacle that stays on it. The commonly used planar world assumption does not hold at larger distances, and small errors in the tilt angle estimated from depth data in front of the car linearly increase with distance. Attempts to estimate the 3D height profile from depth data exist but suffer from the high depth noise at larger distances and the fact that glare and reflections make stable stereo correspondences increasingly difficult at large distances.

The above discussion reveals ways to improve the performance of the stereo analysis. The practical success will depend on their robustness with respect to adverse weather and illumination conditions as well as on their cost/performance relation. As long as FPGAs are the only way to get high computational power at low power dissipation, noniterative algorithms will be the preferred solution.

2.2.3   *Object Recognition*

Pedestrians and cyclists are undeniably among the most endangered traffic participants. In addition, other vehicles as well as traffic lights are relevant for an Autonomous Car. Therefore, these objects have to be recognized fast and reliably. A unique advantage of vision, compared to active sensors such as lasers and radars, is the fact that apart from the 3D shape information, it delivers high-resolution images facilitating additional appearance-based object recognition and image understanding.

Such an appearance based on a real-time vision-based object detection system consists of two main modules: region-of-interest (ROI) generation and object classification. Subsequent tracking helps to reduce the false-positive rate and to increase the detection rate of the single-frame classifier. In the following, we discuss efficient approaches for object recognition that explicitly exploit the depth information delivered by disparity estimation. We distinguish between the near range (up to 40 m away from the vehicle) and the far range.

2.2.3.1 ROI Generation

Naturally, the more one knows about the current environment, the less effort must be spent on extracting the objects of interest.

For a monocular approach, there are no prior clues to exploit except a rough planar road assumption of the 3D environment. Thus, one is forced to test lots of hypotheses spread across the image, covering all possible scales that the objects of interest might have. Approximately 50,000 hypotheses have to be tested per image to obtain reasonable results.

If depth data are available, it can be used to easily sort out unlikely hypotheses in advance, for example, by considering the correlation of depth and scale as suggested in Keller et al. (2011). This strategy allows reduction of the hypotheses set by an order of magnitude, such that about 5000 remaining hypotheses have to be classified (see Figure 2.12 for illustration).

Since Stixels inherently encode where in the scene, at which distance, and at which scale objects are to be expected, it is straightforward to directly use this prior knowledge for the hypotheses' generation step. Enzweiler et al. (2012) prove that it is possible to further reduce the number of required hypotheses by a whole magnitude, resulting in a total number of merely about 500. It also allows reduction in the number of false alarms by almost one order of magnitude, while the detection rate remains constant. The potential of this procedure has also been the focus of the work in Benenson et al. (2011).

Figure 2.12 ROIs overlaid on the gray-scale image. In the monocular case (upper row left), about 50,000 hypotheses have to be tested by a classifier, in the stereo case (upper row right) this number reduces to about 5000. If each Stixel is assumed to be the center of a vehicle at the distance given by the Stixel World (lower row left), only 500 ROIs have to be checked, as shown on the right

2.2.3.2 Pedestrian Classification

Classification in the near range will be explained on the basis of pedestrian recognition. Each ROI from the previous system stage is classified by powerful multi-cue pedestrian classifiers. It is beneficial to use a Mixture-of-Experts scheme that operates on a diverse set of image features and modalities as inspired by Enzweiler and Gavrila (2011). In particular, they suggest to couple gradient-based features such as histograms of oriented gradients (HoG) (see Dalal and Triggs (2005)) with texture-based features such as local binary patterns (LBP) or local receptive fields (LRF) (see Wöhler and Anlauf (1999)). Furthermore, all features operate on both gray-level intensity and dense disparity images to fully exploit the orthogonal characteristics of both modalities, as shown in Figure 2.13. Classification is done using linear support vector machines. Multiple classifier responses at similar locations and scales are fused to a single detection by applying mean-shift-based nonmaximum suppression to the individual detections. For classifier training, the *Daimler Multi-Cue Pedestrian Classification Benchmark* has been made publicly available (see Enzweiler et al. (2010)).

The ROC curves shown in Figure 2.14 reveal that the additional depth cue leads to a reduction of the false-positive rate by a factor of five or an improvement of the detection rate up to 10%.

What is the best operating point? How many pedestrians can be recognized by the classifier? Interestingly, the answers to these questions depend on whether you want to realize a driver assistance system or an Autonomous Vehicle. For an autonomous emergency braking system, you might probably select an operating point far on the left of the ROC curve such that your system will nearly never show a false reaction

Figure 2.13 Intensity and depth images with corresponding gradient magnitude for pedestrian (top) and nonpedestrian (bottom) samples. Note the distinct features that are unique to each modality, for example, the high-contrast pedestrian texture due to clothing in the gray-level image compared to the rather uniform disparity in the same region. The additional exploitation of depth can reduce the false-positive rate significantly. In Enzweiler et al. (2010), an improvement by a factor of five was achieved

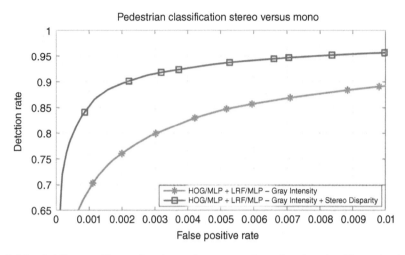

Figure 2.14 ROC curve illustrating the performance of a pedestrian classifier using intensity only (red) versus a classifier additionally exploiting depth (blue). The depth cue reduces the false-positive rate by a factor of five

but still has the potential of saving many lives. For an Autonomous Car, you must ensure that it will never hit a person that it could detect. So you have to accept much more false positives in order to reach the highest possible detection rate. Hopefully, the fusion module as well as the behavior control will be able to manage the problem of many false-positive detections.

The sketched system is highly efficient and powerful at the same time. However, the limited field of view of the used stereo system prohibits the recognition of pedestrians while turning at urban intersections. We used the wide-angled camera installed for traffic light recognition to check for pedestrians in those situations. Traffic light recognition was switched off and an unconstrained pedestrian search process was performed in those situations.

2.2.3.3 Vehicle Detection

For vision-based vehicle detection in the near range, a similar system concept as outlined earlier for pedestrian recognition including Stixel-based ROI generation can be used. However, the high relative velocities of approaching vehicles require a much larger operating range of the vehicle detection module than what is needed for pedestrian recognition. For Autonomous Driving in cities, it is desirable to detect and track oncoming vehicles at distances larger than 120 m (equivalent to 4 seconds look ahead in city traffic) (see Figure 2.15). For highway applications, one aims at distances of 200 m to complement active sensors over their entire measurement range.

Since one cannot apply stereo-based ROI generation for the long range, it has to be replaced by a fast monocular vehicle detector, that is, a Viola–Jones cascade detector

Figure 2.15   Full-range (0–200 m) vehicle detection and tracking example in an urban scenario. Green bars indicate the detector confidence level

(see Viola and Jones (2001b)). Since its main purpose is to create regions of interest for a subsequent strong classifier described earlier, one can easily tolerate the inferior detection performance of the Viola–Jones cascade framework compared to the state of the art and exploit its unrivaled speed.

Precise distance and velocity estimation of detected vehicles throughout the full distance range pose extreme demands on the accuracy of stereo matching as well as on camera calibration. In order to obtain optimal disparity estimates, one can perform an additional careful correlation analysis on the detected object. Pinggera et al. (2013) show that an EM-based multi-cue segmentation framework is able to give a sub-pixel accuracy of 0.1 px and allows precise tracking of vehicles 200 m in front.

2.2.3.4   Traffic Light Recognition

Common Stereo Vision systems obey viewing angles within the range of 40°–60°. However, stopping at a European traffic light requires a viewing angle of up to 120° to see the relevant light signal right in front of the vehicle. At the same time, a comfortable reaction to red traffic lights on rural roads calls for a high image resolution. For example, in case of approaching a traffic light at 70 km/h, the car should react at a distance of about 80 m, which implies a first detection at about 100 m distance. In this case, given a resolution of 20 px/°, the illuminated part of the traffic light is about 2×2 px, which is the absolute minimum for classification. For practical reasons, a 4 MP color imager and a lens with a horizontal viewing angle of approximately 90° were chosen in the experiments presented here as a compromise between performance and computational burden.

Traffic light recognition involves three main tasks: detection, classification, and selection of the relevant light at complex intersections. If the 3D positions of the traffic lights are stored in the map, the region of interest can easily be determined in order to guide the search. Although color information delivered by the sensor helps in this step, it is not sufficient to solve the problem reliably.

Figure 2.16 Examples of hard to recognize traffic lights. Note that these examples do not even represent the worst visibility conditions

The detected regions of interest are cropped and classified by means of a Neural Network classifier. Each classified traffic light is then tracked over time to improve the reliability of the interpretation (see Lindner et al. (2004) for details).

In practice, the classification task turns out to be more complex than one might expect. About 1/3 of the 155 traffic lights along the route from Mannheim to Pforzheim turned out to be hard to recognize. Some examples are shown in Figure 2.16. Red lights in particular are very challenging due to their low brightness. One reason for this bad visibility is the strong directional characteristic of the lights. Lights above the road are well visible at larger distances while they become invisible when getting closer. Even the lights on the right side, which one should concentrate on when getting closer, can become nearly invisible in case of a direct stop at a red light. In these cases, traffic light change detection monitoring the switching between red and green is more efficient than classification.

2.2.3.5 Discussion

The recognition of geometrically well-behaved objects such as pedestrians or vehicles is a well-investigated topic (see Dollár et al. (2012), Gerónimo et al. (2010), and Sivaraman and Trivedi (2013)). Since most approaches rely on learning-based methods, system performance is largely dominated by two aspects: the training data set and the feature set used.

Regarding training data, an obvious conclusion is that performance scales with the amount of data available. Munder and Gavrila, for instance, have reported that classification errors are reduced by approximately a factor of two, whenever the training set size is doubled (see Munder and Gavrila (2006)). Similar beneficial effects arise from adding modalities other than gray-level imagery to the training set, for example, depth or motion information from dense stereo and dense optical flow (see Enzweiler and Gavrila (2011) and Walk et al. (2010)).

Given the same training data, the recognition quality significantly depends on the feature set used. For some years now, there has been a trend emerging that involves a steady shift from nonadaptive features such as Haar wavelets or HoGs toward learned features that are able to adapt to the data. This shift does not only result in better recognition performance in most cases, but it is also a necessity in order to be able to derive generic models that are not (hand-) tuned to a specific object class, but can represent multiple object classes with a single shared feature set. In this regard, deep convolutional neural networks (CNNs) represent one very promising line of research. The combination of such CNNs with huge data sets involving thousands of different object classes and lots of computational power has demonstrated outstanding multi-class recognition performance, for example, see Krizhevsky et al. (2012). Yet, much more research is necessary in order to fully understand all aspects of such complex neural network models and to realize their full potential.

A remaining problem with most object recognition approaches is that they are very restrictive from a geometric point of view. Objects are typically described using an axis-aligned bounding box of a constant aspect ratio. In sliding-window detectors, for example, the scene content is represented very concisely as a set of individually detected objects. However, the generalization to partial occlusion cases, object groups, or geometrically poorly-defined classes, such as road surfaces or buildings, is difficult. This generalization is an essential step to move from detecting objects in isolation toward gaining a self-contained understanding of the whole scene. Possible solutions to this problem usually involve a relaxation of geometric constraints and overall less object-centric representations, as will be outlined in the next section.

2.3   Challenges

Bertha's vision system was intensively tested off-line and during about 6500 km of Autonomous Driving. The gained experience forced us to intensify our research on three topics, namely robustness, scene labeling, and intention recognition, in particular the intention of pedestrians.

2.3.1   Increasing Robustness

The built vision system delivers promising results in outdoor scenes, given suffi-cient light and good weather conditions. Unfortunately, they still suffer from adverse weather conditions. Similarly, the results deteriorate in low-light situations.

As mentioned in the discussion earlier, robustness can be improved if more informa-tion is included in the optimization process. As an example, we consider the disparity estimation task. When the windshield wiper is blocking the view (see Figure 2.17 left), stereo vision algorithms cannot correctly measure the disparity (see Figure 2.17

(a)   (b)

Figure 2.17 Two consecutive frames of a stereo image sequence (left). The disparity result obtained from a single image pair is shown in the second column from the right. It shows strong disparity errors due to the wiper blocking parts of one image. The result from temporal stereo is visually free of errors (right) (see Gehrig et al. (2014))

second from right). However, looking at the whole image sequence as opposed to only the current stereo pair, one can use previous stereo reconstructions and ego-motion information as a prior for the current stereo pair (see e.g., Gehrig et al. (2013)). This temporal stereo approach results in more stable and correct disparity maps. The improvement is exemplified in Figure 2.17 on the right. Since the temporal information just changes the data term of the SGM algorithm, the computational complexity does not increase much.

Similarly, more prior information can also be generated off-line by accurate statistics of typical disparity distributions from driver assistance scenarios. When using such simple information as a weak prior, one can already reduce the number of false-positive Stixels ("phantom objects") under rainy conditions by more than a factor of 2 while maintaining the detection rate (see Gehrig et al. (2014)).

Another option to increase robustness is confidence information. Most dense stereo algorithms deliver a disparity estimate for every pixel. Obviously, the confidence of this estimate may vary significantly from pixel to pixel. If a proper confidence measure that reflects how likely a measurement may be considered to be correct is available, this information can be exploited in subsequent processing steps. When using confidence information in the Stixel segmentation task, the false-positive rate can be reduced by a factor of six while maintaining almost the same detection rate (see Pfeiffer et al. (2013)).

2.3.2 Scene Labeling

A central challenge for Autonomous Driving is to capture relevant aspects of the surroundings and—even more important—reliably predict what is going to happen in the near future. For a detailed understanding of the environment, a multitude of different object classes needs to be distinguished. Objects of interest include traffic participants such as pedestrians, cyclists, and vehicles, as well as parts of the static infrastructure such as buildings, trees, beacons, fences, poles, and so on.

As already mentioned in the discussion, classical sliding window-based detectors do not scale up easily to many classes of varying size and shape, asking for novel generic methods that allow fast classification even for a large number of classes.

One way to approach the problem is scene labeling, where the task is to assign a class label to each pixel in the image. Recent progress in the field is driven by the use of super-pixels. Several of the current top-scoring methods encode and classify region proposals from bottom-up segmentations as opposed to small rectangular windows around each pixel in the image (see Russell et al. (2006)).

Furthermore, in terms of an integrated system architecture, it is "wise" to provide a generic medium-level representation of texture information, which is shared across all classes of interest, to avoid computational overhead. A suitable method for this is the bag-of-features approach, where local feature descriptors are extracted densely for each pixel in the image. Each descriptor is subsequently mapped to a previously learned representative by means of vector quantization, yielding a finite set of typical texture patterns. To encode an arbitrary region in the image, a histogram of the contained representatives is built, which can finally be classified to obtain the object class of the region.

Any super-pixel approach can provide the required proposal regions, while recent work shows that the Stixel representation is a well-suited basis for efficient scene labeling of outdoor traffic (see Scharwächter et al. (2013)). Proposal regions can be generated rapidly by grouping neighboring Stixels with similar depth.

Stereo information not only helps to provide good proposal regions but can also be used to improve classification. In addition to representative texture patterns, the distribution of typical depth patterns can be used as an additional channel of information yielding bag-of-depth features.

In Figure 2.18, a scene labeling result is shown together with the corresponding stereo matching result and the Stixel representation. Stixel-based region candidates are classified into one of five classes: ground plane, vehicle, pedestrian, building, and

Figure 2.18 Scene labeling pipeline: input image (a), SGM stereo result (b), Stixel representation (d), and the scene labeling result (c)

sky. Color encodes the detected class label. This example does not exploit the color information. However, if classes like "tree," "grass," or "water" are of interest, color plays an important role and can easily be added to the classification chain.

2.3.3   Intention Recognition

Video-based pedestrian detection has seen significant progress over the last decade and recently culminated in the market introduction of active pedestrian systems that can perform automatic braking in case of dangerous traffic situations. However, systems currently employed in vehicles are rather conservative in their warning and control strategy, emphasizing the current pedestrian state (i.e., position and motion) rather than prediction to avoid false system activations. Moving toward Autonomous Driving, warnings will not suffice and emergency braking should still be the last option. Future situation assessment requires an exact prediction of the pedestrian's path, for example, to reduce speed when a pedestrian is crossing in front of the vehicle.

Pedestrian path prediction is a challenging problem due to the highly dynamic nature of their motion. Pedestrians can change their walking direction in an instant or start/stop walking abruptly. The systems presented until now only react to changes in pedestrian dynamics and are outperformed by humans (see Keller and Gavrila (2014)) who can anticipate changes in pedestrian behavior before they happen. As shown in Schmidt and Färber (2009), predictions by humans rely on more information than pedestrian dynamics only. Thus, humans are able to differentiate between a pedestrian that is aware of an approaching vehicle and one that is not and use this additional context information. As a consequence, humans are able to predict that a pedestrian aware of the vehicle will probably not continue on a collision course but rather stop or change walking speed. A system relying only on previously observed dynamics will predict that the pedestrian will continue to walk until it observes otherwise.

Future systems for pedestrian path prediction will need to anticipate changes in behavior before they happen and, thus, use context information, just like humans. For example, the motion of the pedestrian when approaching the curb is decisive. Work presented in Flohr et al. (2014) already goes in this direction by additionally estimating head and body orientations of pedestrians from a moving vehicle. Figure 2.19 shows that the resolution of imagers commercially used today is sufficient to determine the pose of the pedestrian. Further work will need to focus on integrating situational awareness (and other context information) into pedestrian path prediction.

2.4   Summary

When will the first Autonomous Vehicle be commercially available? Will it be capable of autonomous parking or Autonomous Driving on highways?

Figure 2.19 Will the pedestrian cross? Head and body orientation of a pedestrian can be estimated from onboard cameras of a moving vehicle. 90° means motion to the left (body), 0° is toward the camera (head)

If you like to have a level 2 system, you can find them already on the market. If you think of a real level 3 system that allows you to forget the driving task on the highway for a while, there is no answer today. But at least three big questions: Can we guarantee that our car can manage every unexpected situation safely? How can we prove the reliability of the complete system if we have to guarantee an error rate of less than 10^{-7} per hour? Can we realize such a system including highly sophisticated sensors and super-reliable fail-safe hardware for a reasonable price that people are willing to pay?

If we cannot answer all these questions positively at the present moment, we could think of alternative introduction strategies. If speed turns out to be the key problem, an automation of traffic jam driving might be a way out of the dilemma. Lower speeds limit the risk of serious hazards and would probably require less sensor redundancy such that the system could be made available at a lower price.

Nevertheless, I do not doubt that Autonomous Driving will become part of our lives in the foreseeable future. People are asking for this possibility as they want to use their time in the car for business and entertainment. Authorities are asking for this mode because they are hoping for fewer accidents. International regulations like the Vienna Convention on Road Traffic have recently been changed to allow Autonomous Driving.

While the DARPA Urban Challenge was dominated by laser scanners and radars, recent research shows that computer vision has matured and become indispensable for Scene Understanding. There is no other sensor that can be used to answer the multitude of questions arising in complex urban traffic. Modern stereo vision delivers precise and complete 3D data with high spatial resolution in real time. Super-pixels like Stixels allow for efficient globally optimal Scene Understanding. Thanks to progress in machine learning and increased computational power on FPGAs and graphical processing units, relevant objects can be detected fast and reliably.

However, there are still important aspects requiring further research.

- It is questionable whether precise localization and feature maps are really necessary for Autonomous Driving. It would be beneficial if a standard map was sufficient to plan the route and to extract all other information from the observed scene. Recent work in Zhang et al. (2013) raises hope that this can be achieved.
- In urban traffic, relevant objects are often partially occluded by other objects or traffic participants. Using the context might help to improve the performance and get closer to the excellence of human vision.
- The field of view of common stereo vision systems is sufficient for highway driving only. In cities we need multicamera systems or significantly higher resolution of automotive compliant imagers. The necessary computational power will become available, thanks to the ongoing progress in consumer electronics.
- An Autonomous Car must be able to stop in front of any obstacle that can cause serious harm. As this requirement limits its maximum speed, the early detection of small objects on the road requires particular attention.

During the last years, deep convolutional neural networks (DCNNs) have shown impressive results in classification benchmarks (see Krizhevsky et al. (2012)). Very recently, a new approach was presented in Szegedy et al. (2013), which does not only classify but also precisely localizes objects of various classes in images. The future will reveal whether these new techniques making use of the available big data will lead to a revolution of computer vision for autonomous vehicles.

Remember, just 25 years ago, researchers started putting cameras and huge computer systems into cars. None of them expected the progress that has been achieved in the meantime. This raises optimism that image understanding will get closer and closer to human visual perception in the future, allowing for Autonomous Driving not only on simply structured highways but also in complex urban environments.

Acknowledgments

The author thanks Markus Enzweiler, Stefan Gehrig, Henning Lategahn, Carsten Knöppel, David Pfeiffer, and Markus Schreiber for their contributions to this chapter.

3

Computer Vision for MAVs

Friedrich Fraundorfer
Institute for Computer Graphics and Vision, Graz University of Technology, Graz, Austria

3.1 Introduction

This chapter discusses recent advances in the use of computer vision for the control of micro aerial vehicles (MAVs). The term MAV typically denotes a class of small-scale unmanned aerial vehicles like multirotor helicopters, for example, a quadrotor helicopter. Figure 3.1 shows such an MAV equipped with digital cameras for control and 3D mapping.

MAVs have a big potential to be used in a various number of applications, for example, search–and-rescue scenario, surveillance, industrial inspection, delivery services, and so on. MAVs can carry a variety of sensors; however, the small scale imposes a strict weight limit. Almost all types of MAVs, however, are able to carry a digital camera and this makes it possible for them to take aerial images or, in general, images from vantage points not reachable otherwise. Already this capability enables an immense variety of applications. Piloting an MAV, however, takes a lot of training and requires constant attention of the pilot. It also requires that the MAV operates within the line of sight. These limitations can be overcome by an autopilot system with the main task of keeping the MAV hovering on a spot. In outdoor environments, this can be achieved using GPS; however, a MAV operating indoors cannot rely on GPS and needs an alternative sensor for the autopilot system. Lately, onboard cameras have been successfully used within such an autopilot system. Computer vision algorithms compute the ego-motion of the MAV from camera images, in most cases then these measurements are fused with measurements of inertial measurement

Computer Vision in Vehicle Technology: Land, Sea, and Air, First Edition.
Edited by Antonio M. López, Atsushi Imiya, Tomas Pajdla and Jose M. Álvarez.
© 2017 John Wiley & Sons Ltd. Published 2017 by John Wiley & Sons Ltd.

Figure 3.1   A micro aerial vehicle (MAV) equipped with digital cameras for control and environment mapping. The depicted MAV has been developed within the SFLY project (see Scaramuzza et al. 2014)

units and used in a control loop to hover the MAV. To achieve these results, some serious challenges have had to be overcome:

• Limited onboard processing power for image processing;
• High frame rate for control is necessary;
• High reliability;
• Ego-motion estimation from a single camera cannot measure metric scale.

A main insight has been that fusing inertial measurement unit (IMU) and camera-based measurements allows for robust and efficient ego-motion estimation algorithms.

In addition to ego-motion estimation, the camera images can also be used for environment sensing and interpretation. From camera images, it is possible to compute a 3D map of the environment that can be used for autonomous navigation and exploration. Having the ability to map the environment in 3D allows collision-free navigation and is a prerequisite for autonomous operation of the MAV. In the following, computer vision methods for MAV control, 3D mapping, autonomous navigation, and scene interpretation are introduced and discussed.

In a number of publications, the astounding flight performances of MAVs have been demonstrated, ranging from acrobatics to fast and dynamic maneuvers (see Mellinger et al. (2011, 2010), Michael et al. (2010a), Mueller et al. (2011), and Schoellig et al.

(2010)). However, until now, these impressive performances could only be performed within a specially instrumented area (see Lupashin et al. (2011) and Michael et al. (2010b)) where a tracking system (typically cameras observing markers on the MAVs) computes the exact position and orientation of the MAV from outside. Systems with onboard sensors are far from reaching these performance parameters. Naturally, MAV control using onboard sensors is a heavily researched area, with the goal to achieve the aforementioned capabilities with onboard sensors. This research not only is limited to digital cameras as onboard sensors but also includes the use of laser range-finder, depth cameras, or combinations of different sensors (see Achtelik et al. (2009, 2011), Ahrens et al. (2009), Bachrach et al. (2009), Bills et al. (2011a), Bloesch et al. (2010), Eberli et al. (2011), Engel et al. (2014), Forster et al. (2014b), Grzonka et al. (2012), Herisse et al. (2008), Hrabar et al. (2005), Klose et al. (2010), Loianno and Kumar (2014), Nieuwenhuisen et al. (2015), Shen et al. (2011, 2012, 2013a), Yang et al. (2014), Zingg et al. (2010), and Zufferey and Floreano (2006)).

3.2 System and Sensors

This section gives a brief overview of system design and sensors of a MAV. The system design described is from the Pixhawk MAV platform (see Meier et al. (2012)), but it is exemplary for many other MAV platforms, for example, see Achtelik et al. (2011), Scaramuzza et al. (2014), and Schmid et al. (2014). The system design is illustrated in Figure 3.2. A main characteristic is the existence of a low-level processing unit for flight control and a high-level processing unit for image processing and high-level tasks (e.g., path planning). The main task of the low-level processing unit is state estimation and control. State estimation has to run with high update rates and takes the measurements of IMU, digital compass, and visual pose as input. An attitude controller and pose controller use these measurements to steer the motors. State estimation and control have to run in real time; thus, it is implemented directly on a microcontroller. Detailed information about the low-level control process can be found in Bouabdallah et al. (2004) and Mahony et al. (2012).

Image processing and high-level tasks, however, need a powerful onboard computer; thus, the MAV is also equipped with a standard, but small scale, Linux computer. These computers run image processing, visual localization, obstacle detection, mapping, and path planning onboard the MAV.

The visual localization module computes the full 6-DOF pose of the MAV. The visual pose is fed to the state estimator for position control. The stereo processing module computes real-time disparity maps from the front-looking stereo pair, which are used by the visual localization module as well as the mapping module.

The minimal sensor set of a MAV comprises an IMU consisting of three-axis accelerometers and three-axis gyroscopes. This IMU can track the attitude of the MAV that is used for attitude control. A digital compass and a barometric pressure sensor are typically used to keep a constant heading and a constant height. For

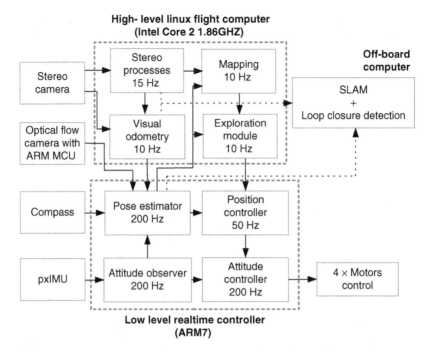

Figure 3.2 The system diagram of the autonomous Pixhawk MAV using a stereo system and an optical flow camera as main sensors

position control that is necessary for automatic hovering and any kind of automatic navigation, a sensor capable of full 6-DOF pose measurements is necessary, which in this case is solved using digital cameras.

3.3 Ego-Motion Estimation

In most approaches, ego-motion estimation is achieved by fusing information from an IMU with visual measurements similar to the work in Scaramuzza et al. (2014). By means of sensor fusion, the pose of the MAV can be computed reliably at high update rates. Visual measurements are essential in this process, as the integration of inertial measurements would accumulate large drifts otherwise.

3.3.1 State Estimation Using Inertial and Vision Measurements

State estimation is a filtering approach using an extended Kalman filter (EKF) for fusing inertial and vision measurements. The inputs for the state estimator are rotational velocities and accelerations from gyroscopes and accelerometers of the IMU at high update rates and camera poses at low update rates. Figure 3.3 illustrates the state estimation process. Camera poses are represented by a 6-DOF transformation consisting of three rotational parameters and three translational parameters and

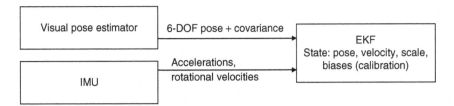

Figure 3.3 The state estimation work flow for a loosely coupled visual-inertial fusion scheme

need to include the uncertainty of the measurement. Depending on the visual pose estimator (monocular, stereo vision), the camera poses could include an unknown scale factor. The IMU measurements consist of three parameters for the rotational velocities and three parameters for the accelerations. The state of the EKF contains the vehicle pose, the scale factor, and biases of the IMU. For state estimation, the vehicle state is propagated forward in time using the high-rate IMU measurements. When a vision measurement becomes available (at low update rates), an EKF update step is performed using the vision pose.

3.3.1.1 Sensor Model

The vehicle pose is represented by the pose of the IMU within the world coordinate frame. The camera sensor is the offset of the IMU coordinate frame by a rotation and translation. This transformation can be computed by a calibration step or it can be included in the state estimation. Figure 3.4 illustrates the different coordinate systems. The IMU measures the angular velocity around each of the three-axis ω_m and the acceleration in each of the three-axis a_m. These measurements are perturbed by noise and contain a bias. The real angular velocity of the system is denoted by ω, and the real acceleration by a. The quantities are modeled by

$$\omega = \omega_m - b_\omega - n_\omega \tag{3.1}$$

$$a = a_m - b_a - n_a \tag{3.2}$$

b_ω and b_a are the biases for the angular velocity and the accelerations, respectively. n_ω and n_a are the noise parameters modeled as additive white Gaussian noise. The biases are nonstatic and are included in the state to be estimated. The noise parameters typically can be taken from the sensor data sheet.

3.3.1.2 State Representation and EKF Filtering

The vehicle state consists of the following necessary parameters:

$$x = \{p_w^i, v_w^i, q_w^i, b_\omega, b_a, \lambda, p_i^c, q_i^c\} \tag{3.3}$$

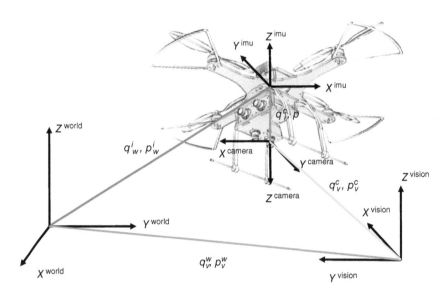

Figure 3.4 A depiction of the involved coordinate systems for the visual-inertial state estimation

- p_w^i: This parameter represents the vehicle's position (i.e., IMU position) in the world coordinate system. It consists of three parameters (x, y, z position).
- v_w^i: This parameter represents the vehicles' velocity. It consists of three parameters, that is, the speeds of all the three axes.
- q_w^i: This parameter represents the vehicles' orientation within the world coordinate system described by a rotation. The world coordinate system typically is chosen to be aligned with the gravity vector.
- b_ω: This parameter is the bias for the gyroscopes and is represented as a three-vector.
- b_a: This parameter is the bias for the accelerometers and is represented as a three-vector.
- λ: This parameter represents the scale factor between the IMU and the camera measurements. If the camera measurements are already in metric scale (e.g., when using a stereo system), then this parameter will converge to 1 (or can be omitted from the state). However, when using a monocular camera system, ego-motion can only be estimated up to an unknown scale factor, which is then represented by λ.
- p_i^c: This parameter represents the translational offset between camera sensor and IMU. When computed by a pre-calibration step, this parameter can be omitted from the state vector.

- p_i^c: This parameter represents the rotational offset between camera sensor and IMU. When computed by a pre-calibration step, this parameter can be omitted from the state vector.

The state transition model of the EKF is used without control input and is defined as

$$x_k = f(x_{k-1}) + w_{k-1} \tag{3.4}$$

The observation model is defined as

$$z_k = h(x_k) + v_k \tag{3.5}$$

The current vehicle state x_k and its uncertainties P_k will be propagated forward in time using inertial measurements of high update rate. On availability of a vision measurement, the vehicle state and its uncertainties will be updated.

The state propagation needs two steps:

1. Propagate state variables $\hat{x}_{k|k-1} = f(\hat{x}_{k-1|k-1})$.
2. Propagate the state covariance matrix $P_{k|k-1} = F_{k-1}P_{k-1|k-1}F_{k-1}^T + Q_{k-1}$.

F_{k-1} is the Jacobian of the state transition function and H_k is the Jacobian of the observation function.

The state transition function f is explained as follows. The new position $p_w^i, k|k-1$ is calculated by adding the doubly integrated accelerations to the current position, and the new orientation $q_w^i, k|k-1$ is calculated by adding the integrated rotational velocities to the current orientation. The biases, scale, and calibration parameters are kept constant in the prediction step. For detailed derivation of F_{k-1} and Q_{k-1}, the reader is referred to Weiss and Siegwart (2011).

On the availability of a visual pose estimate with position p_v^c and orientation q_v^c and its covariances, the filter update consisting of two steps can be carried out:

1. Update state estimate
2. Update covariance estimate.

For the detailed update equations, the reader is referred to Weiss and Siegwart (2011).

Please note that the observation process assumes that the vision system is able to directly observe the 6-DOF full pose. In addition, this means that any computer vision algorithm that delivers a pose estimate plus its uncertainties can be used for the filtering process. In the following sections, three different vision algorithms will be explained that already have been used successfully for the control of a MAV.

3.3.2   MAV Pose from Monocular Vision

It is a fundamental property of computer vision that from multiple images of a scene it is possible to compute a 3D reconstruction of the scene and also to compute the position and orientation of the cameras at the same time. This method is known as structure from motion (SfM) and is also often called Visual SLAM (simultaneous localization and mapping) within the robotics community. By attaching a camera to a MAV, it is therefore possible to keep track of the MAV movements by computing the camera poses using such an algorithm. If one is only interested in the camera poses, such an algorithm is often referred to as visual odometry. A well-known implementation of such an algorithm that also works for high frame rates is the parallel tracking and mapping (PTAM) method (see Klein and Murray (2007)). The basic idea behind such a method is that tracked feature points get triangulated in 3D. For a new camera, image feature points are matched with the so far triangulated 3D points and the camera pose is computed from 3D to 2D point correspondences. Afterwards, bundle adjustment is performed for accuracy and new features get triangulated in 3D. The detailed steps are as follows:

1. Capture two images I_{k-2}, I_{k-1}.
2. Extract and match features between them.
3. Triangulate features from I_{k-2}, I_{k-1}.
4. Capture new image I_k.
5. Extract features and match with previous frame I_{k-1}.
6. Compute camera pose from 3D to 2D matches using the PnP algorithm and RANSAC as a robust estimator.
7. Refine camera pose and 3D points with bundle adjustment.
8. Triangulate all new feature matches between I_k and I_{k-1}.
9. Repeat at step 4.

For the details of the different steps, the reader is referred to Scaramuzza and Fraundorfer (2011)

It is possible to run such an inherently complex algorithm on a low-power computer onboard of an MAV if certain criteria are met. First, robust feature matching between images can be very computationally complex; however, for the case of high frame rate cameras, the feature matching step can be significantly accelerated. For real-time frame rates of about 30 frames per second, the motion between two images is small, which means that image features almost have the same coordinates for a neighboring image pair. In such a case, it is possible to refrain from computing a feature descriptor at all and perform feature matching as a nearest neighbor matching of image coordinates. If in addition a fast feature detector, for example, FAST corners, is used, then the feature detection and matching step can be carried out very fast. Second, it is actually possible to skip the pose estimation from 3D to 2D point correspondences and instead compute the pose by bundle adjustment directly. For real-time frame rates, the camera pose for bundle adjustment can be initialized by the previous camera pose or in particular for MAVs with the propagated pose from the state estimator.

By using a robust cost function in bundle adjustment, outliers can be removed as well. Third, the computational complexity of bundle adjustment would increase with increasing number of 3D points and camera poses. By keeping only the last n frames and 3D points within these frames, the runtime can be kept constant. In Achtelik et al. (2011), an algorithm following these principles was able to compute the pose of an MAV with 30 frames per second and has successfully been used to control the MAV.

However, monocular visual odometry has a significant drawback. The metric scale of the camera position cannot be computed. It is therefore necessary to calibrate the scale upon initialization with a pattern with known metric scale (e.g., a checkerboard) or to estimate the metric scale by fusion with inertial sensors. In addition, the scale estimate also is prone to drift. These problems can be alleviated using a stereo vision system.

3.3.3   MAV Pose from Stereo Vision

The big advantage of stereo vision is that the metric scale of camera poses and 3D points can be computed directly. This means that scale drift as present in a monocular system cannot happen. And in particular for the case of state estimation, it makes the inclusion of a scale factor in the MAV state unnecessary. Furthermore, the triangulation of 3D points always happens from two precisely pre-calibrated image frames. Camera pose from stereo vision can be computed either from 3D to 3D correspondences or 3D to 2D correspondences. The 3D–2D methods recently gained a lot of popularity and is therefore described here. For the 3D–3D method, the reader is referred to Scaramuzza and Fraundorfer (2011).

The basic outline of the 3D–2D method is to use the PnP algorithm to compute camera pose from 3D to 2D correspondences. 3D points are triangulated from each stereo image pair. To compute the current pose, feature matching is performed between one image of the current stereo image pair and one image of the previous stereo image pair. The PnP algorithm is then used to compute the camera pose from corresponding 2D feature points of the current stereo image pair and 3D points from the previous stereo image pair (Figures 3.5 and 3.6).

1. Capture a stereo image pair $I_{l,k-1}$, $I_{r,k-1}$.
2. Extract, match, and triangulate features between $I_{l,k-1}$, $I_{r,k-1}$.
3. Capture new stereo image pair $I_{l,k}$, $I_{r,k}$.
4. Extract features and match between $I_{l,k-1}$ and $I_{l,k}$.
5. Compute camera pose from 3D to 2D matches using the PnP algorithm and random sample consensus (RANSAC) as a robust estimator.
6. Refine camera pose and 3D points with bundle adjustment.
7. Triangulate all new feature matches from stereo image pair $I_{l,k}$, $I_{r,k}$.
8. Repeat at step 3.

Stereo vision processing adds additional computational complexity to the pose estimation process. It is necessary to create matches between the left and right images of the stereo pair and between the current and previous image pair. However,

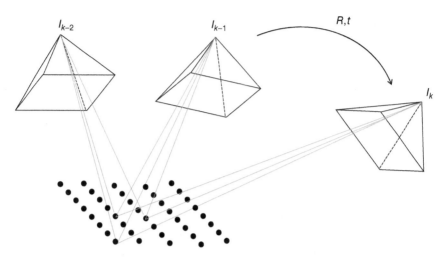

Figure 3.5 Illustration of monocular pose estimation. The new camera pose is computed from 3D points triangulated from at least two subsequent images

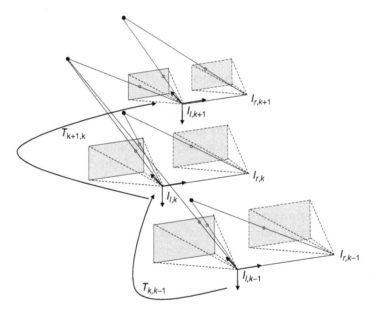

Figure 3.6 Illustration of stereo pose estimation. At each time index, 3D points can be computed from the left and right images of the stereo pair. The new camera pose can be computed directly from the 3D points triangulated from the previous stereo pair

feature matching between the left and right images can be done very efficiently as the camera poses are fixed and pre-calibrated. The corresponding feature needs to lie on the epipolar line and the search for a feature correspondence can be restricted to this epipolar line. Stereo processing, however, has been shown to run in real time on dedicated hardware (e.g., FPGAs; see Schmid et al. (2014)), freeing the main computer from the low-level vision tasks.

The described method is not limited to stereo systems but can be utilized for any RGBD sensor system, that is, a sensor that captures depth (D) and a camera image (RGB). A popular example for such a sensor is the Kinect sensor. Currently, a wide variety of RGBD sensors are developed, and all of these sensors will work as well with the above-described algorithm.

3.3.4   MAV Pose from Optical Flow Measurements

The use of optical flow for controlling MAVs has been popularized with the appearance of Parrot's AR Drone. The AR Drone comes with a position control mechanism based on optical flow (see Bristeau et al. (2011)), which allows it to hover stable on the spot when there is no user input. The main benefits of using the optical flow algorithm for pose estimation are the possibility to achieve very high update rates (e.g., $>100\,\text{Hz}$) and that it can easily be implemented on resource-limited embedded controllers. However, the algorithm comes with some limiting assumptions. The optical flow algorithm measures pixel-shift in the image plane. If the image plane is, for example, parallel to the ground plane, the observed pixel-shift is proportional to the camera motion. If the distance between camera and ground plane gets measured (e.g., by an ultrasound sensor), the pixel-shift can be translated into metric camera movements. To disambiguate optical flow that gets introduced from rotational motion and translational motion, IMU measurements can be used to correct for the rotational part. Necessary components for such a metric optical flow sensor are a camera sensor, a distance sensor (e.g., ultrasound or infrared) and a three-axis gyroscope. The images for the camera sensors are used to compute x and y pixel-shifts using the optical flow algorithm. The distance sensor is used to measure the distance between the camera and the world plane that induces the optical flow to translate the pixel-shifts into metric shifts. Furthermore, the distance sensor is used to track changes in the z-direction (height). The gyroscope is used to measure rotational velocity of the sensor between two image frames. In this way, the rotationally induced part of the optical flow can be computed and subtracted from the measured optical flow. The camera movement (translation) can be computed from the remaining metric optical flow and distance measurements in metric units. The mathematical relation is given in Eq. (3.6). The metric translation of the camera (i.e., the translation of the MAV) is denoted by $\mathbf{t} = [t_x, t_y, t_z]^T$, where the movements are in x, y, and z directions. Eq. (3.6) gives the relation of how to compute $\mathbf{t}$ from the measured optical flow between two images I_0, I_1, the measured rotation between two images and the measured depths. The rotation between two images is measured by the gyroscopes and denoted by the 3×3 rotation matrix $\mathbf{R}$. $\Delta\mathbf{x} = [\Delta x, \Delta y, 0]^T$ is the measured optical flow between the two images in pixels. $\mathbf{x_0} = [x_0, y_0, 1]^T$ is the image coordinate of the location in image I_0 for which the optical flow has been computed. d_0, d_1 are the distance measurements in meters to the ground plane for the images I_0, I_1, respectively, and f is the focal length of the camera in pixels.

$$\mathbf{t} = -\frac{d_1}{f}\mathbf{R}\Delta\mathbf{x} + \frac{d_0}{f}\mathbf{x_0} - \frac{d_1}{f}\mathbf{Rx_0} \tag{3.6}$$

Equation (3.6) can be derived from the simple equation for optical flow given by Eq. (3.7) and substituting the quantities $\mathbf{x_1}$ and $\mathbf{x_0}$ with the terms of Eqs (3.8) and (3.9). Equations (3.8) and (3.9) describe the camera projection of a 3D point before and after the movement of the camera with rotation $\mathbf{R}$ and translation $\mathbf{t}$.

$$\Delta\mathbf{x} = \mathbf{x_1} - \mathbf{x_0} \tag{3.7}$$

$$\mathbf{x_0} = \mathbf{P_0 X} = \frac{f}{d_0}\mathbf{X} \tag{3.8}$$

$$\mathbf{x_1} = \mathbf{P_1 X} = \frac{f}{d_1}(\mathbf{R}^T\mathbf{X} - \mathbf{R}^T\mathbf{t}) \tag{3.9}$$

The geometric relations and quantities used in the derivation are illustrated in Figure 3.7.

Equation (3.6) describes how to compute $\mathbf{t}$ for one image location and the optical flow. In practice, multiple flow vectors within an image are computed (e.g., by KLT feature tracking), which gives rise to multiple estimates of $\mathbf{t}$, which can be averages for robustness. The algorithm can now be summarized as follows:

1. Compute optical flow between consecutive images I_0, I_1 using the KLT method (see Shi and Tomasi (1994)).

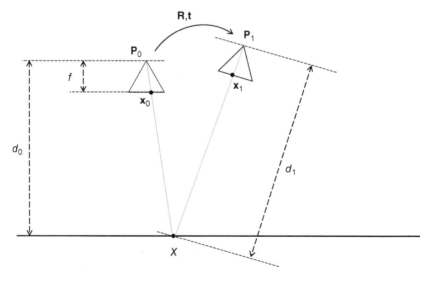

Figure 3.7 Concept of the optical flow sensor depicting the geometric relations used to compute metric optical flow

Figure 3.8   The PX4Flow sensor to compute MAV movements using the optical flow principle. It consists of a digital camera, gyroscopes, a range sensor, and an embedded processor for image processing

2. Measure distances d_0, d_1 with distance sensor.
3. Measure rotation matrix **R** with gyroscopes.
4. Compute **t** using Eq. (3.6).

To achieve the high update rates needed for MAV control, two suggestions can be followed. First, by using a low-resolution camera (e.g., 64×64), a high image capture rate can be achieved. This could, for instance, be done by turning on hardware binning on a standard VGA camera, which will reduce the resolution but increase the image capture rate. Together with a low resolution, a zoom lens is suggested such that small details on the ground plane can be resolved for better feature tracking. Second, by computing KLT feature tracks only for a fixed number of image locations defined on a grid, the computations for the feature detection part of KLT can be avoided and the number of computations will stay constant.

These ideas are actually implemented in the PX4Flow sensor depicted in Figure 3.8. The PX4Flow sensor computes metric optical flow as described earlier. For this, the sensor is equipped with a camera, gyroscopes, an ultrasound ranging device, and an ARM processor that performs the optical flow computation. The PX4Flow sensor is described in detail in Honegger et al. (2013).

3.4   3D Mapping

3D mapping, that is, the generation of 3D data from images, is one of the most prominent tasks for MAVs. MAVs provide unique vantage points for digital cameras as compared to street-level images and traditional aerial images. For building reconstruction in urban scenarios, images can be taken from very close to the building. Images can be taken facing straight down (called nadir images), looking at the facades directly or from general oblique directions at low heights. This however results in nonuniform flight patterns in contrast to the typical regularly sampled grids used in aerial imaging. Computer vision systems that generate 3D data from image sets are known under the term SfM systems. These systems can also be used to process image data taken by MAVs. However, by working only on the image data, these systems neglect the additional information provided by the sensors onboard of the MAV that are used for MAV control. These sensors can be used to improve quality and efficiency of SfM systems in a number of ways.

Figure 3.9 shows the basic building steps that are common to most SfM systems. Depicted by the arrows from the right side are the additional sensor measurements available from the MAV that can be used to improve the individual steps.

In the feature extraction step, a lot of computational power is used to extract viewpoint, scale, and orientation-invariant features and descriptors. Such an invariance, however, can also be achieved by using IMU measurements from the MAV. For the case of a downward-looking camera, the viewpoint invariance can be achieved by aligning all images with the earth's gravity normal. The deviation of the MAV from this normal is measured by the MAV's IMU. The images can be pre-rotated such that all the image planes are parallel, thus removing viewpoint changes. The remaining rotation invariance to the yaw angle can be achieved by utilizing the MAV's absolute compass measurements and by applying an in-plane rotation. Finally, scale invariance can be achieved by measuring the height over ground with the MAV's pressure sensor and correcting for this scale change. After this pre-processing,

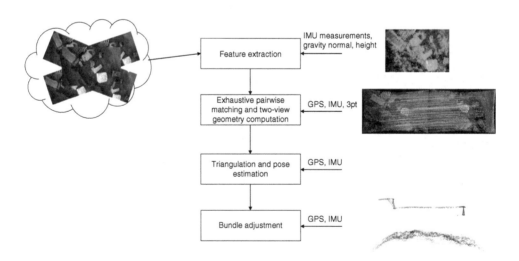

Figure 3.9 The different steps of a typical structure from motion (SfM) pipeline to compute 3D data from image data. The arrows on the right depict the additional sensor data provided from a MAV platform and highlight for which steps in the pipeline it can be used

simpler, less complex features and descriptors can be used. The extraction process is faster and the matching ambiguity gets typically reduced (see Meier et al. (2012)).

In the image matching step, traditionally an exhaustive pairwise matching is computed with the main goal to establish an ordering of how to process the images. This step is extremely time consuming; it consists of descriptor matching and two-view geometry estimation for match verification. Here, additional measures from the MAV's sensor can speed up the process significantly and also increase robustness. The GPS positions of the MAV can be used to avoid full exhaustive matching. With known GPS positions of the images, shortlists of nearby images can be created and matching can be performed on the shortlist images only, avoiding to try to match images that will not match anyway. In the two-view geometry estimation step, the essential matrix between two images is computed to verify the matching. This requires the use of the 5 pt essential matrix estimation algorithm within a RANSAC loop. For the case of MAVs when the gravity normal is measured by the IMU, the more efficient 3 pt essential matrix algorithm, which was developed exactly for this case, can be used instead of the 5 pt algorithm. The 3 pt algorithm takes two rotation measurements directly from the IMU and only estimates the three unknowns that remain. To do this, the algorithm only needs 3 pt correspondences, whereas the 5 pt method needs 5 pt correspondences. This is the reason for its much higher efficiency. When used within a RANSAC loop, the necessary RANSAC iterations depend exponentially on the number of point correspondences, thus 3 or 5 necessary point correspondences make a big difference in runtime.

In the triangulation and pose estimation step, nearby images are registered to each other and 3D points are triangulated. Image registration typically works by computing a pose hypothesis from 3D to 2D matches with the PnP algorithm and then to a nonlinear optimization of the re-projection error. Computing the pose hypothesis from 3D to 2D matches typically is a time-consuming algorithm and can be replaced when IMU measurements of the MAV are used. The pose hypothesis can be computed by integrating IMU measurements of the MAV into a pose hypothesis. It has been shown that such kind of pose hypothesis is sufficiently accurate for subsequent state-of-the-art nonlinear pose optimization.

In the final step, bundle adjustment is used to optimize all the camera poses and 3D points in a global manner. Here, the GPS and IMU measurements can be used as additional constraints, as global pose constraints (GPS), global attitude constraints (IMU), and relative orientation constraints (IMU).

Many of these concepts have already been implemented in the open-source SfM software MAVMAP (see Schönberger et al. (2014)), which has specifically been designed for 3D mapping using MAVs. The main benefits are a major speedup for important computer vision algorithms and increased robustness. In areas with low texture, which leads to a low number of extracted image features, additional information such as GPS or IMU will provide valuable constraints for solving the camera pose estimation problem. Image data from MAVs can be acquired in a highly

(a)

(b)

Figure 3.10 A 3D map generated from image data of three individual MAVs using MAVMAP. (a) 3D point cloud including MAVs' trajectories (camera poses are shown in red). (b) Detailed view of a part of the 3D map from a viewpoint originally not observed from the MAVs

irregular manner, which typically puts the SfM system to the test, and therefore, the SfM process will benefit a lot from using additional constraints. Figure 3.10 shows a 3D map of a rubble field used for the training of search and rescue personal. The 3D map has been computed from more than 3000 images taken by multiple low-flying MAVs. The camera poses have been computed using MAVMAP and the point cloud has been densified using SURE (see Rothermel et al. (2012)). Figure 3.10a depicts the trajectories of the MAVs in red. In this image, the irregularity of the acquisition path is clearly visible. Figure 3.10b shows a detailed view of a part of the 3D map from a viewpoint originally not observed from the MAVs.

3.5   Autonomous Navigation

Digital cameras most likely will be the most important sensors for autonomous navigation of MAVs. Digital cameras allow to map the environment of a MAV in 3D using sophisticated computer vision algorithms. Other options for 3D data generation, including laser range-finders, radar, ultrasound, infrared, still come with significant disadvantages. Full 3D laser range-finders, for instance, are currently simply too heavy to be put on small MAVs. Digital cameras, however, already today, weigh only mere grams and are incredibly tiny. Further miniaturization of both digital cameras and more importantly computer technology will allow to run ever more complex computer vision algorithms onboard of the MAV. Depth cameras in this context are also counted toward the digital camera class, as Kinect-style depth cameras resemble a camera-projector system. Online 3D mapping is a key ability to perform autonomous navigation. The MAV needs to sense obstacles and its surrounding environment in more detail to do path planning and obstacle avoidance for safe navigation. The challenge is real-time, high-fidelity depth sensing on a resource-limited platform with strict weight limitations. The current trend is to use specialized hardware embedded in the sensor to let computer vision algorithms such as stereo processing run in real time. The Kinect sensor, for example, is performing depth estimation within a system-on-a-chip (SoC) system. In other works, the semi-global matching algorithm for stereo processing is running on an FPGA chip to achieve real-time depth sensing for MAVs. The integration of ever more complex algorithms into sensor hardware is already in the works. For example, the Skybotix VI-sensor has its goal to put a complete visual-inertial pose estimation system into the sensor hardware itself, utilizing FPGA processing and dedicated hardware.

The sensor measurements have to be fused together into a common map representation of the environment that facilitates path planning, obstacle avoidance, and higher level AI operations such as exploration strategies. In this context, methods that have been developed for ground robots cannot directly be used, they have to be first extended from 2D representation to 3D representation as a MAV can navigate freely in 3D. 3D occupancy grids represent the state of the art of environment representation. They allow the incremental fusion of different depth scans into a common map of user-defined accuracy. 3D occupancy maps can efficiently be used for path planning and navigation. However, one quickly runs into scalability problems on memory-limited computers onboard of MAVs and typically tiling approaches have to be developed.

Figure 3.11 shows a 3D occupancy grid used for MAV navigation as described in Heng et al. (2014). Grid cells that are occupied by an object (walls, floor, furniture, etc.) are visualized as blue cubes. The occupancy grid was computed by fusing a large number of individual depth sensor measurements. Each grid cell further holds a probability that indicates the certainty about the measurement.

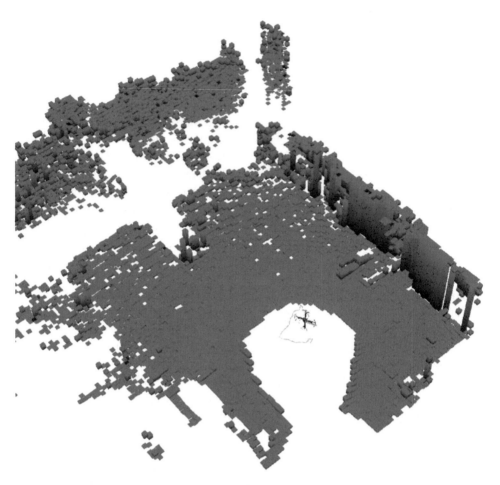

Figure 3.11 Environment represented as a 3D occupancy grid suitable for path planning and MAV navigation. Blue blocks are the occupied parts of the environment

3.6   Scene Interpretation

In the previous section, the focus was on how to use digital images for MAV navigation and mapping mainly by extracting 3D information from image data. However, the analysis of the image content itself by computer vision methods to perform scene interpretation is of importance for MAVs as well. Fully autonomous task-driven operation of a MAV needs knowledge about not only the geometry of its environment but also a semantic description and interpretation. The MAV needs to be able to detect and identify objects, people, and so on. It needs to be able to semantically localize itself, that is, recognize if it is in a kitchen, bathroom, or living room. It needs to identify people and understand gestures to interact with them. And it needs to be able to identify passageways, doors, windows, or exits. Computer vision is the most promising technology to achieve this necessary semantic interpretation.

Figure 3.12   Live view from a MAV with basic scene interpretation capabilities. The MAV detects faces and pre-trained objects (e.g., the exit sign) and marks them in the live view

Figure 3.12 shows an example for scene interpretation by a MAV (see Meier et al. (2012)). The system uses a face detector to detect and identify persons in its vicinity. This lets the system always keep a safe distance from people. The system also identifies objects from a pre-trained database. One of these objects is the exit sign attached above the door. The system can use information like this for path planning and navigation.

3.7   Concluding Remarks

Computer vision proved to be a key enabling technology for autonomous MAVs. Digital cameras are used for pose estimation and for navigation of MAVs using onboard sensors. The possibility to do pose estimation of a MAV with onboard sensors immensely widened the scenarios in which MAVs can be used. Without onboard pose estimation, autonomous operation would be restricted to outdoor areas where GPS reception is available or to instrumented areas (e.g., areas equipped with a tracking system). Applications like search and rescue in partially collapsed buildings, plant inspection tasks, or indoor metrology for documentation would otherwise just not be possible. In addition, the emergence of autonomous MAV can be considered as a new driving force for new developments in computer vision. Computer vision systems used for autonomous MAVs need to be highly reliable and robust. Many computer vision algorithms still lack in this respect. One promising route to more reliable computer vision algorithms is visual-inertial fusion, which is currently heavily investigated. Interest in this direction is largely due to the fact that a MAV is naturally equipped with an IMU and as such there is a big incentive to look into these approaches further. And of course, new insights into computer vision algorithms for MAVs can readily be transferred to other kinds of autonomous systems as well.

4

Exploring the Seafloor with Underwater Robots

Rafael Garcia[1], Nuno Gracias[1], Tudor Nicosevici[1], Ricard Prados[1], Natalia Hurtos[1], Ricard Campos[1], Javier Escartin[2], Armagan Elibol[3], Ramon Hegedus[4] and Laszlo Neumann[1]

[1] *Computer Vision and Robotics Institute, University of Girona, Girona, Spain*
[2] *Institute of Physics of Paris Globe, The National Centre for Scientific Research, Paris, France*
[3] *Department of Mathematical Engineering, Yildiz Technical University, Istanbul, Turkey*
[4] *Max Planck Institute for Informatics, Saarbruecken, Germany*

4.1 Introduction

The ocean covers nearly 75% of our planet. Surprisingly, humans have explored a very small fraction of this unbelievably vast extent of the globe. The main reason for this is that the deep sea is a hostile environment, with absence of light and extreme pressures, making the ocean a dangerous place for human beings. Therefore, deep sea exploration, beyond the capacity of human divers, requires the use of underwater vehicles. Initially, such vehicles were operated by a pilot while carrying one or more scientists. Since all these manned submersibles have hovering capabilities, a skilled pilot would be able to survey the seafloor at very low altitude (i.e., distance from the vehicle to the seafloor) while studying target areas. Having the pilot on the survey loop allows real-time re-planning of the survey depending on the interests of the onboard

Computer Vision in Vehicle Technology: Land, Sea, and Air, First Edition.
Edited by Antonio M. López, Atsushi Imiya, Tomas Pajdla and Jose M. Álvarez.
© 2017 John Wiley & Sons Ltd. Published 2017 by John Wiley & Sons Ltd.

scientists. However, human-operated vehicles have the limitation of restricted diving time (as a function of battery life, and air reserves for the crew).

These limitations have led to the development of unmanned underwater vehicles (UUVs), which represent a safer alternative since no human personnel need to dive into the ocean. UUVs can be classified into remotely operated vehicles (ROVs) and autonomous underwater vehicles (AUVs). ROVs are connected to a mother vessel through a tether, from which a pilot operator remotely controls the vehicle. The tether provides both control feedback signals and power, allowing real-time control and mission re-planning for the scientists. However, one of the greatest disadvantages of ROVs is the fact that the tether is generally affected by water currents, which in turn affects the motion of the vehicle. In addition, when working at depths beyond 500 m, the ship requires a tether management system (TMS), which acts as a "garage" to eliminate the effect of drag of the long length of umbilical attached to the ROV, increasing the design and operational complexity of the ship. Moreover, such vehicles require the supporting vessel to move in coordination with the ROV; thus, the ship should be equipped with dynamic positioning systems to automatically maintain its position and heading, which involves additional expenses associated with the cost of ship time.

AUVs do not require a pilot, nor do they require a tether. Therefore, they can be launched from smaller (and less expensive) vessels. AUVs are usually pre-programmed to carry out a specific trajectory. Their diving time is limited only by the autonomy of the on-board batteries, which often allow them to work for at least a whole day. Some AUVs are connected to the mother ship by means of an ultrasound link, providing communications and positioning cues (e.g., through an ultra short base line (USBL), while other AUVs navigate fully autonomously. As such, AUVs need to make their own decisions, within the mission parameters, based on the readings of the on-board sensors and their control architecture, without the (useful) feedback and decisions of a human operator. Due the aforementioned reasons, most AUVs are nowadays employed mostly for bathymetric mapping of the ocean floor (i.e., using a multibeam sonar to obtain a 2.5D digital terrain model of the seafloor). This allows the robot to travel at a relatively safe altitude—from 50 to 100 m above the ocean floor. In some cases, AUVs may also carry a side-scan sonar that aims to provide an understanding of the different types of textures and materials present on the seafloor. In such cases, the AUV needs to travel at lower altitude (between 10 and 15 m), increasing the associated risks.

Acquiring optical images with an AUV is an even more dangerous endeavor since the robot needs to get very close to the seafloor, which may lead to accidents that range from hitting the seafloor to being trapped by a fishing net. Most commercial AUVs nowadays typically navigate at 1.5–3 knots and do not have hovering capabilities (i.e., remaining in one place while keeping constant altitude). This makes them adequate for bathymetric mapping, and it also limits their capabilities for safely acquiring optical images. However, some scientific AUVs are able to move at much lower speeds, while others are even able to hover—for example, Seabed (WHOI) or Girona-500 (UdG)—enabling them to travel at very low altitudes (less than 2 m). These types of AUVs are, thus, more adequate for visual data acquisition.

4.2 Challenges of Underwater Imaging

When acquiring images of the ocean floor, the main challenges are caused by the special transmission properties of the light in the underwater medium (Wozniak and Dera 2007). The interaction between the light and the aquatic environment includes basically two processes: absorption—where light is gradually attenuated and eventually disappears from the image-forming process; scattering—a change in the direction of individual photons, mainly due to the various particles suspended in water. These transmission particularities of this medium result in additional challenges in underwater imaging, such as blurring of image features, limited range due to light absorption, clutter, and lack of structure in the regions of interest. Sometimes, small floating particles create a phenomenon called "marine snow" (essentially a backscattering effect), which makes image processing even more challenging.

Additionally, natural light is often not sufficient for imaging the sea floor. In such cases, one or more light sources are usually attached to the submersible, providing the necessary lighting. Such light sources, however, might increase the backscattering effect and tend to illuminate the scene in a nonuniform manner (producing a bright spot in the center of the image with a poorly illuminated area surrounding it). Moreover, the motion of the light source creates a shift of the shadows induced in the scene, generating a change in the brightness pattern as the vehicle moves. For this reason, application of standard computer vision techniques to underwater imaging requires first dealing with these inherent challenges (see Figure 4.1).

In summary, numerous challenges need to be addressed when dealing with underwater vision: light scattering, light absorption, color shifts since absorption happens as a function of wavelength, shape distortions, visibility degradation, blurring effects, and many others. Among these many other situations, a good example would be *sunflicker*. This effect is produced when acquiring images of the seafloor in shallow waters on sunny days. In this situation, the images suffer from strong light fluctuations due to refraction, corrupting image appearance and altering human perception of the scene. These artifacts are caused by the intersection of the sunlight rays with the water surface waves and appear in the image as bright stripes that change quickly in both space and time (see Figure 4.2). Refracted sunlight generates dynamic patterns, which degrade the image quality and the information content of the acquired data. Therefore, the sunflickering effect creates a difficult challenge to any image processing pipeline, affecting the behavior of further image processing algorithms (mosaicing, segmentation, classification, etc.). For this reason, the development of online techniques to reduce or eliminate these artifacts becomes crucial in order to ensure optimal performance of underwater imaging algorithms (Gracias et al. 2008; Shihavuddin et al. 2012).

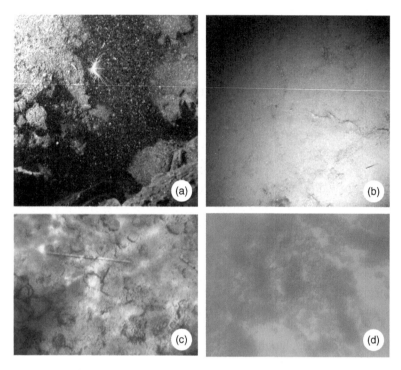

Figure 4.1   (a) Example of *backscattering* due to the reflection of rays from the light source on particles in suspension, hindering the identification of the seafloor texture. (b) Image depicting the effects produced by *light attenuation* of the water resulting in an evident loss of luminance in the regions farthest from the focus of the artificial lighting. (c) Example of the image acquired in shallow waters showing sunflickering patterns. (d) Image showing a generalized blurred appearance due to the small-angle forward-scattering phenomenon

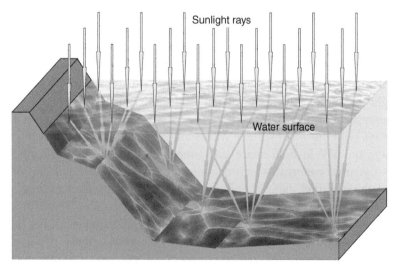

Figure 4.2   Refracted sunlight creates illumination patterns on the seafloor, which vary in space and time following the dynamics of surface waves

4.3 Online Computer Vision Techniques

4.3.1 Dehazing

Since underwater image processing has first to deal with the challenging processes described earlier, several image enhancement and restoration techniques have been proposed in the past few years. The term *dehazing* originates from the scientific literature that addresses restoration of images compromising atmospheric haze, which is essentially an effect of light scattering. Later this term, albeit somewhat inaccurately, developed a broader usage by denoting a similar image restoration scheme in other scenarios such as enhancement of underwater images. The underlying image formation model is based on single scattering with a single and unidirectional illumination source as depicted in Figure 4.3. Excluding absorption, in such a scheme (Bohren and Clothiaux, 2006) it can be shown that the wavelength-dependent radiance reaching the observer from a distant object in the presence of molecular/particulate scatterers can be formulated by a simple formula that clearly expresses the observed radiance $I(\lambda, d)$ being the sum of two components: the attenuated light coming from the object situated at distance d and the veiling light, that is, light scattered by all the molecules and particles along the line of sight between the object and observer. $I(\lambda, d) = J(\lambda)t(\lambda, d) + V(\lambda)(1 - t(\lambda, d))$, where $J(\lambda)$ is the direct scene radiance transmitted from the object and $V(\lambda)$ is the veiling light parameter, which means the radiance that could be measured when source illumination scattered into the line of sight through an infinite optical depth and $t(\lambda, d)$ is the transmission.

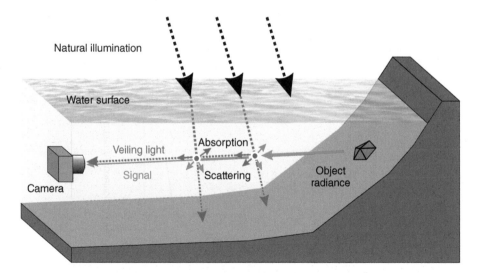

Figure 4.3   Scheme of underwater image formation with natural light as main illumination source. The signal reaching the camera is composed of two main components: attenuated direct light coming from the observed object and water-scattered natural illumination along this propagation path. Attenuation is due to both scattering and absorption

In the most general case, transmission is given by the following expression: $t(\lambda, d) = \exp\left(-\int_0^d \beta(\lambda, z)dz\right)$, where $\beta(\lambda, z)$ is the extinction coefficient characteristic at distance z, λ is the wavelength, and d is the distance of the observed object. In general, the extinction coefficient is the sum of scattering and absorption coefficients. As for atmospheric image restoration cases, the effect of absorption can be deemed negligible (although this is only true in the presence of haze proper, but not in the case of dense fog, e.g., when absorption plays a major role). Hence, in this scheme, attenuation of the direct light from the observed object is merely due to scattering. The $\int \beta(\lambda, z)dz$ integral is called the optical depth, which is thus the natural-scale factor of the hazing phenomenon. In dehazing methods, it is usually assumed that the scattering coefficient is constant across the field of view and the line of sight, so that transmission becomes as simple as $t(\lambda, d) = \exp(-\beta(\lambda) \cdot d)$. This simplification carries the underlying assumption that the distribution of various scattering particles within the volume of the environment falling in the observer's field of view would be homogeneous. This may be more or less justified in a terrestrial scene, especially with a narrow field of view it seems reasonable to assume a spatially invariant scattering coefficient in a hazy atmosphere. The advantage of such a simple model is obvious: if a per-pixel depth map of the scene were known, then only a handful of unknown parameters remain, the estimation of which would presumably lead to a good restoration of the image. However, in reality, and this applies *a fortiori* to the underwater environment, the image formation is more subtle and complicated. First of all, within the water medium one should not neglect absorption, which has a different spectral behavior compared to that of scattering (see Figure 4.4). In this aspect, one of the inherent problems in underwater imaging is that due to the high absorption of water in the visible red spectral range, sometimes there is simply no signal recorded in the red-filtered pixels of a camera for anything but the closest objects. Another complication is that in a hazy atmosphere, Rayleigh scattering is the singlemost dominant factor creating the veiling effect on

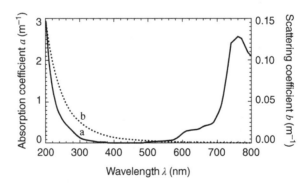

Figure 4.4   Absorption and scattering coefficients of pure seawater. Absorption (solid line (a)) and scattering (dotted line (b)) coefficients for pure seawater, as determined and given by Smith and Baker (1981) and reproduced from Mobley (1994)

scene objects, whereas in seawater usually there is a significant concentration of floating particles exhibiting Mie scattering. As a consequence, there can be a wide variety of scatterers present bearing different characteristics (spectral and angular dependence) on the scattering process, with a possibly inhomogeneous distribution. On top of these, multiple scattering cannot be neglected, either. For further details, we refer the reader to Mobley (1994). Considering only a couple of such factors, the image formation model quickly becomes so complex that it becomes impossible to use it for any kind of reverse-engineering, what one would wish for by performing underwater image enhancement. Therefore, it is not for chance that the above-mentioned simple image formation model is directly or indirectly used in most dehazing approaches, as this level of model complexity is still tractable, despite its limited validity.

In order to put the single-scattering model to work, we see that it is crucial to have a scene depth estimation. Early methods of dehazing primarily rely on additional depth information or multiple observations of the same scene. Schechner et al. (2001) and Schechner and Karpel (2005) exploit the fact that the scattered veiling light (in both the atmosphere and underwater) is partially polarized, whereas the direct light coming from the object can be considered practically unpolarized. Hence, if per-pixel polarization data are acquired from the scene, one can separate well the direct and veiling signals. Based on this observation, they developed a quick method to reduce the veiling effect by using two images taken through a polarizer at different angles. Narasimhan and Nayar (2002, 2003) propose a physics-based scattering model, using which the scene structure can be recovered from two or more weather images. Kopf et al. (2008) propose to dehaze an image by using the scene depth information directly accessible in georeferenced digital terrain and urban models. The inherent limitation of these approaches is that they require multiple, geometrically registered images of the same scene and/or special optical elements beyond a simple camera–lens combination. Hence, they are not usable on an arbitrary image or video footage acquired in scattering media. Furthermore, by relying on extra measurement/data, the applied technique may impose additional unknown parameters into the model used for image enhancement. For instance, polarization can provide valuable information about the veiling light component even though the degree of its partial polarization is not known *a priori*; it can be highly wavelength-dependent and, in general, it is a function of the scattering process.

In recent years, a new concept called *Single Image Dehazing* has emerged. Under this concept, novel algorithms have been proposed that attempt to carry out image restoration (in both terrestrial and underwater imaging) without requiring any additional information. This is a highly desired procedure since no other equipment is needed, apart from a standard camera, to acquire images. However, restoring the original scene to its true colors from a single image is a heavily underconstrained problem due to the fact that both attenuation of the object-reflected light and the intensity of the additional veiling light are dependent on the optical depth of the given object (Schechner and Karpel 2004). Consequently, such an ill-posed problem can only be resolved by imposing additional constraints through exploiting natural limits of the physical phenomena themselves, invariances, and statistics of certain natural image features. Extracting and leveraging these constraints also implies the need for sophisticated algorithms, often with a significant computational cost, such as image-matting methods, independent component analysis, or Markov random fields.

Fattal (2008) proposes an image formation model that accounts for surface shading and scene transmission. Under the assumption that the two functions are locally statistically uncorrelated, a haze image can be broken into regions of constant albedo, from which the scene transmission can be inferred. Tan (2009) proposes to enhance the visibility of a haze image by maximizing its local contrast. He et al. (2009) present an approach introducing the *dark channel prior*. This prior comes from an observation that most local patches in haze-free images often contain some low intensity, almost completely dark pixels. Ancuti et al. (2011) improved upon the dark channel prior method comparing the hue of the original image with the hue of the inverse image to estimate the airlight color and applying a layer-base dehazing technique. Tao et al. (2012) also extended the dark channel method considering the influence of multiple scattering in the atmosphere. This method needs the evaluation of the atmospheric point spread function and includes convolution and deconvolution steps, which increase the computational time. Kratz and Nishino (2009) model an image as a factorial Markov random field, in which the scene albedo and depth are two statistically independent latent layers. A canonical expectation maximization algorithm is implemented to factorize the image. Kratz's method can recover a haze-free image with fine edge details; however, it has high computational costs. Tarel and Hautiere (2009) present a single image dehazing algorithm that has the main advantage of speed: its complexity is a linear function of the number of image pixels. The method is controlled only by a few parameters and consists of atmospheric veil inference, image restoration and smoothing, and tone mapping. Luzon-Gonzalez et al. (2015) propose an image enhancement method that works in several adverse weather conditions based on the RGB response ratio constancy under illuminant changes. Their algorithm restores visibility, contrast, and color in degraded images with low computational times.

As for single image dehazing methods in the underwater environment, they mostly reiterate the ideas developed for atmospheric cases, with some variations. Carlevaris-Bianco et al. (2010) proposed an underwater dehazing algorithm using a prior based on the difference in attenuation among the different color channels, which allows for estimating the per-pixel scene depth. Then the scene radiance is recovered from the hazy image by modeling the true scene radiance as a Markov random field using the estimated depth map. Ancuti et al. (2012) developed a multiresolution method based on image fusion principles. They define two inputs that represent color-corrected and contrast-enhanced versions of the original underwater image and the associated weight maps for the fusion process, which evaluate several image qualities by specifying spatial pixel relationships. Chiang and Chen (2012) introduced a novel approach to enhance underwater images by compensating the attenuation discrepancy along the propagation path, which also takes the influence of the possible presence of an artificial light source into account. They evaluated the performance of their algorithm utilizing ground-truth color patches and have shown results with significantly enhanced visibility and good color fidelity. Serikawa and Lu (2013) also use a simple prior based on the difference in attenuation among the different color channels and estimate the depth map through the red-colored channel in underwater images. They propose to apply fast joint trilateral filtering on the depth map, for achieving an edge-preserving smoothing with a narrow spatial window in only a few iterations. Hitam and Awalludin (2013) present a method called mixture contrast limited adaptive histogram equalization (CLAHE). The method operates CLAHE on RGB and HSV color spaces, and the results are combined together using Euclidean norm. Anuradha and Kaur (2015) focus on the problem of uneven illumination often encountered in the underwater environment that is usually neglected in previous works. They propose a new LAB-color-space- and CLAHE-based image enhancement algorithm and they use image gradient-based smoothing to account for the illumination unevenness within the scene. They improve the performance of the underwater image enhancement techniques that utilize CLAHE.

From the recent literature, one can observe that *single image dehazing* remains a very much researched topic and particularly for underwater scenes there is definitely room for improvement. We can mainly distinguish two different approaches in the currently available techniques:

1. Physics-based algorithms, which aim at recovering per-pixel object radiance directly from an equation that models attenuation of the object signal and backscattered veiling light, according to a scheme identical or similar to Figure 4.3 and using certain priors that help estimation of unknown parameters.
2. Nonphysical algorithms, which rather attempt to enhance/change certain properties of the image, such as color balance and contrast, so that it looks less affected by the attenuation/scattering phenomena in the medium and provides a plausible appearance of the scene. Physics-based approaches can be beneficial in those scenarios, where the applied image formation model and additional priors resemble well the given circumstances where the images were taken, and especially when there is a way to physically validate certain parameters (e.g., measuring attenuation coefficients, calibrating against a target with known reflectance). In such cases, a physics-based algorithm may restore well the direct object signal. However, their performance also tends to be strongly limited for exactly the same reason. Take for example the scheme of Figure 4.3: this is only valid with natural light in shallow waters, and particularly when sunlight is present and dominating, so that illumination can be considered unidirectional. Once we go into very shallow waters, it is not sufficient anymore, as there are sunflickering effects seen on the seafloor. And once we submerge into deep water, where there is not enough natural light and we have to use artificial illumination to record images, the model becomes invalid and needs to be significantly altered.

In contrast, nonphysical algorithms, if well designed and not tied too strongly to a given image formation model, can be applied in a more robust way with varying illumination, scattering, and attenuation conditions. The challenge with such an approach is that an unnaturally looking result can be as easily achieved as a visually pleasing one, depending on certain adjustable parameters of the algorithm, the setting of which can be completely arbitrary and these might also need user interaction. Nevertheless, our team also opted for such a nonphysical, formal approach to underwater image enhancement that can be equally well applied in both shallow and deep waters, with natural and artificial or even mixed illumination sources, and it does not require prior information about the image content or scattering and absorption parameters. This method utilizes ideas from Tarel and Hautiere (2009) as well as the guided imaging filter of He et al. (2010) along with the principles of color constancy. Some sample results are illustrated in Figure 4.5, which highlight the significance of this approach under low to extreme low visibility conditions.

Beyond the need for further improvement, open problems also remain in underwater image enhancement. For instance, it is a question: what is the best strategy to retrieve the object signal with proper contrast while combating the increasing noise. Ultimately, there are physical limits for restoring visibility since contrast of objects and image features is decreasing exponentially with the distance from the camera, and at some point they necessarily fall under the noise level of the camera sensor. Another question is what can be optimally done for restoring colors, when absorption in the red spectral range is so strong that there are only blue- and green-filtered signals recorded by the camera. More research could be done also on video applications, where temporal coherence could be exploited for better estimation of unknown parameters in the applied physical model or for better designed, nonphysical approaches.

4.3.2 Visual Odometry

Accurate vehicle localization and navigation are crucial to the successful completion of any type of autonomous mission. To this end, terrestrial applications typically employ GPS sensors that enable constant positioning estimation with no drift accumulation. In the underwater medium, however, GPS information is not available, increasing the complexity of autonomous navigation. As a result, extensive research efforts have been dedicated to this topic. Underwater navigation usually involves fusing the information from multiple sensors, such as long baseline, short baseline, Doppler velocity log, and inertial sensors, which allow estimations of the position, speed, and accelerations of the UUVs. More recently, advances in the area of computer vision, in terms of both hardware and software, have led to the development of vision-based navigation and positioning systems. Such systems employ one or more cameras mounted on the vehicle, typically coupled with artificial illumination systems for deep-sea missions. The images acquired by the cameras are processed in order to estimate the motion of the vehicle in real time using either

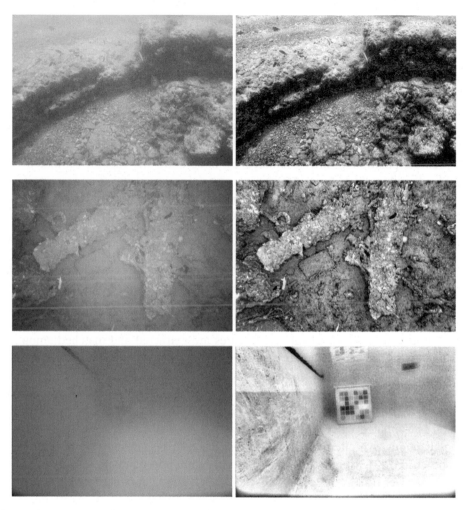

Figure 4.5 Image dehazing. Example of underwater image restoration in low to extreme low visibility conditions

two-dimensional (2D) mapping (mosaicing) or three-dimensional (3D) mapping techniques. Mosaicing was primarily developed as a technique that allows widening the coverage of the scene by aligning (stitching) images taken by a moving camera. This is particularly relevant in underwater mapping applications (Garcia et al. 2001, 2003a, 2005; Gracias and Santos-Victor 2000; Jaffe et al. 2002; Pizarro and Singh 2003; Singh et al. 2004, 2007), where the field of view of the camera is very narrow due to the limited distance between the camera and the seafloor. Positioning based on mosaicing represents by far the most commonly used vision-based technique in underwater navigation, employing either image feature analysis or spatiotemporal image analysis. Image feature-based approaches (Eustice 2005; Fleischer 2000; Garcia et al. 2003b; Gracias 2002; Gracias et al. 2003) involve the extraction of features such as SURF (Bay et al. 2006), SIFT (Lowe 1999), FAST (Rosten and Drummond 2006), ORB (Rublee et al. 2011), and so on. These features are then characterized using descriptors (Bay et al. 2006; Lowe 1999) exploiting neighboring visual information. This enables feature matching between two time-consecutive images or feature tracking across multiple consecutive images, and ultimately the estimation of the camera motion. The motion of the camera is modeled by means of planar homographies (Hartley and Zisserman 2003; Negahdaripour et al. 2005), allowing estimation in up to 6 degrees of freedom (3 rotations + 3 translations). The vehicle position is then estimated by integrating the motion estimated from the homographies over time. Alternative mosaicing-based positioning systems use spatiotemporal image gradients in order to directly measure interframe vehicle motion (Madjidi and Negahdaripour 2006; Negahdaripour 1998; Negahdaripour and Madjidi 2003a). When the area surveyed by the vehicle exhibits prominent 3D variations, mosaicing-based approaches tend to yield low accuracy motion estimation due to the scene parallax. This shortcoming of mosaicing techniques has led to the development of 3D mapping-based UUV localization and navigation. Three-dimensional navigation techniques may involve multiple camera systems or a single camera for acquisition. When multiple-camera configurations are used (which are generally intercalibrated), image features are extracted and matched among the camera views. The 3D position of these image features is then recovered using triangulation techniques (Hartley and Zisserman 2003). Authors have proposed different approaches in stereo-based navigation. In Eustice et al. (2006b), Negahdaripour and Madjidi (2003b), Park et al. (2003), and Zhang and Negahdaripour (2003), the vehicle motion is estimated by recovering the 3D position of the features over consecutive image captures. An alternative strategy proposed in Ferrer and Garcia (2010), and Filippo et al. (2013) provides a 3D position estimation of image features for each stereo pair over time, registering the sets of 3D features in consecutive acquisitions. The relative camera motion is then recovered from the registration of the 3D points. In the case where a single camera is used for visual navigation (monocular vision), structure from motion (SfM) strategies are employed. Such techniques are similar to stereo navigation, except that the 3D camera motion has to be estimated during the 3D feature reconstruction. Initial SfM approaches used motion computation based on fundamental matrix (Beardsley et al. 1994; Longuet-Higgins 1981) and trifocal tensor (Fitzgibbon and Zisserman 1998). A more accurate alternative to these methods enables the recovery of vehicle position by directly registering the camera with 3D feature sets, using direct linear transformation (DLT) (Klein and Murray 2007). The use of direct camera registration is proposed by Pizarro (2004) and Pizarro et al. (2004) to deal with the problem of error accumulation in the large-area vehicle navigation. Here, the 3D map of the surveyed area is divided into submaps. Within the submaps, the camera pose is recovered directly by using resection methods and the submaps are registered using global alignment techniques. More recently, Nicosevici et al. (2009) proposed a framework for online navigation and mapping for UUVs employing a novel direct camera registration technique. This technique uses a dual-model DLT approach that is able to accurately cope with both planar and high 3D relief scenes.

4.3.3   SLAM

Vision-based navigation is essentially a *dead-reckoning* process. During navigation and map building, the vision system estimates the camera pose relative to either previous poses or an environment map, while it builds the map from observations relative to camera poses. All estimations are prone to aliasing, noise, image distortions, and numerical errors, leading to inaccuracies in both pose and map inferences. Although generally small, these inaccuracies build up in time, leading to significant errors over large camera trajectories (Nicosevici et al. 2009). These errors can be reduced by taking advantage of the additional information resulting from *cross-overs*. Cross-overs (or loop-closures) are situations that appear when the robot revisits a region of the scene previously mapped during a visual survey. If correctly detected, these situations can be exploited in order to establish new constraints, allowing both camera pose and map errors to be decreased (see Figure 4.6) using either offline approaches, such as

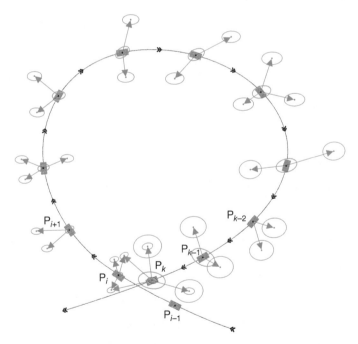

Figure 4.6   Loop-closure detection. As the camera moves, there is an increasing uncertainty related to both the camera pose and the environment map. At instant t_k, the camera revisits a region of the scene previously visited at instant t_i. If the visual observations between instants t_k and t_i can be associated, the resulting information not only can be used to reduce the pose and map uncertainties at instant t_k but also can be propagated to reduce the uncertainties at prior instants

BA (Capel 2004; Madjidi and Negahdaripour 2005; McLauchlan and Jaenicke 2002; Sawhney et al. 1998; Triggs et al. 1999), or online approaches employing Gaussian filters, such as the popular Kalman filter (Caballero et al. 2007; Fleischer 2000; Garcia et al. 2002; Richmond and Rock, 2006) or nonparametric methods, such as those using particle filters (M. Montemerlo 2007; Montemerlo et al. 2003). In this context, the main open issue is the correct and efficient detection of loop closures.

A brute force loop-closure detection, where the current visual observations are compared to the entire map, would be much too computationally expensive, especially for online applications, due to the extremely large number of features that need to be matched.

As an alternative, the complexity of the loop-closure problem can be reduced by narrowing the search to the vicinity of the current camera pose. This is a widely used approach in the SLAM community, where the vision system is modeled as a sensor with a known uncertainty (Eustice et al. 2004, 2005; Ila et al. 2007; Paz et al. 2008). However, an accurate estimation of the vehicle uncertainty is a complex problem and is generally affected by linearization approximations. To counterbalance this shortcoming, assuring the detection of the cross-over, current observations may be compared with a region of the map corresponding to a higher covariance than the estimated one (Jung and Lacroix 2003; Matthies and Shafer 1987). Doing so becomes computationally expensive, especially over large trajectory loops, where the covariance of the camera is high. Moreover, the noise model used for covariance estimation does not account for inaccuracies resulting from obstruction, temporary motion blur, sensor failures, and so on. These situations lead to poor vehicle pose estimation, not reflected in the uncertainty estimation, in which case the loop closure may not be detected.

Goedeme et al. (2006), Wahlgren and Duckett (2005), and Zhang (2011) propose a loop-closing detection method that computes the visual similarity using features. During navigation, they extract key points from each image (e.g., SIFT; Lowe (2004)). These features are matched among images, and the visual similarity is proportional to the number of successfully matched features. Generally, such methods are sensitive to occlusions while being computationally expensive, limiting their application over large navigation trajectories.

A more robust and computationally efficient alternative is to represent entire images as observations rather than individual image features. In this context, cross-overs are detected on the basis of image similarity, drastically decreasing the amount of data that need to be processed. The reduced computational cost related to such approaches enables brute force cross-over detection, even for large camera trajectories. This allows correct detection of trajectory loops, independent of camera pose and covariance estimation accuracy.

Initial proposals on image similarity cross-over detection use image representations based on a single global descriptor, embodying visual content such as color or texture (Bowling et al. 2005; Kroese et al. 2001; Lamon et al. 2001; Ramos et al. 2005;

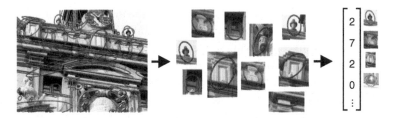

Figure 4.7 BoW image representation. Images are represented by histograms of generalized visual features

Torralba et al. 2003). Such global descriptors are sensitive to camera viewpoint and illumination changes, decreasing the robustness of the cross-over detection.

The emergence of modern feature extractors and descriptors has led to the development of new appearance-based cross-over detection techniques that represent visual content in terms of local image descriptors (Angeli et al. 2008a, 2008b; Cummins and Newman 2007, 2008; Wang et al. 2005). Inspired by advances in the fields of object recognition and content-based image retrieval (Opelt et al. 2004; Sivic 2006; Zhang et al. 2006), recent examples of such approaches describe images using bag of words (BoW) (see Figure 4.7). BoW image representation employs two stages: (i) in the training stage, sets of visual features are grouped or clustered together to generate *visual vocabularies*—collections of generalized visual features or *visual words*; (ii) in the second stage, the images are represented as histograms of visual word occurrences. While discarding the geometric information in images, BoW proved to be a very robust method for detecting visual similarities between images, allowing efficient cross-over detection even in the presence of illumination and camera perspective changes, partial occlusions, and so on.

In terms of clustering strategies, Schindler et al. (2007) proposed the use of kd-trees to build a visual vocabulary as proposed by Nister and Stewenius (2006). The vocabulary is then used for SLAM at the level of a city with good results. Galvez-Lopez and Tardos (2011) proposed the use of a vocabulary based on binary features for fast image matching.

Konolige et al. (2010) proposed a two-stage method in which visual vocabularies are first used to extract candidate views followed by a feature-based matching.

The main shortcoming of the above-mentioned methods is the use of a static vocabulary: the vocabulary is built *a priori* and remains constant during the recognition stage, failing to accurately model objects or scenes not present during training (Yeh et al. 2007). This shortcoming is particularly critical in the case of mapping and navigation, where a robot should be able to successfully detect loop-closure situations in uncontrolled environments. As a consequence, a series of authors in the SLAM community have proposed alternatives to address this problem. Notably, Filliat (2007) and Angeli et al. (2008a, 2008b) assumed an initial vocabulary that is gradually incremented with new image features in an agglomerative manner using a user-defined distance threshold as the merging criterion. Alternatively, Cummins and

Newman (2007, 2008, 2009), and later Paul and Newman (2010) and Glover et al. (2011), proposed a large-scale loop detection probabilistic framework based on BoW. They show good results employing k-means-based static vocabularies built from large sets of visual information, not necessarily acquired in the same areas where the robot navigation takes place. As an alternative, Zhang (2011) proposed a workaround to the off-line vocabulary building stage by describing images directly using visual features, instead of vector-quantized representation of BoW. Here, the complexity of raw feature matching for loop-closure detection is partially reduced by means of a feature selection method that reduces the number of features extracted from images.

Nicosevici and Garcia (2012) proposed a method aimed at increasing the efficiency and accuracy of loop detection in the context of online robot navigation and mapping called online visual vocabularies (OVV). It requires no user intervention and no *a priori* information about the environment. OVV creates a reduced vocabulary as soon as visual information becomes available during the robot survey. As the robot moves, the vocabulary is constantly updated in order to correctly model the visual information present in the scene.

OVV presents a novel incremental visual vocabulary building technique that is both scalable (thus suitable for online applications) and automatic (see Figure 4.8). In order to achieve this goal, it uses a modified version of agglomerative clustering. Agglomerative clustering algorithms begin with each element as a separate cluster—called hereafter *elementary clusters*—and merge them using some similarity measurement into successively larger clusters until some criterion is met (e.g., minimum number of clusters, maximum cluster radius).

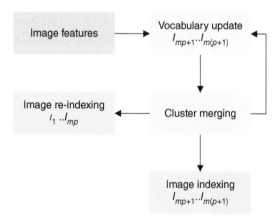

Figure 4.8 Flowchart of OVV and image indexing. In every m frames, the vocabulary is updated with new visual features extracted from the last m frames. The complete set of features in the vocabulary is then merged until convergence. The obtained vocabulary is used to index the last m images. Also, the previously indexed frames are re-indexed to reflect the changes in the vocabulary

The convergence criterion is based on an objective function inspired by Fisher's linear discriminant (McLachlan 2004), maximizing the repetitiveness and discriminative power of the resulting vocabulary. Moreover, using a natural convergence criterion, the process eliminates the need of user-set parameters such as cluster radius or number of clusters, specific to other vocabulary building algorithms.

This OVV is of particular interest in underwater SLAM, especially in autonomous applications, due to its robustness, scalability, and its capacity to continuously adapt to new environmental elements on the journey with no human intervention.

4.3.4   Laser Scanning

The goal of deploying laser systems in underwater imaging applications is twofold: (i) increasing the effective range of the imaging devices and (ii) obtaining high-resolution 3D reconstructions. The use of finely controlled illumination devices based on lasers allows reducing the backscatter effect, making their deployment especially suitable in high-turbidity waters. These systems are usually comprised of a pulsating laser coupled with a range-gated camera. The backscatter effect is reduced by capturing the photons reflected from the target rather than the ones reflected by suspended particles. The selective photon capturing is carried out by finely synchronizing the electronic camera shutter with the laser pulses, taking into account the distance to the target and the time of flight of the light into the water medium (Caimi et al. 2008). Some implementations use spatially broadened lasers with range-gated intensified cameras allowing imaging of target with up to 40 degree field of view (Fournier et al. 1993, 1995; Seet and He 2005). More recent implementations, such as LUCIE2, provide more compact configurations of such systems, allowing deployment on AUVs and ROVs (Weidemann et al. 2005). Other proposals employ off-the-shelf hardware. In this scenario, planar continuous lasers are typically coupled with one-dimensional (1D) or 2D cameras. Using specific camera-laser setups (e.g., mounting the laser at a certain distance from the camera), the backscatter effect can be reduced (Narasimhan et al. 2005). A hybrid approach is reported in Moore et al. (2000), where a pulsating laser system is coupled with a linear CCD camera. The pulsed laser allows short camera integration times, thereby reducing the influence of the ambient daylight signal in shallow waters and increasing the contrast in turbid environments. Three-dimensional reconstruction techniques employ lasers as structured light sources and 1D or 2D cameras as capture devices. Such techniques typically involve three main stages: (i) accurate calibration of the laser–camera setup, (ii) image filtering for detecting the laser scanline, and (iii) 3D reconstruction using triangulation algorithms (DePiero and Trivedi 1996). Roman et al. (2010) proposed a structured light system deployed on a ROV to create high-resolution bathymetric maps of underwater archeological sites. The system employs a 532-nm planar laser system to create sea-bottom profiles that are merged using the navigation data provided by the ROV. A similar approach is proposed in Tetlow and Spours (1999), where the authors used a laser scanning system to generate a model of an underwater site for ROV docking activities. A high-resolution seafloor scanning system is presented in Moore and Jaffe (2002), resulting in sub-millimeter bathymetric maps with a transect coverage of 1.35 m. The authors report good results in using the system for characterization of the spatial variability and temporal evolution of the seafloor.

4.4   Acoustic Imaging Techniques

Given the limitations of optical devices, underwater operations have long relied on sonar technology. Acoustic waves are significantly less affected by water attenuation, facilitating operation at greater ranges and allowing work in turbidity conditions, thanks to longer wavelengths. Thus, sonar devices address the main shortcomings of optical sensors although at the expense of providing, in general, noisy data of lower resolution and more difficult interpretation.

Sonars delivering range measurements, such as single-beam echosounders, profiling sonars, or multibeam echosounders, have been successfully employed for obstacle avoidance, navigation, localization, and mapping (Fairfield et al. 2007; Kinsey et al. 2006; Leonard et al. 1998; Roman and Singh 2005), the latter being especially popular for the creation of seafloor bathymetric charts. Imaging sonars, such as mechanically scanning sonars or side-scan sonars, have also been widely used in obstacle avoidance, in localization, and particularly in mapping applications (Aulinas et al. 2010; Mallios et al. 2014; Ribas et al. 2008; Tena et al. 2003), thanks to its ability to represent the returning acoustic intensities from an insonified area. Recently, a new generation of imaging sonars (Blu 2015a; Sou 2015; Tri 2015), namely the 2D forward-looking sonar (FLS), are emerging as a strong alternative for those environments with reduced visibility given their capabilities of delivering high-quality acoustic images at a near-video frame rate. FLS provides significant advantages over other imaging sonars, thanks to the use of advanced transducer arrays that allow simultaneous sampling of multiple acoustic returns and render them in a 2D image. By directly providing a 2D image, they offer a closer rendition of what the eye naturally sees and minimize the required level of processing and interpretation when compared to other sonar modalities. Thus, they can be regarded as the analogous tool of optical cameras for turbid waters (see Figure 4.9). However, due to the inherent differences between optical and acoustic cues, issues arise in trying to leverage the techniques used on optical images, and often different approaches are required.

4.4.1   Image Formation

Two-dimensional FLSs, sometimes also referred to as acoustic cameras, provide high-definition acoustic imagery at a fast refresh rate. Although the specifications regarding operating frequency, acoustic beam width, frame rate, and the internal beam-forming technology depend on the specific sonar model and manufacturer,

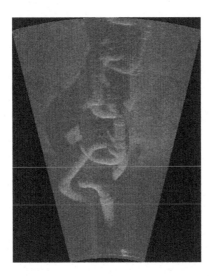

Figure 4.9 Sample 2D FLS image of a chain in turbid waters

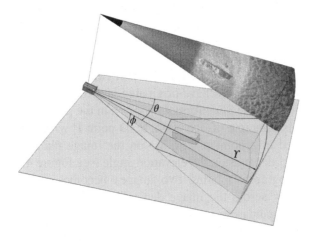

Figure 4.10 FLS operation. The sonar emits an acoustic wave spanning its beam width in the azimuth (θ) and elevation (ϕ) directions. Returned sound energy is sampled as a function of (r, θ) and can be interpreted as the mapping of 3D points onto the zero-elevation plane (shown in red)

the principle of operation is the same for all of them. The sonar insonifies the scene with an acoustic wave, spanning its field of view in the azimuth (θ) and elevation (ϕ) directions (see Figure 4.10). Then, the intensity of the acoustic return is sampled by an array of transducers as a function of range and bearing in a polar image. Therefore, the dimensions of a raw frame correspond to the number of beams in the angular direction and the number of range samples in the range axes. This representation is then converted to the final 2D image in the Cartesian coordinates for an easier

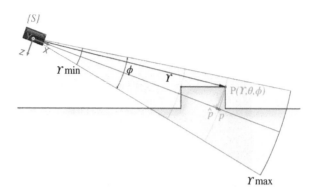

Figure 4.11   Sonar projection geometry. A 3D point $\mathbf{P}(r, \theta, \phi)$ is mapped onto a point p on the image plane along the arc defined by the elevation angle. Considering an orthographic approximation, the point $\mathbf{P}$ is mapped onto $\hat{p}$, which is equivalent to considering that all scene points rest on the plane $X_s Y_s$ (in red)

interpretation. It is worth noting that this process produces images with nonuniform resolution as one pixel in polar domain is mapped onto multiple pixels with the same intensity in the Cartesian coordinates as the range increases.

Because of the sonar construction, it is not possible to disambiguate the elevation angle of the acoustic return originating at a particular range and bearing. In other words, the reflected echo could have originated anywhere along the corresponding elevation arc. Therefore, the 3D information is lost in the projection into a 2D image.

According to this principle of operation, a 3D point $\mathbf{P}$ with spherical coordinates (r, θ, ϕ) is projected in a point $\mathbf{p} = (x_s, y_s)$ on the image plane $(X_s Y_s)$ following a nonlinear model that depends on the elevation angle (see Figure 4.11).

Hence, the homography relating two images becomes an affine homography whose elements vary across the image depending on the range and the unknown elevation angles (Negahdaripour 2012b). Therefore, this geometry model requires the estimation of the sonar elevation angles by using surface normals computed either from the imaging configuration (Negahdaripour 2012a) or from object–shadow pairs identified in the images (Aykin and Negahdaripour 2013). An easier approach to describe the FLS imaging geometry is to consider the narrow elevation angle that typically characterizes FLS devices (around 7-10 deg). Approximating this narrow elevation to the limit (i.e., considering only the zero-elevation plane), leads to a linear model in which the sonar can be seen as an orthographic camera (Johannsson et al. 2010). Hence, the projection $\mathbf{p}$ of a 3D point $\mathbf{P}$ is approximated by the orthogonal projection $\hat{\mathbf{p}}$, and the motion between two sonar frames can be related by a 2D rigid transformation comprising the x and y translations (t_x, t_y) and the plane rotation (θ).

Analogously to the parallax problem in optical imaging, this approximation holds as long as the relief of the scene in the elevation direction is negligible compared to the range. The imaging geometry under a typical operation scenario falls within this consideration since the sonar device is usually tilted to a small grazing angle to cover a large portion of the scene.

4.4.2 Online Techniques for Acoustic Processing

Some of the computer vision techniques described in the previous section (e.g., visual odometry, SLAM) can be applied on acoustic FLS images so that they can be performed regardless of the water visibility conditions. However, due to the different nature of the image formation, these techniques require alternative processing methodologies. Two of the most characteristic and differentiated processing techniques are described later.

4.4.2.1 FLS Image Registration

Techniques such as SLAM, visual odometry, or mosaicing approaches, similar to the techniques described in Chapter 7, often require to address a previous and fundamental step: the registration of sonar images (i.e., finding the spatial transformation that relates one sonar frame with another). Although registration is a broadly studied field in other modalities, notably the optical one (Zitova and Flusser 2003), it is still a premature field with regard to sonar data. The particularities of FLS imagery, such as low resolution, low signal-to-noise ratio (SNR), and intensity alterations due to viewpoint changes, pose serious challenges to the feature-based registration techniques that have proved very effective at aligning optical images.

Some feature-based approaches have been applied to the pairwise registration of spatially close acoustic images, in particular Harris corner detector (Harris and Stephens 1988) has been used by several researchers to extract corner-like features in FLS images (Kim et al. 2005, 2006; Negahdaripour et al. 2005). These features are later matched by cross-correlation of local patches and once correspondences are established, the transformation estimation is performed with a RANSAC-like method to reject outliers. Negahdaripour et al. (2011) have also highlighted the difficulties of registering FLS frames from a natural environment by using the popular SIFT detector and descriptor (Lowe 2004). In general, due to the inherent characteristics of sonar data, pixel-level features extracted in sonar images suffer from low repeatability rates (Hurtós et al. 2013b). Consequently, extracted features lack stability and are prone to originate erroneous matches and yield wrong transformation estimations. Moreover, the difficulties in accurately extracting and matching stable features are exacerbated when dealing with spatially or temporally distant sonar images.

In view of these difficulties, other researchers have proposed alternatives involving features at regional level rather than at pixel scale, which are presumably more stable. Johannsson et al. (2010) proposed the extraction of features in local regions located on sharp intensity transitions (i.e., changes from strong- to low-signal returns as in the boundaries of object–shadow transitions). Feature alignment is formulated as an optimization problem based on the normal distribution transform (NDT) algorithm (Biber and Straßer 2003), which adjusts the clustered regions in grid cells, thus removing the need to get exact correspondences between points and allowing for possible intensity variations. A similar approach has been recently presented in Aykin and Negahdaripour (2013). The authors propose to extract blob features comprising high-intensity values and negative vertical gradients (that ensure object–shadow transitions). As an alternative to the NDT algorithm, Aykin and Negahdaripour (2013) used an adaptive scheme where a Gaussian distribution is fitted to each blob feature. Afterwards, an optimization is formulated to seek the motion that best fits the blob projections from one Gaussian map to the other.

To overcome the instability and parameter sensitivity of feature-based registration approaches, and at the same time mitigate the requirement of prominent features in the environment, Hurtós et al. proposed to use a Fourier-based registration methodology (Hurtós et al. 2014b). Instead of using sparse feature information, they take into account all image content for the registration, thus offering more robustness to noise and the different intensity artifacts characteristic of the sonar image formation. By assuming a simplified imaging geometry, a global area technique can be used to perform 2D FLS registration, thus estimating a translation and rotation that relates two given frames. The method takes advantage of the phase-correlation principle that estimates translational displacements, thanks to the disassociation of the energy content from the structure shift in the frequency domain. The phase-correlation algorithm is adapted to cope with the multiple noise sources that can jeopardize the registration, introducing a specific masking procedure to cope with the spectral leakage caused by the sonar fan-shaped footprint edges and an adaptive frequency filtering to conform to the different amounts of noise of the phase-correlation matrix. The rotation estimation between frames is computed by also applying phase correlation, but in this case directly on the polar sonar images. Given that rotation is not decoupled from translational motions in the polar domain, this is regarded as an approximation. However, it has shown better behavior on the low SNR sonar images than other popular global rotation estimation approaches. Figure 4.12 shows the outline of the Fourier-based registration of FLS images. A further advantage of the Fourier-based registration is that given an image size the computation time is constant, while in feature-based methods computation time fluctuates depending on the number of features found. Moreover, the availability of efficient fast Fourier transform (FFT) implementations together with the method's resilience to noise, which alleviates the need of pre-processing the images, makes it suitable for real-time applications.

4.4.2.2 FLS Image Blending

Another common processing applied on underwater optical images is the fusion of the content of two overlapping frames to achieve a visually pleasant composition (Prados et al. 2012). Regardless of the particular techniques, optical blending generally deals with a low number of images at a given position (most of the times pairwise) and

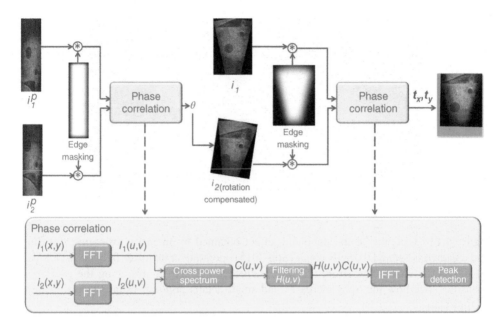

Figure 4.12   Overall Fourier-based registration pipeline

treats only their intersecting region. This prevents direct leverage from blending techniques designed for video images since blending acoustic images requires dealing with multiple overlapping frames involving high overlap percentages. High overlap is usual in FLS data because of the high frame rate of the FLS sensors; in addition, when acquiring images in an across-range manner, high overlap is a must to achieve good coverage due to the sonar fan-shaped footprint. Moreover, presuming that transformations between images are known with accuracy, it is of interest to keep as much of overlapping images as possible to be able to improve the SNR of the final image. This is again opposed to other approaches typically adopted on optical mosaicing, such as trying to select only the best image portion for a given location. Therefore, to blend FLS mosaics it is necessary to deal with not only the seam areas but also the whole image content.

In addition to this main divergence of the blending approach, there are some sonar-specific photometric irregularities that can also have a strong impact on the blending process (inhomogeneous insonification, nonuniform illumination, blind areas, seams along tracklines, etc.). The state of the art does not include precise solutions to cope with all these factors and, in fact, little work can be found in the literature regarding sonar image blending. In Kim et al. (2008), a probabilistic approach was proposed in the context of a super-resolution technique for FLS frames. The blending problem of fusing a low-resolution sonar image into a high-resolution image is modeled in terms of a conditional distribution with constraints imposed by the illumination profile of the observed frames so as to maximize the SNR of

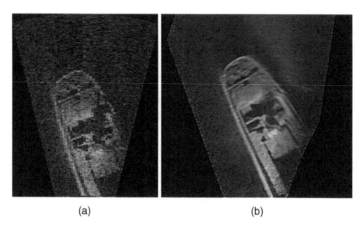

(a)   (b)

Figure 4.13 Example of the denoising effect obtained by intensity averaging. (a) Single frame gathered with a DIDSON sonar (Sou 2015) operating at its lower frequency (1.1 Mhz). (b) Fifty registered frames from the same sequence blended by averaging the overlapping intensities. See how the SNR increases and small details pop-out. Data courtesy of Sound Metrics Corp

the resulting image. Hurtós et al. (2013a) proposed a compendium of pre-processing strategies that are targeted to address each of the photometric irregularities that can be present when blending FLS images. However, this kind of treatment is intended for offline use, as often all the images are required to estimate the correction for a given artifact. For the online blending of FLS images, a simple but effective strategy is to perform an average of the intensities that are mapped onto the same pixel location. Assuming that a correct image alignment has been found, averaging the overlapping image intensities yields the denoising of the final image. Thus, the resulting image will have a better SNR compared to a single image frame (see Figure 4.13).

4.5 Concluding Remarks

Mapping and navigation are difficult tasks due to the complexity of the environment and the lack of absolute positioning systems such as GPS. Moreover, in this chapter, we have seen that underwater imaging is a difficult endeavor due to the transmission properties of the medium. Light is absorbed and scattered by water, producing images with limited range, blurring, color shift, sunflicker or marine snow, among other effects. As a result, mapping using standard computer vision techniques tends to fail in underwater imaging due to these very specific peculiarities of the medium. However, with the adequate processing pipeline, vision can be a powerful tool for underwater robots to explore the ocean. Careful image enhancement can effectively improve image visibility, partially restore color, and remove haze. These techniques, in combination with robust SLAM techniques, are able to yield accurate mapping and navigation, improving remote operations and enabling autonomous tasks in underwater robotics. Mapping by means of laser systems can drastically improve the mapping capabilities, particularly when accurate 3D mapping is required. Complementary to optical sensing, acoustic sensors can drastically increase the mapping range and coverage of underwater vehicles, especially in underwater environments with low visibility.

Acknowledgments

László Neumann is thankful to ICREA, Barcelona, Spain. Ramon Hegedüs is grateful to the Alexander von Humboldt Foundation and acknowledges the support through his fellowship for experienced researchers.

5

Vision-Based Advanced Driver Assistance Systems

David Gerónimo[1], David Vázquez[1] and Arturo de la Escalera[2]

[1]*ADAS Group, Computer Vision Center, Universitat Autònoma de Barcelona, Barcelona, Spain*
[2]*Laboratorio de Sistemas Inteligentes, Universidad Carlos III de Madrid, Madrid, Spain*

5.1 Introduction

Since the early ages of the automotive industry, motor companies have continuously pursued new technologies to improve the passengers' safety. First, relatively simple mechanical artifacts such as the turn signals or seat belts have led to more complex ones such as airbags or pop-up hoods. Then, with the development of electronics, new technologies such as the electronic stability control (ESC) or the advanced brake warning have provided more protection using signal processing. In the last decade, the development of computation has led to a new kind of protection systems: the advanced driver assistance systems (ADAS). The ADAS are intelligent systems that help the driver in the driving action by providing warnings, assist to take decisions, and take automatic actions to protect the vehicle passengers and other road users. The main difference between these systems and the former technologies is that while seat belts, airbags, or ESC deploy their functionality after the accident has happened or in the best cases while the dangerous situation is taking place, ADAS are aimed at predicting and avoiding the accident itself.

Computer Vision in Vehicle Technology: Land, Sea, and Air, First Edition.
Edited by Antonio M. López, Atsushi Imiya, Tomas Pajdla and Jose M. Álvarez.
© 2017 John Wiley & Sons Ltd. Published 2017 by John Wiley & Sons Ltd.

Figure 5.1 Typical coverage of cameras. For the sake of clarity of the illustrations, the actual cone-shaped volumes that the sensors see are shown as triangles

Such a new technology requires new sensors, different from the traditional mechanical devices, wheel speed sensor, or accelerometers. These sensors are cameras, radar, lidar (light detection and ranging), and so on. In this chapter, we put the focus on ADAS making use of cameras (Figure 5.1), that is, exploiting computer vision techniques.

We divide the different ADAS into three types, depending on the direction of the camera: forward assistance, lateral assistance, and inside assistance.

5.2   Forward Assistance

5.2.1   Adaptive Cruise Control (ACC) and Forward Collision Avoidance (FCA)

Rear-end crash is one of the most frequent types of traffic accident. In the United States, during 2002 light vehicles (passenger cars, vans, minivans, sport utility vehicles, and light trucks) were involved in 1.8 million rear-end crashes. This is 29% of all light-vehicle crashes and with a consequence of 850,000 injured people (see Najm et al. (2006)). In addition to its frequency, another characteristic is the absence of driver reaction before the accident. A report from 1999 showed that in more than 68% of rear-end collisions, the driver made no avoidance maneuver (braking or steering) to avoid it.

Figure 5.2   Forward assistance

Two systems are related with this type of accident: adaptive cruise control (ACC) and forward collision avoidance (FCA). Figure 5.2 shows the forward-facing sensors employed in these systems. ACC keeps the vehicle at a fixed speed until there is a slower vehicle in front of it. At that moment, it keeps a safe distance between the driver's car and vehicles ahead. The driver can adjust the distance, and the system makes sure it is maintained using throttle and brake control. When the slower vehicle disappears, the system resumes the fixed speed. ACCs are designed for highways. FCA provides warning of an impending accident, mainly at low speeds, alerting the driver and if it does not react, some of them can even brake the vehicle at a full stop.

Nearly all the ACC or FCA commercial systems are based on radar or laser sensors. Nevertheless, as lane departure warning (LDW) sensors are increasingly appearing on vehicles, it is convenient and cheaper to use the same sensor for both tasks. Lexus was a pioneer manufacturer that added a stereo camera to its Advanced Pre-Collision System in 2006. In 2007, Volvo's collision warning with auto brake (CWAB) developed in cooperation with Mobileye. Mobileye has developed a FCA system based on computer vision (see Raphael et al. (2011)). Subaru developed a stereo system on the Legacy called EyeSight in 2008. Recent systems performed sensor fusion, as in the Audi A8 in 2010, between a video and radar sensor. In 2012, General Motors provide a system where the same camera warns the driver when there is a vehicle ahead or there is a lane departure. Using four different exposure settings, satisfactory images across a wide range of lighting and weather conditions are obtained. The first step in the image analysis algorithm is obtaining regions of interest (ROI), where possible vehicles can be located. ROI are found where rectangles having vehicle-like characteristics are present in the image. During the night, pairs of light sources are looked for and classified as tail lights of a lead vehicle. The ROI are classified as vehicles through their appearance. Later on, they are tracked over time along with metrics (classification scores, consistency across time, etc.) that measure the likelihood that the tracked candidate is indeed a real vehicle. Knowing also the vehicle status (speed, pitch changes), a hidden Markov model filter generates and updates the estimated real-world position and dynamics of each target vehicle and determines whether they are stationary, moving, or oncoming. The last step is to determine which vehicles are within the trajectory of the ego-vehicle. The ego-vehicle path is calculated using steering angle, yaw, and speed, and also a vision sensor is used to detect the road lane markings.

5.2.2 Traffic Sign Recognition (TSR)

The speed of the vehicle plays a crucial role in many traffic accidents, and also the severity of injuries is proportional to the vehicle speed. Therefore, several measures have been taken in order to impose a low speed when necessary. Some of them are roundabouts and speed humps. Apart from that, on-board sensors can obtain the vehicle speed and check against GPS information or traffic signs detected using computer vision techniques. Although GPS navigators include speed limit information, sometimes it is not updated, there are highways where maximum speed depends on the time of day and road works may change the speed limit. Therefore, detecting traffic signs is always useful for ADAS. Figure 5.3 shows a sketch of a typical scenario where TSR is useful.

Besides being part of one ADAS, traffic sign recognition is useful for road maintenance and inventory (see Pelaez et al. (2012)). Nowadays, a human operator has to watch a recorded video sequence and check frame by frame the presence of the traffic signs. An automatic system has the advantage of releasing humans from this tedious task, it has no real-time constraint, but it has to deal with the whole set of traffic signs and sometimes in harder environments than the ADAS counterpart.

As this ADAS has to deal with object recognition in outdoor environments, there are many difficulties involved in the process due to the changes in lighting conditions, shadows, and the presence of other objects that can cause partial occlusions. Particular problems associated with traffic sign recognition are the color fading of the traffic signs depending on their age, perspective distortions, the different pictograms among countries, and the huge number of different sign pictograms. Many proposed algorithms and all the commercial systems recognized only a limited number of types and signs.

Usually, traffic sign recognition algorithms have two steps: detection and classification. The detection can help the classification step limiting the number of classes due to the shape and/or color information used for the detection.

Figure 5.3   Traffic sign recognition

For the detection, two approaches are possible depending on whether the color information is used or not. Traffic sign colors and shapes have been chosen to be easily distinguished from their background by drivers and, therefore, can be segmented in the images by their color and detected by their shape but, in practice, their colors depend a lot on the lighting conditions, the age and state of the signs, and, primarily in urban environments, there are many objects with similar colors. For these reasons, some authors preferred to analyze black and white images and used the shape or the appearance of the signs. Several color spaces have been used: RGB in Timofte et al. (2009), HSI in Liu et al. (2002), HSV in Ruta et al. (2010), and LCH in Gao et al. (2006). If no color information is used, the shape can be detected using the Hough transform as in Garcia-Garrido et al. (2011) or radial symmetry as in Barnes et al. (2008). The appearance can be described using Haar features (see Moutarde et al. (2007)) or HOG (see Xie et al. (2009)).

For the final step, the recognition of the detected signs, most of the methods are based on template matching using cross-correlation (see Piccioli et al. (1996)) or neural networks. Although there are many different approaches using neural networks, the most used are the radial basis functions (see Lim et al. (2009)) and the multilayer perceptron (see Broggi et al. (2007)), where a set of artificial samples is constructed to train the neural network.

One of the first image data sets was the *German Traffic Sign Recognition Benchmark* (see Stallkamp et al. (2011)) created for a competition held at the International Joint

Conference on Neural Networks 2011. A detailed state of the art review with many references can be found in Mogelmose et al. (2012).

In 2008 through a cooperation between Mobileye and Continental AG, a commercial system was created, appearing on the BMW 7-series and in the Mercedes-Benz S-Class (2009), although only a restricted number of traffic signs were detected: round speed limit signs. Other systems increased the number of traffic signs detected, for example, overtaking restrictions in the Opel and Saab vehicles in 2009. Other automakers have recently started to offer this ADAS such as Volkswagen in 2011 and Volvo in 2012.

5.2.3 Traffic Jam Assist (TJA)

Driving in traffic jams is boring and monotonous. In these situations, drivers suffer stress due to the constant acceleration and braking. Being stuck in a traffic jam produces frustration and distraction to the drivers that can cause fender-bender crashes. In addition, traffic jams represent a waste of time for the drivers.

Traffic jam assistant is a device that controls the vehicle speed, steering, and the distance to the car ahead in heavy traffic at relative low speeds. It takes over the vehicle control in these monotonous traffic situations. This system simply guides along the vehicle with the other cars in dense traffic situations, making traffic jams less frustrating. However, some systems still require the driver to keep his/her hands on the wheel.

This technology provides a combination of the individual's own comfort with automated travel and helps to drive more comfortably and safe in heavy-driving situations. It could potentially cut down on accidents by reducing the fender-bender-type crashes in heavy traffic. The TJA system also offers moderate energy savings over regular driving, and takes up less space on the road than the same number of vehicles would occupy if each were driving independently. So it could reduce the pollution and alleviate traffic jams. However, it is as much of a luxury feature as it is a safety one. It frees the driver to take the control of the vehicle in this situation and allows them to find some other ways to make use of the time.

The traffic jam assistance system is a natural next step from advanced cruise control technology. It is similar to cruise control, except it is specifically designed to work in heavy traffic instead of on an open road. It is limited to use at slow speeds having systems that allow even 60 km/h. It combines automatic cruise control with lane assist and automatic braking technology to help your car glide smoothly along in the most annoying road conditions. The ACC system uses a combination of cameras and radar to maintain a safe, set distance behind the car in front, and Lane Keeping Aid uses a network of cameras and sensors to keep the car centered within its lane. So, this automotive innovation makes the use of available vehicle cameras and sensors to help all traffic flow more smoothly.

The car will monitor the vehicle in front of you, and pace it to automatically maintain a steady following distance. It will also steer to stay within the lane. If the car in front swerves to avoid an obstacle, your car can mimic the same swerve path by following the tire treads. Overall, the TJA system actuates over the engine, steering, and brakes. So by activating the system, the driver entrusts the car to make the most important judgment calls of heavy-traffic driving: steering, deciding when to accelerate and decelerate, and determining how much of a distance cushion to maintain around other vehicles and obstacles.

It has been available in Volvo's cars since 2014. Similar systems are in development by Audi, VW, Cadillac, Mercedes, and Ford. So far, it seems like most will operate in a comparable way, as they are also designed to allow completely hands-free operation in these low-speed scenarios. Owners of Mercedes equipped with TJA systems have fewer options to pass the time, though—these drivers have to maintain contact with the steering wheel for the system to work. If a driver pulls his or her hands off the wheel, the system will not engage. The Ford version of the system, which is similar to Volvo's, has a different plan in place. It uses audio warnings to alert the driver to take back control if the car determines that there is too much nearby activity, such as frequent changes in adjacent lanes, lots of obstacles, or erratic and therefore unpredictable speeds of travel.

5.2.4   Vulnerable Road User Protection

During most of the history of the vehicles, safety technologies developed by the motor companies have been focused on its occupants, while other road users such as pedestrians or cyclists have not received the same attention. However, statistics show that the number of accidents involving these actors is not to be neglected. For example, 150,000 pedestrians are injured and 7000 are killed every year in the European Union (see UN – ECE (2005)); and 70,000 injured and 4000 killed in the United States (see NHTSA (2007)). Even though these numbers are progressively decreasing through the years in developed regions, thanks to the new safety measures and awareness, emerging countries such as China or India are likely to be greatly increasing these numbers as a result of the already high accidents over vehicles ratio and the increasing number of vehicles (see Gerónimo and López (2014)).

The first papers addressing pedestrian protection using computer vision were presented in the late 1990s by Poggio, Gavrila, and Broggi research groups in MIT, University of Amsterdam, and Parma University, respectively. The first approaches made use of the knowledge in object classification and worked in very constrained scenarios (e.g., fully seen well-illuminated pedestrians in flat roads). Papageorgiou and Poggio (2000) introduced the use of Haar wavelets in pedestrian classification and the first pedestrian data set. Gavrila and colleagues introduced a template-based hierarchical classification algorithm known as the Chamfer System (see Gavrila (2001)). Bertozzi et al. (2003) and Broggi et al. (2000) proposed different approaches to specific problems of on-board pedestrian detection, for example, camera stabilization, symmetry-based models, and tracking.

Input → raw image stereo ego etc.

Candidate generation
• Road position and profile estimation
• General object detection
• Obstacle detection

Pedestrian classification
• Object classification
• Fusion of overlapped detections
• Scene understanding

Pedestrian tracking
• Inidividual /multiple object tracking
• Path estimation and prediction

→ Output detections directions behavior

Figure 5.4 The main steps of pedestrian detection together with the main processes carried out in each module

The human image class is one of the most complex in computer vision: nonrigid shape, dynamic, and very heterogeneous in size and clothing, apart from the typical challenges that any forward-looking ADAS application must tackle, for example, illumination changes, moving targets. Since 2000, the number of papers addressing pedestrian detection has grown exponentially. The emergence of computer vision as a hot research field has helped to improve the systems' robustness and pursue new challenges, that is, going from holistic classification (detect the silhouette as a whole) in simple scenarios to multipart classification in cluttered streets. The standard pedestrian detector can be divided into three steps (see Figure 5.4):

- Candidate generation selects image windows likely to contain a pedestrian. The selection is made using both prior constraints such as the position of the camera and the expected size and aspect ratio of pedestrians; and online detection of free space, obstacles, and the road profile.
- Pedestrian classification labels the selected windows as pedestrian or nonpedestrian (e.g., background, vehicles).
- Pedestrian tracking adds temporal coherence to the frame-based pedestrian detections, linking each pedestrian window with a specific identity that has a correspondence among the video frames. The last trend is to predict the pedestrian behavior.

Some of the major milestones in candidate generation are the flat-world assumption (see Gavrila et al. (2004)), which takes advantage of the knowledge of the camera position with respect to the road in order to avoid scanning the whole image. As its name says, the assumption is that the road is flat, which only holds in certain streets and roads. The next step was to extend this to sloppy roads (see Labayrade et al. (2002) and Sappa et al. (2008)) making use of stereo cameras. One of the latest and most relevant innovations in this is the *stixels* model (see Badino et al. (2007) and Benenson et al. (2012)) presented by researchers at Daimler AG. It consists of a 3D occupancy grid that represents objects as vertical bars placed on the road where its pixels have a coherent disparity.

Candidate classification is the most researched component, given its connection with general visual object detection. The first approaches used a holistic model composed of local features such as Haar filters (see Papageorgiou and Poggio (2000) and Viola and Jones (2001a)) or HOG (see Dalal and Triggs (2005))—there are many more such as edge orientation histograms, local binary patterns, shapelets, and so on,—and a learning machine such as SVM, AdaBoost, or Random Forest, which label each selected window in the candidate generation step. Then, these classifiers evolved to parts-based ones, in which individual parts were also part of the model in a fixed (see Mohan et al. (2001)) or flexible manner (see Felzenszwalb et al. (2008) and Marin et al. (2013)). It is worth highlighting other approaches such as the aforementioned Chamfer System (see Gavrila (2001)) or the ISM (Implicit Shape Model; see Leibe et al. (2008)), the latter approach omitting the window generation stage or data-driven features that avoid the handcrafted ones (e.g. HOG, Haar) by the use of neural networks (see Enzweiler and Gavrila (2009)). The latest works aim at detecting occluded pedestrians (see Tang et al. (2009)), fusing and combining different features (see Dollár et al. (2009) and Rao et al. (2011)), using nonvisible spectrum cues (e.g., IR; see Krotosky and Trivedi (2007) and Socarras et al. (2013)), and using online adaptation to new scenarios (see Vazquez et al. (2014) and Xu et al. (2014a)), that is, improve the classifier as the vehicle captures new pedestrians.

Tracking approaches have traditionally used the well-known Kalman filtering (see Franke and Joos (2000) and Grubb et al. (2004)) or particle filtering (see Arndt et al. (2007)) techniques, although other approaches have also been proposed. Examples are the event cone by Leibe et al. (2007), tracking-by-detection by Adnriluka et al. (2008), the contour-based tracking by Mitzel et al. (2010), or the long-term 3D-tracklets model in Wojek et al. (2014). As previously mentioned, state-of-the-art works try to extend the tracking information with higher-level information such as action classification or face orientation in order to predict the pedestrian's behavior (see Keller and Gavrila (2014)). This information is crucial in order to avoid false alarms, for example, even if the predicted pedestrian's path collides with the vehicle path, an alarm may not need to be triggered if his/her face points to the vehicle, that is, the pedestrian is aware of the vehicle and is likely to stop in time.

Once the pedestrian or cyclist has been detected, this information is sent to a high-level component that triggers the alerts or actions to the vehicle. There exist many example applications, especially in the past years, where vulnerable road users' protection is being commercialized. One of the most illustrative systems is that presented in the SAVE-U European project (see Marchal et al. (2005)). It divides the application in three phases. The first one is called early detection, in which the pedestrians are just tracked and detected but no protection measure is activated. The second phase occurs when a pedestrian is estimated to enter the vehicle trajectory, but there is no predicted collision. In this case, an acoustic warning is triggered. Finally, the third phase is activated when a high risk of collision is identified. In this case, the brakes automatically activate in order to avoid the collision. In recent years, some interesting studies in evasive actions, that is, steering around the pedestrian when full braking is not enough to avoid the accident, have been being researched by Daimler AG (see Dang et al. (2004)).

One of the first vehicles to commercialize a pedestrian protection system was the Volvo S60, which used a radar and a visible-spectrum camera engineered by the ADAS company Mobileye. From 2013, a class of Mercedes-Benz incorporates the result of the research developed in Daimler AG, able to detect obstacles up to 200 m using a radar and pedestrians up to 35 m using a stereo camera. It incorporates emergency brake assist (EBA), which stops the car at speeds up to 70 km/h and emergency steer assist (ESA), which maneuvers the car around the obstacle if there is insufficient time to stop. Other motor companies such as BMW, Ford, and Toyota are planning to present similar systems in their top cars in the following years. The latest research directions are focused on intention estimation in pedestrians and cyclists.

The reader can refer to review papers such as by Dollár et al. (2012), Enzweiler and Gavrila (2009) and Gerónimo et al. (2010), and to books such as Gerónimo and López (2014) for detailed information.

5.2.5 *Intelligent Headlamp Control*

Driving in nighttime has its specific difficulties when compared to daytime, obviously as a result of poor lighting. Headlamps were introduced with the invention of the car around 1890, and very soon incorporated low- and high-beam capability. The two, sometimes three, position headlamps allow the driver to illuminate long distances taking advantage of the absence of approaching cars from the front and lowering them when a car approaches and there is danger of dazzling other drivers. Often, drivers prefer to use low beams and only switch to high beams when it is absolutely needed, in order to not blind others. This behavior is reflected in statistics, which state that high beams are used less than 25% of the time in which they should be used (see Mefford et al. (2006)). However, incorrectly setting high beams is a well-known source of accidents, and low beams also are a source of accidents due to the limited visibility and hence slow reaction time.

Intelligent Headlamp Control provides an assisted control of the lights aimed at automatically optimizing their use without inconveniencing other drivers. The typical approach is to analyze the image searching for vehicles. Oncoming vehicles are distinguished by white lights, while preceding vehicles are distinguished by the rear lights, which are red. As can be seen, it is important not to dazzle oncoming vehicles but also preceding ones, as they could be dazzled via their rear mirror. In Schaudel and Falb (2007), both preceding and oncoming vehicles and also the presence of sufficient illumination are detected. If none of these conditions apply, the high beams are turned on.

A more sophisticated approach was introduced by the A. López et al. team in 2007 (Figure 5.5). The vehicles were detected by using blob, gray-level statistics, and red-channel statistics as features and AdaBoost as a classifier (see Lopez et al. (2008a, 2008b) and Rubio et al. (2012)). These systems typically use a continuous range of beam, instead of just switching from high to low. The light cone is adjusted dynamically as the oncoming vehicles approach and moved further as far as 300 m

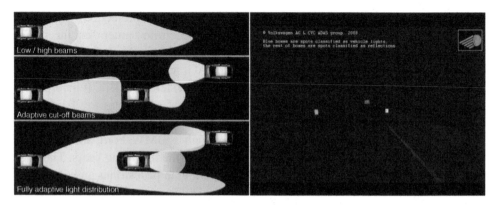

Figure 5.5 Different approaches in Intelligent Headlamp Control (Lopez et al. (2008a)). On the top, traditional low beams that reach low distances. In the middle, the beams are dynamically adjusted to avoid glaring the oncoming vehicle. On the bottom, the beams are optimized to maximize visibility while avoiding glaring by the use of LED arrays

when no vehicles are detected. This is feasible by the use of LED lights that illuminate or not according to the content of the position they are pointing at. The state-of-the-art research is focused on selectively illuminating all the road, shading only the spots where there is a vehicle.

Daimler AG and Volkswagen AG, among other companies, have incorporated a similar technology in their high-end vehicles since 2009.

5.2.6   Enhanced Night Vision (Dynamic Light Spot)

Most of the applications presented in both ADAS and autonomous driving require specific solutions to work in nighttime (Figure 5.6). For example, while reflecting objects such as traffic signs are specially engineered to be visible in nighttime, pedestrians or nonreflective obstacles are barely distinguishable with regular headlamps, and often they are too close to the vehicle to avoid them in the case of danger.

Figure 5.6 Enhanced night vision. Thanks to infrared sensors the system is capable of distinguishing hot objects (e.g., car engines, pedestrians) from the cold road or surrounding natural environment

Enhanced night vision systems take advantage of the fact that for most of the objects of interest (i.e., pedestrians, cyclists, vehicles) their fingerprint temperature is different from the background, which can be captured by analyzing the infrared spectrum of the scene. The infrared spectrum ranges from 0.8 to 1000 μm, dividing itself into near infrared (NIR) from 0.8 to 2.5 μm, mid–infrared (MIR) from 2.5 to 25 μm, and far infrared (FIR) from 25 to 1000 μm. Regular visible spectrum cameras often also capture NIR together with the visible spectrum range, which goes from 0.4 to 0.75 μm, making them a lower cost version of this technology. In fact, night vision technology can be divided into active and passive approaches, depending on the range that is captured. In the active systems, the camera emits a pulse of NIR, which is captured by the sensor (see Andreone et al. (2005)). Passive systems capture FIR (also referred to as thermal infrared) directly emitted by hot objects (see Olmeda et al. (2011) and Socarras et al. (2013)). These latter cameras tend to be more expensive and higher in dimensions, but capture longer distances and work well under cold weather.

In any case, nighttime visibility always depends on the available illumination on the road. For instance, an urban scene full of lampposts probably can make these systems irrelevant while a poorly illuminated highway or a countryside road will show their whole potential. Using infrared can also be challenging because the scene can be full of hot objects (hot lamps illuminated during the day, vehicles, etc.). Two interesting examples of the use of this technology are Ge et al. (2009) and Zhou et al. (2012). In the former, they use a two-stage pedestrian classifier consisting of Haar-like HOG features extracted from infrared imagery. In the latter, the authors extract HOG features also from thermal imagery to detect deer in the context of traffic safety.

One of the first companies incorporating such technology was General Motors in 2000–2004 with a head-up display that showed the raw infrared image acquired by the camera. This is the simplest setup: the driver has to switch often from the front-shield view to the head-up in order to analyze the potential hazards. In 2002, Toyota developed a similar head-up display but based on an active IR system. In 2004, Honda performed pedestrian detection and highlighted (framed) them in the head-up display. This system had an audio warning that triggered when some danger existed to the pedestrian, alleviating the driver from checking the display when there was no danger. Toyota has incorporated such a pedestrian detection system since 2008.

Other motor companies such as BMW, Mercedes-Benz, and Audi also featured these systems in their top models in the early years of development and added pedestrian detection several years later (around 2009). Currently, they are including animal detection and visual/audio alerts, exploiting either active or passive systems, depending on the company.

5.2.7 Intelligent Active Suspension

Suspension was incorporated in automobile design right after invention of the car. It provides not only comfort to the passengers but also improves handling and braking safety, given that it holds the wheels on the road by overcoming road irregularities or vehicle dynamics (e.g., braking or cornering). Suspension, as a system that absorbs bumps, has been used not only in vehicles of the modern industrialized era but also on old carts and carriages. The systems slowly evolved from leaf strings to shock absorbers, but it was not until the 1980s that active suspension was developed, thanks to the use of electronic control. Active suspension incorporates sensors, which analyze the road surface, and actuators, which control the vertical movement of each wheel, even raising and lowering the chassis, depending on the system. These systems provide a smoother driving experience than previous suspension systems that just absorbed the bumps mechanically.

The current developments in this field are pioneered by the use of vision in order to model the road surface in advance. Even though current active suspension systems incorporate different sensors that handle each vehicle movement (i.e., lateral movement, bumps, braking), vision has the capability of anticipating the needed suspension actions. The idea is that instead of rapidly reacting to the current road profile, the system scans and models the road surface by the use of a camera and raises or lowers each wheel accordingly. For instance, on a typical bumpy road, a regular active suspension system reacts instantaneously to the current surface just below the wheels. An intelligent active suspension system predicts the wheels and chassis movements in the road ahead, providing a much smoother suspension than the former. Singh and Agrawal (2011) made use of camera and lidar sensors in order to get a 3D contour of the road, providing cues to a servo drive managed by a neural network. Interestingly, the shock absorber oil is replaced by a magnetized fluid that allows the system to extend and retract the suspension cylinder.

Mercedes-Benz has recently presented a pioneering system, named Magic Body Control (Figure 5.7), which scans the road surface with a stereo camera mounted in the windscreen. It scans the road up to 15 m ahead with a vertical precision of 3 mm.

5.3 Lateral Assistance

5.3.1 Lane Departure Warning (LDW) and Lane Keeping System (LKS)

Lane detection has been studied for around 30 years (see Dickmanns (2007), Crisman and Thorpe (1993), and Pomerleau (1995)). As a high percentage of traffic accidents are related with unintended lane departures, the first commercially available ADAS were related for this task. First, they were implemented on trucks and, later on, on cars. Lane departures mostly happen on long trips on highways where the monotony of driving produce lapses of attention or drowsiness, leading to lane departures and collision with another vehicle or a stationary obstacle, or a rollover accident. This is an advantage for perception systems as the highway is a very structured environment. One example is shown in Figure 5.8, where a computer vision algorithm has detected both lane boundaries. From this information, as it will be described later, some warning to the driver or action on the steering wheel can be done.

Figure 5.7 Intelligent active suspension. Image courtesy of Daimler AG

Figure 5.8 Lane Departure Warning (LDW) and Lane Keeping System (LKS)

Most of the algorithms have the same steps in common: after extracting some features from the images, they are fitted into a lane/road model and time integration is used in order to reject errors and refine the results. As human drivers detect the road depending on color or texture and the presence of road boundaries and lane markings, these are the features detected on images. The lane boundaries are detected using the gradient steerable filters (see McCall and Trivedi (2006)), the top-hat shape of the marks (see Wu et al. (2008)), and the Euclidean distance transform (see Danescu and Nedevschi (2009)). Appearance is used for road detection. Color is used in Alvarez et al. (2007), Alon et al. (2006), and Nefian and Bradski (2006); Gabor filters are used to describe the road texture. Different models have been proposed to describe the lanes or the road. Straight lines are the most common in highway scenarios or when only the part of the road close to the vehicle is needed (see Alon et al. (2006) and Xu and Shin (2013)). More complex shapes have been described using arcs (see Zhou et al. (2010), McCall and Trivedi (2006), Linarth and Angelopoulou (2011), and Meuter et al. (2009)), polylines (see Romdhane et al. (2011)), clothoids (see Dickmanns (2007) and Danescu and Nedevschi (2011)), and splines (see Wang et al. (2003)). Temporal integration is based on Kalman (see McCall and Trivedi (2006) and Loose and Franke (2009)) or particle filtering (see Danescu and Nedevschi (2009) and Liu et al. (2011)).

Although cameras are the most frequent type of sensor used for road and lane detection, light detection and ranging (lidar) has also been used (Huang et al. 2009). The advantages are as follows: they provide very accurate 3D information of the scene in front of the vehicle so curbs can be detected; some give information about the amount of intensity reflected by the surfaces so lane marks or different types of terrains can be recognized. Nevertheless, their price and size make them unsuitable for commercial application at the moment. There are some states-of-the-art accounts about road and lane detection, such as McCall and Trivedi (2006), Hillel et al. (2014), and Shin et al. (2014).

There are two main types of ADAS that perceive the lanes of the highways: LDW and LKS. The main difference is the output action of the system, whereby LDW only warns the driver when an unintended departure is going to happen whereas LKS warns and helps the driver to keep the vehicle on track by controlling the steering wheel.

LDW can take into account several types of information: the lateral distance to the lane boundary or distance to line crossing (DLC), where no information about the vehicles or shape of the line is taken into account, or the actual time for the departure of the vehicle or time to line crossing (TLC), where the vehicle's speed and orientation with respect to the lane has to be known. And additional source of information is the turn signal state in order not to warn the driver when changing lanes.

One of the first systems was developed by Iteris for Mercedes Actros trucks in 2000, and later on the Japanese manufacturers Nissan in 2001 and Toyota in 2002 used this technology in sedan vehicles. Although Citroën, in 2004, mounted several infrared sensors under the vehicle for lane detection, computer vision is the preferred technology for LDW and LKS. A camera mounted behind the windshield gives more information of the geometry of the road, and the driver can be warned with more anticipation. Nowadays, LDW is the most widely available ADAS.

LKS needs the information previously explained and in addition they actuate on the heading, producing and assisting torque on the steering wheel, although the driver remains in charge of the control of the vehicle. In some systems, additional action is on the braking system of the vehicle. The geometry of the road, as a clothoid or polynomial approximation, has to be computed in order to obtain its curvature. Again, this ADAS was firstly introduced in Japan by Honda in 2003 and Toyota in 2004 and later on in Europe by Volkswagen in 2008.

5.3.2 Lane Change Assistance (LCA)

LCA is a collection of technologies taking care of blind spots and rear-view problems. It uses sensors to detect objects and vehicles that usually cannot be seen by the driver because of obstructed view. In addition, approaching vehicles from behind can be detected in time, and the driver can be informed of this.

Nearly all car manufacturers offer an ADAS that monitors the blind spots of the vehicle. Through the change in the color of one optical display, the system indicates to the driver if an obstacle is present or not. The kind of accident this ADAS tries to avoid is collision with another vehicle being driven at the blind spot when the driver changes lane on a highway, or collision with another vehicle not in the blind spot but whose speed is faster than the driver estimates. Therefore, this ADAS supports drivers when changing lanes because either they have not used the exterior and rear-view mirrors properly or they have incorrectly estimated the speed of approaching overtaking vehicles.

Two sensors can be used: radar and vision based. As radar sensor does not have information of the location of the lane, depending on the radius of the road they can give false warnings misplacing a vehicle as being in an adjacent lane when it is in the same lane or a following vehicle that is two lanes away and not in the next lane. Due to the sensor placement, a mounted trailer might interfere with the radar. Nevertheless, radar is more reliable in adverse weather conditions than vision and most manufacturers use 24 GHz radars mounted behind the rear bumper and cameras integrated in the exterior side-view mirrors.

Some Peugeot and Citroën models have used the system developed by FICOSA (see Sartori et al. (2005)) since 2002. It analyses the presence of objects in the blind spot providing a qualitative idea of the speed and position of them relative to the car. The system detects vehicles and computes optical flow. The movement is obtained through a phase difference approach and the vehicles are detected as rectangular structures in the image of edges. Fusing both types of information, approaching and receding objects can be differentiated and the distance and relative speed of the vehicles at different levels of risks can be determined. Volvo installed a system in 2005 based on computer vision but in 2007 started to offer a radar-based system.

5.3.3 Parking Assistance

The Parking Assistance system looks like LCA, but it is meant for low speed and short distance, for example, when parking a car (Figure 5.9). By using sensors, a car can measure available space and show this information to the driver. Current systems have limited use because of the low range these sensors operate with. Future developments will let the system take over control of the car during parking, thus letting the car park itself.

All car manufacturers offer some kind of Parking Assist system, varying from offering only visual and audio information to the driver to automatic parking free place detection or semiautomatic self-parking. The sensor in charge of this belongs to a kind of system that is based on the ring of ultrasound sensors around the vehicle. Vision-based systems are very simple. They offer the image provided by a camera placed in the rear of the vehicles. The most complex ones perform a calibration of the intrinsic and extrinsic parameters of the camera, and therefore they can show images without geometrical aberration and draw the obstacle detected by the ultrasound in the image. Knowing the pose of the camera and the dynamic constraints of the vehicle, the system can also draw the intended path of the vehicle in order to park and the existing one.

Figure 5.9 Parking Assistance. Sensors' coverages are shown as 2D shapes to improve visualization

5.4   Inside Assistance

5.4.1   Driver Monitoring and Drowsiness Detection

Most traffic accidents have a human cause. Some studies establish that more than 80% of road accidents are due to human error (see Treat et al. (1979)). Among several factors, inattention can be established as the most important one (see Beirness et al. (2002)). For example, the NHTSA estimates that approximately 25% of police-reported crashes involve some form of driving inattention, including fatigue and distraction (see Ranney et al. (2001)). In Europe, driver inattention is the cause of 34,500 deaths and 1.5 million injured, with associated costs representing 2% of the EU GDP. Data gathered for several decades have shown that inattention, which includes drowsiness and distractions, is behind 80% of crashes (see Juliussen and Robinson (2010) and Mahieu (2009)).

Therefore, driver drowsiness and distraction have received a lot of attention from the scientific community in recent years in order to alert the driver before a dangerous situation happens. Most of the research can be classified within one of the following three groups. The first two groups pay attention to the driver and the last group to the vehicle itself:

- **Driver physiological information:** one or several biological signals of the driver are collected such as electrocardiogram (ECG), electromyogram (EMG), electro-oculogram (EoG), and electroencephalogram (EEG) in order to detect driver drowsiness.
- **Driver appearance:** The driver is monitored through one or several cameras and depending on several facial expressions such as yawning, eye closure, eye blinking, head pose, and so on, drowsiness and distraction are detected. Toyota developed its Driver Monitoring System in 2006. The system, when a dangerous situation is detected, checks if the driver is looking in front of the vehicle or not and warns it in that case. Several OEMs have developed systems that can be installed on board the vehicle such as LumeWay, Seeing Machines, or Smart Eye, which use computer vision to monitor drivers.
- **Vehicle information:** The vehicle is monitored instead of the driver, including deviations from lateral lane position, time-to-line crossing, movement of the steering wheel, pressure on the acceleration pedal, and changes in a normal behavior indicating driver drowsiness or distraction. This last approach has been used by Volvo for its Driver Alert Control since 2007 and by Daimler since 2009 for its Attention Assist.

All the approaches have some advantages and shortcomings. On the one hand, biological signals are direct measurements of the driver state but are intrusive and nonpractical. On the other hand, driver observation is not intrusive and drowsiness can also be detected through computer vision. However, illumination changes and the diversity in driver appearance is a challenge, making this approach not suitable for every time of the day. Vehicle information is easier to obtain but the correlation with the state of the driver is complex, and in some important environments, such as driving within cities, the absence of lanes avoids the calculation of two of their most important parameters: lateral lane position and time-to-line crossing.

EEG has been used for drowsiness detection for more than four decades (see Volow and Erwin (1973)). Although its results are considered valid (Lal and Craig (2002) detected fatigue with an error rate of approximately 10%, and Golz et al. (2010) obtained microsleep detection errors of 10%), the excessive intrusiveness, where the driver has to wear electrodes connected by wires to a computer, makes it physiologically unsuitable for real applications.

PERCLOS (PERcentage of eye CLOSure), the proportion of time interval that the eyes are 80–100% closed, was described by Skipper and Wierwille (1986) as an index of driver drowsiness and received a lot of promotion, such as in 1998 when it was supported by the Federal Highway Administration (see Dinges and Grace (1998)) as an accepted standard for alertness measures. Using NIR illumination (Figure 5.10) has the advantages of the pupil effect, similar to the red-eye effect of flash cameras, and the capability of obtaining an independent image with respect to external illumination (see Ji and Yang (2002) and Bergasa et al. (2004)). However, if the driver wears sunglasses, the PERCLOS cannot be computed and the illumination change is a challenge for the robustness of the image analysis algorithms.

Computer vision is also useful for driver monitoring as the orientation of the head and the gaze can be obtained, in this way distraction can also be detected. In Jiménez et al. (2009), a stereo camera system automatically builds a 3D rigid model of the face. At the beginning of a video sequence, salient features of the face are detected and used to build the model, which was consequently tracked. It was developed by Jiménez et al. (2012a) for 90 yaw rotations and under low-light conditions. The driver

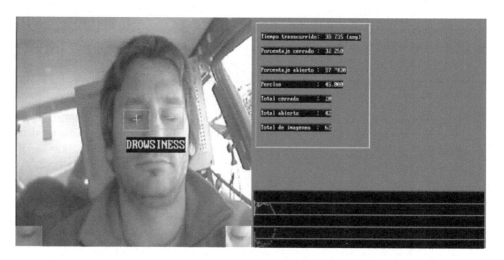

Figure 5.10   Drowsiness detection based on PERCLOS and an NIR camera

head model was initially made upon a set of 3D points derived from stereo images. As new areas of the subject face appear, the model was updated. It was validated on sequences recorded in a naturalistic truck simulator, on driving exercises designed by a team of psychologists (see Jiménez et al. (2012b)).

Several signals on the vehicle reflect the driver intentions and actions so that the driver's behavior can be inferred by analyzing them, with the additional advantages of being a nonintrusive method and their availability through the CAN (controller area network) bus. This way several parameters can be obtained such as speed, steering angle, position of the accelerator, and brake pedals. If the vehicle is perceiving the lane, additional parameters are time-to-collision, time-to-lane crossing, and lateral shift (see Tango et al. (2010)).

This has been the technological choice for the first automotive company systems installing driver drowsiness or attention systems into their vehicles. The disadvantages are as follows: the systems require a training period for each person driver so that they are not useful for occasional drivers and they are not able to detect when the driver falls asleep for a few seconds on a straight road without changing the direction of the vehicle.

5.5 Conclusions and Future Challenges

Computer vision is a key component for understanding the scene around the car. It has the potential of providing higher level information than other techniques that use radar or lidar information. This high level of understanding is crucial when engineering systems such as pedestrian detection in complex environments, driver monitoring, or traffic sign recognition. As has been explained throughout this chapter, there are many commercial ADAS making use of vision as a key component already in the market. However, each one is at its own stage of maturity and has its specific problems. For instance, although vision-based ACCs are being researched mainly in order to improve the success case of radar-based ones, pedestrian protection is starting its commercialization and still has a long journey not only to increase its robustness but also to add extra functionalities (e.g., estimate their behavior to anticipate actions), as previously explained.

In this section, we overview the main challenges present in ADAS as a whole. We divide the challenges into two aspects: systems robustness and cost. These aspects correspond to the factors that must be addressed by researchers, industry, and governments in order to achieve the integration of ADAS with other vehicle safety measures such as airbags or seat belts.

5.5.1 Robustness

One of the ways to measure the robustness of any on-board safety system is the standard safety performance assessments such as the Euro NCAP (European New Car Assessment Program), the Japanese NASVA (National Agency for Automotive

	Stereo	Optical flow	Detection	Classification	Tracking	Lidar
Adaptive cruise control and forward collision avoidance	Useful	Low	High	High	High	Useful
Traffic sign recognition	Null	Null	High	High	Useful	Null
Traffic jam assist	Useful	Low	High	High	High	Useful
Vulnerable road user protection	High	Useful	High	High	High	Null
Intelligent headlamp control	Null	Useful	High	High	Useful	Null
Enhanced night vision	Null	Null	High	High	Low	Null
Intellignt active suspension	High	Null	High	Useful	High	Useful
Lane departure warning and lane keeping system	Null	Null	High	High	Useful	Null
Lane change assistance	Useful	Null	High	High	Useful	Useful
Parking assistance	High	Null	Useful	Useful	Null	Useful
Driver monitoring and drowsiness detection	Useful	Null	High	High	High	Null

Figure 5.11 Summary of the relevance of several technologies in each ADAS: in increasing relevance as null, low, useful, and high

Safety and Victims Aid), or the American NHTSA (National Highway Traffic Administration).

Even though ADAS are still in the process of being included in these demanding assessments, very solid steps have already been made in this direction. As an example, the Euro NCAP has a rewards program for the best advanced safety systems in the market that complements the usual star-rating scheme (see EURO NCAP (2014)). This program includes blind spot, lane assist, speed alert, emergency braking, and pre-crash systems, among others. These systems include most of ADAS and are quite specific in the applications addressed. For example, in the case of the Autonomous Emergency Braking (AEB) program, it is again divided into city, interurban, and pedestrian systems. Different commercial vehicles from 2010 to 2013 have been rewarded. It is worth to highlight Ford's Driver Alert (an indirect way of driver monitoring through forward-looking cameras); Ford, Audi, and SEAT's lane assist systems; and Volkswagen Group's FCA systems. From 2014 onwards, standard protocols to assess the safety rating of some of these systems have been in use, which gives an idea of the maturity of the field.

5.5.2   Cost

Perhaps the most difficult barrier nowadays to the global deployment of ADAS is their cost. Night vision systems were commercialized as early as the year 2000, and vulnerable road users' protection is being integrated by the top tier vehicles of different motor companies nowadays. However, the real challenge is to integrate different ADAS at lower cost in the average cost vehicles. The approach that must be taken here is to be able to use the same sensors for different ADAS (i.e., using the same forward-looking camera for detecting vehicles at long distances, pedestrians at short distances, and lanes). This can be problematic nowadays given that most classifiers, trackers, and so on require cameras with fields of view and resolutions in a given range. Furthermore, another important point to be taken into account is to provide an easy and inexpensive maintenance of these systems. For example, the calibration of the vision system has to be performed once a year as for other parts of the vehicle, not once per month. In this direction, self-calibration is an interesting way to solve this potential problem (see Dang et al. (2009)). Finally, Figure 5.11 summarizes the relevance of several technologies in each ADAS: in increasing relevance as null, low, useful, and high.

Acknowledgments

This work is supported by the Spanish MICINN projects TRA2011-29454-C03-01 and TRA2014-57088-C2-1-R by the Secretaria d'Universitats i Recerca del Departament d'Economia i Coneixement de la Generalitat de Catalunya (2014-SGR-1506), and by DGT project SPIP2014-01352. Our research is also kindly supported by NVIDIA Corporation in the form of different GPU hardware.

6

Application Challenges from a Bird's-Eye View

Davide Scaramuzza

Robotics and Perception Group, University of Zurich, Zurich, Switzerland

6.1 Introduction to Micro Aerial Vehicles (MAVs)

An unmanned aerial vehicle (UAV), commonly known as a drone, is an aircraft without a human pilot aboard. The international civil aviation organization (ICAO) of the United Nations classifies UAVs into two types: (i) autonomous aircrafts and (ii) remotely piloted aircrafts. UAVs were initially conceived for military applications, but in recent years we have witnessed also a growing number of civil applications, such as law enforcement and firefighting, security and surveillance, agriculture, aerial photography, inspection, and search and rescue.

6.1.1 Micro Aerial Vehicles (MAVs)

The term micro aerial vehicle (MAV) means a miniature UAV that is less than 1 m in size and below 2 kg in weight. Some MAVs can even be as small as a few centimeters and weigh only a few grams (cf. Ma et al. (2013) and Troiani et al. (2013)).

MAVs can be seen as the logical extension of ground mobile robots. Their ability to fly allows them to easily avoid obstacles on the ground and to have an excellent bird's-eye view. MAVs can be classified into rotorcrafts (or rotary wing), fixed or flapping wing, or hybrid (cf. Figure 6.1).

Figure 6.1   A few examples of MAVs. From left to right: the senseFly eBee, the DJI Phantom, the hybrid XPlusOne, and the FESTO BioniCopter

6.1.2   Rotorcraft MAVs

Small rotorcrafts have several advantages compared to those based on fixed wings: they are able to take off and land vertically, hover on a spot, and even dock to a surface (cf. Kumar and Michael (2012)). This capability allows them to navigate easily in unstructured, indoor environments (Shen et al. 2012), pass through windows (Achtelik et al. 2009), traverse narrow corridors (Zingg et al. 2010), climb stairs (Bills et al. 2011b), and navigate through or over damaged buildings for rescue or inspection operations (Faessler et al. 2015b; Michael et al. 2012b). Thus, they are the ideal platforms for exploration, mapping, and monitoring tasks in search-and-rescue and remote-inspection scenarios.

Multirotor MAVs come usually in the form of quadrotors (also known as quadcopters), hexacopters, or octocopters and have matched sets of rotors turning in opposite directions. The smaller the number of rotors, the better the efficiency of the vehicle. On the other hand, the achievable dynamics and, therefore, the maneuverability of the vehicle can be enhanced by a larger number of propellers and a smaller ratio between rotor surface and total weight (Achtelik et al. 2012). Additionally, hexacopters and octocopters offer redundancy against single-rotor failure. However, quadrotors have become very successful nowadays because of their relatively simple design.

6.2   GPS-Denied Navigation

To date, most autonomous MAVs rely on GPS to navigate outdoors. However, GPS may not be reliable in cases of low satellite coverage or multipaths: two phenomena that are very frequent in urban settings when flying at low altitudes and close to buildings. Furthermore, GPS is completely unavailable indoors, thus limiting the use of drones in search-and-rescue or remote-inspection operations. At the current state, most MAVs used in search-and–rescue and remote-inspection scenarios are teleoperated under direct line of sight with the operator (cf. Murphy (2014)). If wireless communication with the MAV can be maintained, there is the possibility to teleoperate the MAV by transmitting video streams from onboard cameras to the operator. However, teleoperation from video streams is extremely challenging in indoor environments. Furthermore, wireless communication cannot be guaranteed after a certain range. For these reasons, there is a large need of flying robots that can navigate autonomously, without any user intervention.

The key problem in MAV navigation is attitude and position control. Today's systems handle well the attitude control using proprioceptive sensors such as inertial measurement units (IMU). However, without position control, they are prone to drift over time. In GPS-denied environments, this can be solved using offboard sensors (such as motion-capture systems) or onboard sensors (such as cameras and laser range-finders). Motion-capture systems (e.g., Vicon or OptiTrack) consist of a set of external cameras mounted on the ceiling, which track the position of the robots with submillimeter accuracy and at high frame rates (more than 350 Hz). They are very appropriate for testing and evaluation purposes (cf. Lupashin et al. (2014) and Michael et al. (2010b)), such as prototyping control strategies or fast maneuvers, and serve as a ground-truth reference for other localization approaches. However, for truly autonomous navigation in unknown, unexplored environments, sensors should be installed onboard.

A journal special issue on MAV onboard perception and control was published by Michael et al. (2012a). The literature can be divided into approaches using range sensors (e.g., lidars or RGB-D sensors) and camera sensors.

6.2.1   Autonomous Navigation with Range Sensors

Lidars have been largely explored for ground mobile robots (cf. Thrun et al. (2007)) and similar strategies have been extended to MAVs (cf. Achtelik et al. (2009) and Bachrach (2009)). Using an RGB-D camera and a 2D laser, multifloor mapping results have recently been demonstrated using an autonomous quadrotor (cf. Shen et al. (2012); Figure 6.2). Although lidars and RGB-D sensors are very accurate and robust, they are still too heavy and consume too much power for lightweight MAVs. Therefore, cameras are the only viable sensors in the medium to long term; however, they require external illumination to "see" and a certain computing power to extract meaningful information for navigation.

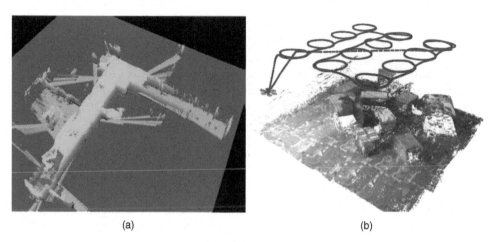

Figure 6.2   (a) Autonomous MAV exploration of an unknown, indoor environment using RGB-D sensor (image courtesy of Shen et al. (2012)). (b) Autonomous MAV exploration of an unknown, indoor environment using a single onboard camera (image courtesy of Faessler et al. (2015b))

6.2.2   Autonomous Navigation with Vision Sensors

6.2.2.1   Reactive Navigation

Most works on vision-based reactive navigation of MAVs have relied on biologically inspired vision algorithms, such as optical flow (cf. Floreano et al. (2009), Hrabar and Sukhatme (2009), Ruffier and Franceschini (2004), and Zufferey (2009)). Optical flow has been applied to MAVs for tasks such as on-spot hovering, take-off, landing, and, more generally, reactive navigation (e.g., for obstacle avoidance or to keep the MAV in the center of a canyon by balancing the optical flow on both sides of the robot field of view). While optical flow is crucial for reactive navigation, it cannot be used for precise maneuvers, such as trajectory following. Furthermore, optical flow only measures the relative velocity, leading the MAV to inevitably drift over time. Nevertheless, due to the limited computational power required by optical flow, this approach has been successfully integrated in several commercial drones, such as the Parrot AR Drone and the senseFly products, for autonomous hovering and landing.

6.2.2.2   Map-based Navigation

The alternative to reactive navigation is a map-based navigation, which proved very successful for ground mobile robots equipped with laser range-finders (cf. Thrun et al. (2007)). Breakthrough work on vision-controlled map-based navigation of MAVs was done within the European project SFLY (Scaramuzza et al. 2014), where visual-SLAM (Simultaneous Localization And Mapping) pipelines (e.g., Chiuso et al. (2002), Davison et al. (2007), Forster et al. (2014b), and Klein and Murray

(2007)) were used in combination with inertial sensors to enable autonomous basic maneuvers, such as take-off and landing, trajectory following, and surveillance coverage. Building upon that work, several vision-based systems have been proposed using both monocular (cf., Achtelik et al. (2011), Brockers et al. (2014), Forster et al. (2014b), and Weiss et al. (2013)) and stereo camera configurations (cf. Achtelik et al. (2009), Fraundorfer et al. (2012), Meier et al. (2012), Schmid et al. (2014), and Shen et al. (2013b)).

6.2.3 SFLY: Swarm of Micro Flying Robots

The Swarm of Micro Flying Robots (SFLY) project,[1,2] (Scaramuzza et al. 2014) was an EU-funded project with the goal of creating a swarm of vision-controlled MAVs capable of autonomous navigation, 3D mapping, and optimal surveillance coverage in GPS-denied environments. The SFLY MAVs did not rely on remote control, radio beacons, or motion-capture systems but could fly all by themselves using only a single onboard camera and an IMU.

The first contribution of the SFLY was the development of a new hexacopter equipped with enough processing power for onboard computer vision. The hexacopter was designed and manufactured by Ascending Technology and later sold under the name of Firefly, which has become very popular. The second contribution of the SFLY was the development of a local navigation module based on the parallel tracking and mapping (PTAM) framework by Klein and Murray (2007) that run in real time onboard the MAV (an Intel Core 2 Duo). The output of PTAM was fused with inertial measurements (cf. Weiss et al. (2012)) and was used to stabilize and control the MAV locally without any link to a ground station. The third contribution was an offline dense-mapping process that merges the individual maps of each MAV into a single global map that serves as input to the global navigation module (cf. Forster et al. (2013)). Finally, the fourth contribution was a cognitive, adaptive optimization (CAO) algorithm to compute the positions of the MAVs, which allowed the optimal surveillance coverage of the explored area (cf. Doitsidis et al. (2012)). Experimental results demonstrating three MAVs navigating autonomously in an unknown GPS-denied environment and performing 3D mapping and optimal surveillance coverage were presented. A detailed description of the SFLY can be found in Scaramuzza et al. (2014). Open-source code is publicly available to the robotics community.[3]

6.2.4 SVO, a Visual-Odometry Algorithm for MAVs

A visual-odometry and mapping algorithm, named SVO, specifically designed for MAV navigation with computationally limited computers, such as Odroid, was recently proposed by Forster et al. (2014b). Contrary to state-of-the-art

---

[1] Project website: www.sfly.org
[2] YouTube Channel: https://www.youtube.com/sFlyTeam/videos
[3] http://wiki.ros.org/asctec_mav_framework

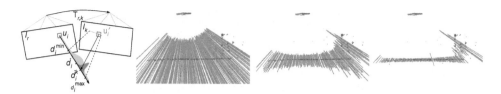

Figure 6.3 Probabilistic depth estimate in SVO. Very little motion is required by the MAV (marked in black at the top) for the uncertainty of the depth filters (shown as magenta lines) to converge. Image courtesy of Faessler et al. (2015b)

visual-odometry and SLAM algorithms relying on costly feature extraction and matching pipelines (cf. Davison et al. (2007) and Klein and Murray (2007)), SVO (semi-direct visual odometry) uses a combination of features and direct methods (from which derives the nickname "semi-direct") to achieve unprecedented real-time performance (up to 70 fps on Odroid boards and more than 400 fps on an i7 laptop) and high-precision visual odometry (less than 1% drift). The semi-direct approach eliminates the need for costly feature extraction and robust matching techniques for motion estimation. The algorithm operates directly on pixel intensities, which results in subpixel precision at high frame rates. Motion estimation of precise and high frame rate brings increased robustness in scenes characterized by little, repetitive, and high-frequency textures.

SVO uses a probabilistic mapping method that explicitly models outlier measurements to estimate 3D points; this results in fewer outliers and more reliable points (cf. Figure 6.3). Image points are triangulated from multiple views using recursive Bayesian estimation. This probabilistic depth estimation allows using every image for incremental depth estimation and provides a depth uncertainty that can be directly used for path planning.

SVO has so far been used for MAV state estimation in GPS-denied environments in combination with inertial sensors and runs on the onboard embedded computer. The integration of SVO onboard an MAV, its fusion with the IMU, and use for closed-loop control and navigation are detailed in Faessler et al. (2015b). Open-source code is publicly available to the robotics community.[4] Instructions on how to integrate the SVO position measurements into the popular PX4 autopilot are provided on the PX4 webpage.[5]

6.3 Applications and Challenges

6.3.1 Applications

Drones have several applications in search-and-rescue, remote inspection, law enforcement, video surveillance, agriculture, aerial photography, photogrammetry,

---

[4] https://github.com/uzh-rpg/rpg_svo.
[5] https://pixhawk.org/dev/ros/visual_estimation.

mapping, entertainment, and parcel delivery. However, localization and position tracking is not the sole use of vision sensors. In agriculture, for instance, drones with high-resolution spectral imaging devices are used to gather insight of crops, thus allowing for targeted fertilizing and better use of water and labor. This information can then be used to reduce the need of common fertilizers, which typically pollute local waterways. The main drone-based observation technique is called Normalized Difference Vegetation Index, a measure that assesses the crop productivity, which is calculated on the basis of visible and infrared radiation. When crops are viewed from a standard camera, crops normally look like an indistinct green and brown mass; however, when viewed with an infrared camera many colors suddenly pop out, such as yellow, orange, red, and green; software then stitches together hundreds of images to form a complete picture. In architecture, archeology, geography, and nature conservation, drones are used as mapping tools to get high-resolution 3D models of a construction, building, or terrain. The drones are usually set to take pictures at regular time intervals and a trajectory is planned through GPS. The images must be then downloaded to a laptop PC and powerful photogrammetry software, such as Pix4D or Agisoft, which uses state-of-the-art structure-from-motion (SfM) tools to build dense, photorealistic 3D models with centimeter accuracy. This mapping technology is also used for disaster management to get an overview picture after a flood or an earthquake. Finally, drones are also used as a remote camera in video surveillance and inspection. A live video stream is sent wirelessly from the drone to a tablet screen or video glasses, which are utilized as a feedback to the operator.

In the applications listed earlier, drones use GPS to navigate autonomously or are remotely operated by an expert pilot. In order to authorize the operation of autonomous drones in different countries in the near future, several challenges need to be overcome in terms of safety and robustness. Furthermore, additional sensors should be used other than cameras and GPS, such as lidars, radars, sonars, thermal cameras, and so on. Redundancy allows coping with sensor failures and operation in harsh conditions, such as night, low light, smoke, and so on. Since the focus of this book is on computer vision, we will review works dealing with safety and robustness of MAVs using mainly vision sensors.

6.3.2   Safety and Robustness

If a quadrotor's vision pipeline fails, there is typically a small set of options left: (i) a pilot must take over; (ii) the quadrotor must land immediately; (iii) the quadrotor must use simple fall-backs for stabilization in order to continue its mission. In the following two sections, the state-of-the-art research on failure recovery and emergency landing is reviewed.

6.3.2.1   Failure Recovery

In Shen (2014), a linear sliding window formulation for monocular visual-inertial systems was presented to make a vision-based quadrotor capable of failure recovery and on-the-fly initialization. The approach assumed that visual features could be extracted and correctly tracked right from the beginning of the recovery procedure.

Along with possible failures of their state-estimation pipeline, monocular vision-based quadrotors present the drawback that they typically require an initialization phase before they can fly autonomously. This initialization phase is usually performed by moving the quadrotor by hand or via remote control. Since this is time consuming and not easy to perform, attempts have been made to perform the initialization automatically. For instance, in Brockers et al. (2014) and Weiss et al. (2015), the authors presented a system that allows the user to toss a quadrotor in the air, where it then initializes a visual-odometry pipeline. Nevertheless, that system still required several seconds for the state estimate to converge before the toss and several more seconds until the visual-odometry pipeline was initialized. A closed-form solution for state estimation with a visual-inertial system that does not require initialization was presented in Martinelli (2012). However, at the current state of the art, this approach is not yet suitable for systems that rely on noisy sensor data.

A system enabling a monocular vision-based quadrotor to autonomously recover from any initial attitude and quickly re-initialize its visual-inertial system was recently proposed by Faessler et al. (2015a) and demonstrated in a scenario where a quadrotor is thrown in the air (cf. Figure 6.4). In contrast to Shen (2014), their system did not require the observation of visual features at the beginning of the recovery procedure but only once its attitude is stabilized, which simplifies feature tracking greatly and reduces computational complexity. In contrast to Brockers et al. (2014) and Weiss et al. (2015), no preparation time before launching the quadrotor was required and the entire recovery was performed more quickly.

6.3.2.2 Emergency Landing

Early works on vision-based autonomous landing for UAVs were based on detecting known planar shapes (e.g., helipads with "H" markings) in images (cf. Saripalli et al. (2002)) or on the analysis of textures in single images (cf. Garcia-Pardo et al. (2002)). Later works (e.g., Bosch et al. (2006), Desaraju et al. (2014) and Johnson et al. (2005)) assessed the risk of a landing spot by evaluating the roughness and inclination of the surface using 3D terrain reconstruction from images.

One of the first demonstrations of vision-based autonomous landing in unknown and hazardous terrain is described in Johnson et al. (2005). SfM was used to estimate the relative pose of two monocular images and, subsequently, a dense elevation map was computed by matching and triangulating regularly sampled features. The evaluation of the roughness and slope of the computed terrain map resulted in a binary classification of safe and hazardous landing areas. This approach detected the landing spot solely based on two selected images rather than continuously making depth measurements and fusing them in a local elevation map.

(a) t = 0 ms   (b) t = 80 ms   (c) t = 440 ms

(d) t = 1120 ms   (e) t = 1640 ms   (f) t = 2000 ms

Figure 6.4   Autonomous recovery after throwing the quadrotor by hand: (a) the quadrotor detects free fall and (b) starts to control its attitude to be horizontal. Once it is horizontal, (c) it first controls its vertical velocity and then (d) its vertical position. The quadrotor uses its horizontal motion to initialize its visual-inertial state estimation and uses it (e) to first break its horizontal velocity and then (f) lock to the current position. Image courtesy of Faessler et al. (2015a)

In Bosch et al. (2006), homography estimation was used to compute the motion of the camera as well as to recover planar surfaces in the scene. A probabilistic two-dimensional grid was used as a map representation. The grid stored the probability of the cells being flat.

While previously mentioned works were passive in the sense that the exploration flight was pre-programmed by the user, recent work by Desaraju et al. (2014) was done on how to *actively* choose the best trajectory autonomously to explore and verify a safe landing spot. However, due to computational complexity, the full system could not run entirely onboard in real time. Thus, outdoor experiments were processed on data sets. Additionally, only two frames were used to compute dense motion stereo; hence a criterion, based on the visibility of features and the interframe baseline, was needed to select two proper images.

A real-time approach running fully onboard an MAV was recently proposed by Forster et al. (2015) (cf. Figure 6.5). The authors proposed to generate a 2D elevation map that is probabilistic, of fixed size, and robot-centric, thus, always covering the area immediately underneath the robot. The elevation map is continuously updated at a rate of 1 Hz with depth maps that are triangulated from multiple views using recursive Bayesian estimation. This probabilistic depth estimation not only allows using every image for incremental depth estimation but also provides a depth uncertainty that can be directly used for planning trajectories minimizing the depth uncertainty as fast as possible, as proposed by Forster et al. (2014a).

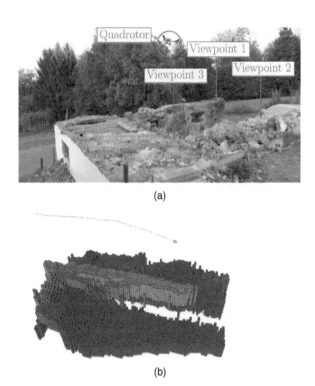

(a)

(b)

Figure 6.5   (a) A quadrotor is flying over a destroyed building. (b) The reconstructed elevation map. (c) A quadrotor flying in an indoor environment. (d) The quadrotor executing autonomous landing. The detected landing spot is marked with a green cube. The blue line is the trajectory that the MAV flies to approach the landing spot. Note that the elevation map is local and of fixed size; its center lies always below the quadrotor's current position. Image courtesy of Forster et al. (2015)

(c)

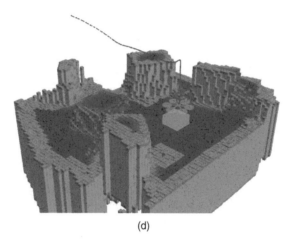

(d)

Figure 6.5   (*Continued*)

6.4   Conclusions

This chapter gave a description of the challenges of GPS-denied autonomous navigation of drones. Laser-based SLAM can outperform by several orders of magnitude of
the precision of GPS; however, laser range-finders consume too much power and are
too heavy for lightweight micro drones. The chapter then presented alternative techniques based on visual-odometry and SLAM technologies as a viable replacement
of laser-based navigation. However, they require external illumination and sufficient
texture in order to work reliably. The optimal sensor suit of a drone should be a combination of GPS, laser, ultrasound, and vision sensors (both standard and infrared) to
provide sufficient redundancy and success in different environment conditions. However, robustness to changes in the environment and how to handle system failures still
remains an open challenge for both engineers and researchers.

7

Application Challenges of Underwater Vision

Nuno Gracias[1], Rafael Garcia[1], Ricard Campos[1], Natalia Hurtos[1], Ricard Prados[1], ASM Shihavuddin[2], Tudor Nicosevici[1], Armagan Elibol[3], Laszlo Neumann[1] and Javier Escartin[4]

[1]*Computer Vision and Robotics Institute, University of Girona, Girona, Spain*
[2]*École Normale Supérieure, Paris, France*
[3]*Department of Mathematical Engineering, Yildiz Technical University, Istanbul, Turkey*
[4]*Institute of Physics of Paris Globe, The National Centre for Scientific Research, Paris, France*

7.1 Introduction

Underwater vehicles, either remotely operated or autonomous, have enabled a growing range of applications over the last two decades. Imaging data acquired by underwater vehicles have seen multiple applications in the context of archeology (Eustice et al. 2006a), geology (Escartin et al. 2009; Zhu et al. 2005), or biology (Pizarro and Singh 2003) and have become essential in tasks such as shipwreck inspection (Drap et al. 2008), ecological studies (Jerosch et al. 2007; Lirman et al. 2007), environmental damage assessment (Gleason et al. 2007a; Lirman et al. 2010), or detection of temporal changes (Delaunoy et al. 2008), among others. Despite their acquisition constraints, which often require the underwater vehicle to navigate at a close distance to the seafloor or the structure of interest, imaging sensors have the advantage of purveying higher resolution and lower noise when compared with the traditional sensors for seafloor surveying such as multibeam echosounders or side-scan sonars. Such higher resolution naturally promotes easier interpretation of finer-scale benthic features.

One of the most useful tools to carry out the above-mentioned scientific studies is the generation of optical maps. These maps provide the scientists with short-range, high-resolution visual representations of the ocean floor, enabling a detailed analysis of the structures of interest. Additionally, these offline-generated maps can be used by the vehicle to precisely locate themselves in the environment with respect to previously visited areas.

Rather than reviewing particular application cases, this chapter focuses on describing computer vision techniques that are common to most real-world applications. These techniques address the use of the collected data *after mission*, without the constraints of real-time operation, and are offline by nature.

We start by addressing the creation of 2D mosaics, which is currently the most widely used method for organizing underwater imagery in mapping and inspection applications. Key challenges here are the efficient co-registration of potentially very large image sets and the adequate blending of the images into seamless visual maps that preserve the important visual content for the applications at hand. The inclusion of 2.5D information is addressed next, in the context of multimodal mapping, using acoustically derived bathymetry and optical images. For fine-scale estimation of 3D models of benthic structures, structure from motion (SfM) and multiview stereo techniques are discussed. A key challenge for underwater applications is the generation of meaningful object surfaces from point clouds that are potentially very noisy and highly corrupted. The interpretation of optical maps is addressed next by reviewing some of the recently proposed techniques for image segmentation. These techniques are motivated by the large volume of image data that modern underwater vehicles can provide, which is beyond what is feasible for human experts to analyze manually. Finally, the topic of mapping with modern high-frequency imaging sonars is addressed, motivated by the fact that they allow for the use of computer vision techniques that have been developed for optical images.

7.2 Offline Computer Vision Techniques for Underwater Mapping and Inspection

7.2.1 2D Mosaicing

Building a 2D mosaic is a task that involves two main steps. From a geometrical point of view, the acquired images should be aligned and warped accordingly into a single common reference frame. From a photometric point of view, the rendering of the mosaic should be performed through blending techniques, which allow dealing with differences in appearance of the acquired stills and reduce the visibility of the registration inaccuracies between them (see Figure 7.1).

Large-scale deep-ocean surveys may be composed of hundreds to hundreds of thousands of images, which are affected by several underwater phenomena, such as scattering and light attenuation. Furthermore, the acquired image sets may present small or nonexistent overlaps between consecutive frames. Navigation data coming

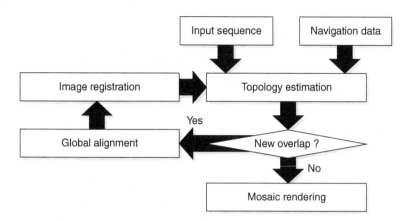

Figure 7.1 Underwater mosaicing pipeline scheme. The *Topology Estimation, Image Registration*, and *Global Alignment* steps can be performed iteratively until no new overlapping images are detected

from acoustic positioning sensors (ultra short base line (USBL), long base line (LBL)), velocity sensor Doppler velocity log (DVL), inclinometers, or gyroscopes become in that case essential to estimate the vehicle trajectory.

7.2.1.1 Topology Estimation

Unfortunately, if positioning data coming from USBL, LBL, or DVL are not available, using time-consecutive image registration, assumed to have an overlapping area, becomes the only method to estimate the trajectory of the robot. This dead-reckoning estimate suffers from a rapid accumulation of registration errors, which translates into drifts from the real trajectory followed by the vehicle. However, it does provide valuable information for non-time-consecutive overlapping between the involved images. The matching between non-time-consecutive images is fundamental to accurately recover the path followed by the vehicle. This task is performed using global alignment methods (Capel 2004; Elibol et al. 2008, 2011a; Ferrer et al. 2007; Gracias et al. 2004; Sawhney et al. 1998; Szeliski and Shum 1997). The refined trajectory can be used to predict additional overlapping between nonsequential images, which can be consequently attempted to match. The iterative process involving the registration of the new image pairs and the subsequent optimization is known as *topology estimation* (Elibol et al. 2010, 2013). Even when navigation data are available, performing a topology estimation step is required to guarantee recovering accurate estimates of the vehicle path, and its value becomes even higher when dealing with large-scale surveys involving hundreds of thousands of images (Figure 7.2).

When dealing with data sets of thousands of images, all-to-all image pair matching strategies are unfeasible to carry out the topology estimation. Consequently, the use of more efficient techniques is required. Elibol et al. (2010) proposed an extended

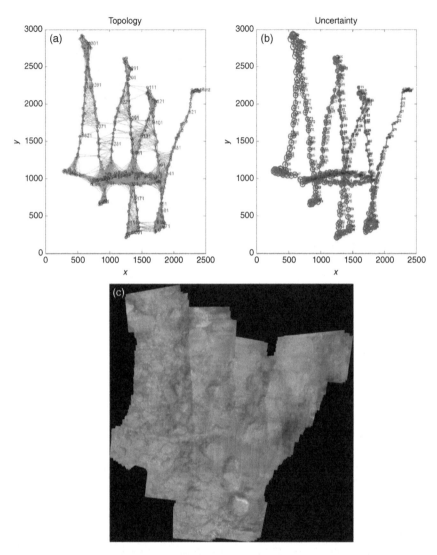

Figure 7.2 Topology estimation scheme. (a) Final trajectory obtained by the scheme proposed in Elibol et al. (2010). The first image frame is chosen as a global frame, and all images are then translated in order to have positive values in the axes. The x and y axes are in pixels, and the scale is approximately 150 pixels per meter. The plot is expressed in pixels instead of meters since the uncertainty of the sensor used to determine the scale (an acoustic altimeter) is not known. The red lines join the time-consecutive images while the black ones connect non-time-consecutive overlapping image pairs. The total number of overlapping pairs is 5412. (b) Uncertainty in the final trajectory. Uncertainty of the image centers is computed from the covariance matrix of the trajectory (Ferrer et al. 2007). The uncertainty ellipses are drawn with a 95% confidence level. (c) Mosaic built from the estimated trajectory

Kalman filter (EKF) framework, aimed at minimizing the total number of matching attempts while obtaining the most accurate trajectory. This approach predicts new possible image pairs considering the uncertainty of the recovered path. Another solution to the topology estimation problem based in a bundle adjustment (BA) framework was proposed by Elibol et al. (2011b). The approach combines a fast image similarity criterion with a minimum spanning tree (MST) solution to obtain an estimate of the trajectory topology. Then, image matching between pairs with high probable overlap is used to improve the accuracy of the estimate.

7.2.1.2   Image Registration

The image registration problem (Brown et al. 2007) consists of finding an appropriate planar transformation, which allows aligning in two or more 2D images taken from different viewpoints. The aim is to overlay all of them into a single and common reference frame (see Figure 7.3).

There are two main groups of image registration methods: *direct methods* and *feature-based methods*. The first group, also known as featureless methods, relies on the maximization of the photometric consistency over the overlapping image regions and is known to be appropriate to describe small translations and rotations (Horn and Schunck 1981; Shum and Szeliski 1998; Szeliski 1994). Nevertheless, in the context of underwater imaging using downward-looking cameras attached to an autonomous underwater vehicle (AUV) or remotely operated vehicle (ROV), it is common to acquire stills using stroboscopic lighting. This is due to power consumption restrictions affecting vehicle autonomy and leads to a low-frequency image acquisition. Consequently, the images do not have enough overlap to be registered using direct methods. For that reason, feature-based methods are most widely used to register not only underwater but also terrestrial and aerial imagery in the literature. Feature-based methods use a sparse set of salient points (Bay et al. 2006; Beaudet 1978; Harris and Stephens 1988; Lindeberg 1998; Lowe 1999) and correspondences between image pairs to estimate the transformation between them.

Image registration using feature-based methods involves two main stages. First, in the *feature detection* step, some interest or salient points should be located in one or both images of an image pair. Next, in the *feature matching* step, these salient points should be associated according to a given descriptor. This procedure is also known as the resolution of the correspondence problem. Depending on the strategy used to detect and match the features, two main strategies can be distinguished.

A first feature-based registration strategy relies on detecting salient points in one image using a feature detector algorithm, such as Harris (Harris and Stephens 1988), Laplacian (Beaudet 1978), or Hessian (Lindeberg 1998), and recognizing the same features in the other. In this case, the identification is performed using cross-correlation or a sum of squared differences (SSD) measure, involving the

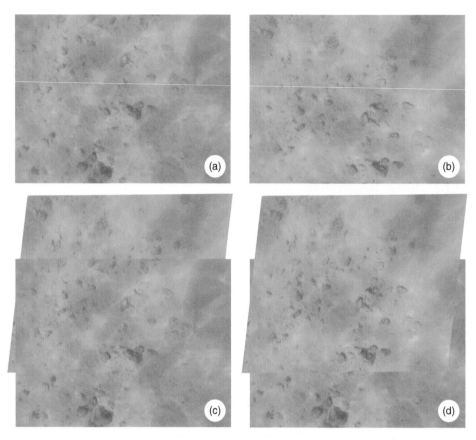

Figure 7.3 Geometric registration of two different views (a and b) of the same underwater scene by means of a planar transformation, rendering the first image on top (c) and the second image on top (d)

pixel values of a given area surrounding the interest point. A second method consists of detecting interest points on both images using some invariant image detectors/descriptors, such as SIFT (Lowe 1999), its faster variant SURF (Bay et al. 2006), or others, and solving the correspondence problem comparing their descriptor vectors. The descriptors have demonstrated to be invariant to a wide range of geometrical and photometric transformations between the image pairs (Schmid et al. 1998). This robustness becomes highly relevant in the context of underwater imaging, where viewpoint changes and significant alterations in the illumination conditions are frequent. Furthermore, the turbidity of the medium has been proven to have an impact in the performance of the feature detectors (Garcia and Gracias 2011) (Figure 7.4).

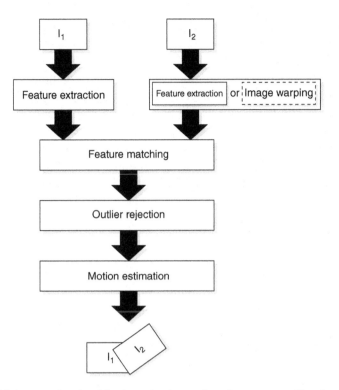

Figure 7.4 Main steps involved in the pairwise registration process. The feature extraction step can be performed in both images of the pair, or only in one. In this last case, the features are identified in the second image after an optional image warping based on a transformation estimation

7.2.1.3   Motion Estimation

Once a set of correspondences has been found on an image pair, they can be used to compute a planar transformation describing the motion of the camera between both. This transformation is stored in a homography matrix H (Hartley and Zisserman 2003; Ma et al. 2003), which can describe a motion with up to eight degrees of freedom (DOF).

The homography matrix H encodes information about the camera motion and the scene structure, a fact that facilitates establishing correspondence between both images. H can be computed, in general, from a small number of corresponding image pairs.

The homography accuracy (Negahdaripour et al. 2005) is strongly tied to the quality of the correspondences used for its calculation. The homography estimation algorithms assume that the only source of error is the measurement of the locations of the points, but this assumption is not always true inasmuch as mismatched points may also be present. There are several factors that can influence the goodness of the correspondences detected. Images can suffer from several artifacts, such as nonuniform illumination, sunflickering (in shallow waters), shadows (specially in the presence of artificial lighting), and digital noise, among others, which can produce a failure of the matching. Furthermore, moving objects (including shadows) may induce correspondences which, despite being correct, do not obey the dominant motion between the two images. These correspondences are known as *outliers*. Consequently, it is necessary to use an algorithm able to discern right and wrong correspondences. There are two main strategies to reject outliers widely used in the bibliography (Huang et al. 2007): RANSAC (Fischler and Bolles 1981) and LMedS (Rousseeuw 1984). LMedS efficiency is very low in the presence of Gaussian noise (Li and Hu 2010; Rousseeuw and Leroy 1987). For this reason, RANSAC is the most widely used method in the literature in the underwater imaging context.

7.2.1.4   Global Alignment

Pairwise registration of images acquired by an underwater vehicle equipped with a downward-looking camera cannot be used as an accurate trajectory estimation strategy. Image noise, illumination issues, and the violation of the planarity assumption may unavoidably lead to an accumulative drift. Therefore, detecting correspondences between nonconsecutive frames becomes an important step in order to close a loop and use this information to correct the estimated trajectory.

The homography matrix $^1\mathbf{H}_k$ represents the transformation of the kth image with respect to the global frame (assuming the first image frame as a global frame) and is known as *absolute homography*. This $^1\mathbf{H}_k$ matrix is obtained as a result of the concatenation of the *relative homographies* $^{k-1}\mathbf{H}_k$ between the kth and ^{k-1}kth images of a given time-consecutive sequence. As mentioned earlier, relative homographies have limited accuracy and computing absolute homographies by cascading them results in cumulative error. This drift will cause, in the case of long sequences, the presence of misalignments between neighboring images belonging to different transects (see Figure 7.5).

The main benefit of *global alignment* techniques is the use of the closing-loop information to correct the pairwise trajectory estimation by reducing the accumulated drift.

There are several methods in the literature intended to solve the global alignment problem (Szeliski 2006). Global alignment methods usually require the minimization of an error term based on the location of the image correspondences. These methods can be classified according to the domain where this error is defined, leading to two main groups: image frame methods (Capel 2001; Ferrer et al. 2007; Marzotto et al. 2004; Szeliski and Shum 1997) and mosaic frame methods (Can et al. 2002; Davis 1998; Gracias et al. 2004; Kang et al. 2000; Pizarro and Singh, 2003; Sawhney et al. 1998).

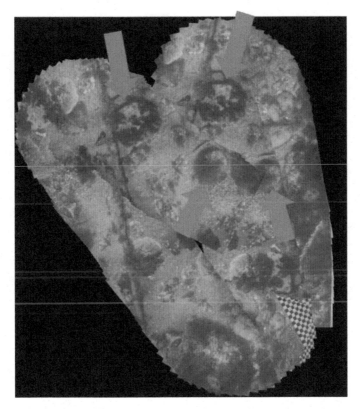

Figure 7.5   Example of error accumulation from registration of sequential images. The same benthic structures appear in different locations of the mosaic due to error accumulation (trajectory drift)

7.2.1.5   Image Blending

Once the geometrical registration of all the mosaic images has been carried out, during the global alignment step, the photomosaic can be rendered. In order to produce an informative representation of the seafloor that can be used by the scientists to perform their benthic studies, the use of blending techniques to obtain a seamless and visually pleasant mosaic is required (see Figure 7.6).

On the one hand, the geometrical warping of the images forming the mosaic may lead to inconsistencies on their boundaries due to registration errors, moving objects, or the presence of 3D structures of the scene violating the planarity assumption in which the 2D registration relies. On the other hand, differences in the image appearance due to changes in the illumination conditions, oscillations in the distance to the seafloor, or the turbidity of the underwater medium cause the image boundaries to be easily noticeable (Capel 2004). Consequently, the consistency of the global appearance of the mosaic can be highly compromised. The main goal of image blending

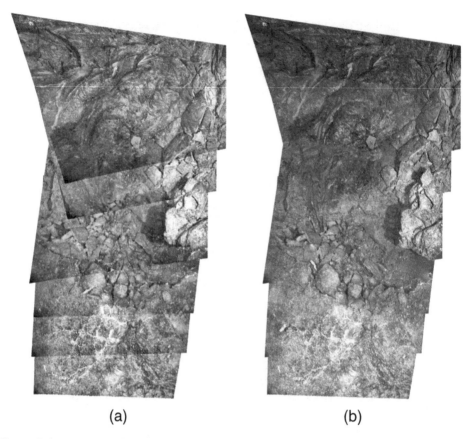

(a)   (b)

Figure 7.6   Photomosaic built from six images of two megapixels. The mosaic shows notice-able seams in (a), where the images have only been geometrically transformed and sequentially rendered on the final mosaic canvas, the last image on top of the previous one. After apply-ing a blending algorithm, the artifacts (image edges) disappear from the resulting mosaic (b). Images courtesy of Dan Fornari (Woods-Hole Oceanographic Institution)

techniques is to obtain a homogeneous appearance of the generated mosaic, not only from the esthetic but also from the informative point of view, enhancing the visual data when needed, to obtain a continuous and consistent representation of the seafloor.

There are two main groups of blending algorithms depending on their main working principle (Levin et al. 2004): *transition smoothing* methods and *optimal seam finding* methods. The *transition smoothing* methods (also known as *feathering* (Uyttendaele et al. 2001) or *alpha blending* methods (Porter and Duff 1984)) are based on reducing the visibility of the joining areas between images combining the overlapping infor-mation. The *optimal seam finding* methods rely on searching the optimal path to cut the images along their common overlapping area in which the photometric differences between both are minimal (Davis 1998; Efros and Freeman 2001). The combination of the benefits of both groups of techniques lead to a third group (e.g., Agarwala et al.

(2004) and Milgram (1975)), which can be called *hybrid methods*. These methods reduce the visibility of the seams, smoothing the common overlapping information around a photometrically optimal seam.

Image blending methods can be classified according to their capabilities and weaknesses, which may make them appropriate for certain applications but unfeasible for others. Considering the main principle of the techniques, the combination of a transition smoothing around an optimally found boundary (i.e., the use of hybrid methods) seems to be the most adopted approach in the recent bibliography. The tolerance of the techniques to moving objects is strongly tight to the principle, being all the optimal seam finding based methods able to deal with this issue up to a certain degree. This is due to the fact that optimal seam finding methods place the cut path on areas where photometric differences are small. As a consequence, overlapping areas with moving objects are cut. Concerning the domain in which the blending is performed, both luminance and gradient domains are widely used, the second having gained a special importance in recent years (Mills and Dudek 2009; Szeliski et al. 2008; Xiong and Pulli 2009). One of the benefits of the gradient domain is the easy reduction of exposure differences between neighboring images, which does not require additional pre-processing, due to the fact that image gradients are not sensitive to differences in exposure. Ghosting and double contouring effects arise when fusing information between images affected by registration errors or a strong violation of the planarity assumption. The ghosting effect occurs when wrong-registered low-frequency information is fused, while double contouring affects the high-frequency information. Given that all transition smoothing methods are affected by this artifact, the restriction of the fusion to a limited width area is required to reduce its visibility. Concerning the color treatment, it is similar in most of the techniques in the literature. Concretely, the blending is always performed in a channel-wise manner independent of the number of channels of the source images (i.e., color or gray-scale images). There are few methods in the literature conceived to work in real time (Zhao 2006), which therefore requires sequential processing to be performed. However, methods working in a global manner are better conditioned to deal with problems such as the exposure compensation so as to ensure global appearance consistency. The sequential processing tends to accumulate drift on the image corrections, which may strongly depend on the first processed and stitched image. Few blending methods are claimed to work with high dynamic range images. Nevertheless, gradient-based blending methods are able to intrinsically deal with them due to the nature of the domain. Methods able to process high dynamic range images require the application of tone mapping (Neumann et al. 1998) algorithms in order to appropriately display the results. The high dynamic range should be stretched in order to allow its visualization into low dynamic range devices, such as screen monitors or printers.

Large-scale underwater surveys often lead to extensive image data sets composed from thousands to hundreds of thousands of stills. Given the significant computational resources that the processing of this amount of data may require, the use of specific optimal techniques such as that proposed by Prados et al. (2014) is needed. The first stages of the pipeline involve the input sequence pre-processing, required to reduce artifacts such as the inhomogeneous lighting of the images, mainly due to the use of limited-power artificial light sources and the phenomenon of light attenuation and scattering. In this step, a depth-based non-uniform-illumination correction is applied, which dynamically computes an adequate illumination compensation function depending on the distance of the vehicle to the seafloor. Next, a context-dependent gradient-based image enhancement is used, allowing to equalize the appearance of neighboring images when those have been acquired at different depths or with different exposure times. The pipeline follows with the selection of each image contribution to the final mosaic based on several criteria, such as image quality (i.e., image sharpness and level of noise) and acquisition distance. This step allows getting rid of redundant and low quality image information, which may affect in a counterproductive way the surrounding contributing images. Next, the optimal seam placement between all the images is found, minimizing the photometric differences around the cut path and discarding moving objects. A gradient blending in a narrow region around the optimally computed seams is applied, in order to minimize the visibility of the joining regions as well as to refine the appearance equalization along all the involved images. The usage of a narrow region of fusion reduces the appearance of artifacts, such as ghosting or double-contouring, due to registration inaccuracies. Finally, a strategy allowing to process gigamosaics composed of tens of thousands of images in conventional hardware is applied. The technique divides the whole mosaic in tiles, processing them individually, and seamlessly blending all of them again using another method that requires low computational resources.

7.2.2   2.5D Mapping

Apart from the optical images acquired at a close distance to the seafloor, AUVs and ROVs can acquire bathymetric information when traveling further from the scene. Acoustic information has a lower resolution than optical imagery, but provides a rough approximation of the seabed relief, which may become highly informative during the scene interpretation. Both optical and acoustic data can be combined, projecting the detailed 2D high-resolution photomosaics into a low-resolution triangle mesh generated from the bathymetry, leading to what can be named as 2.5D mosaics (see Figure 7.7). Formerly, these mosaics cannot be considered 3D inasmuch as acoustic data can only provide elevation information.

There is a great deal of literature on the different uses of this scanning configuration for sonar mapping, and automatic methods to build these maps out of raw sonar readings have been a hot research topic in recent years (Barkby et al. 2012; Roman and Singh 2007). The application of these techniques has proven to provide key benefits for other research areas such as archeology (Bingham et al. 2010) or geology (Yoerger et al. 2000). Given the depth readings, retrieving a surface representation is

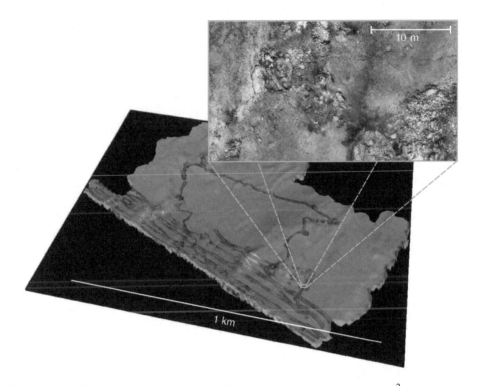

Figure 7.7 2.5D map of a Mid-Atlantic Ridge area of approximately $1\,km^2$ resulting from the combination of a bathymetry and a blended photomosaic of the generated high-resolution images. The obtained scene representation provides scientists with a global view of the interest area as well as with detailed optical information acquired at a close distance to the seafloor. Data courtesy of Javier Escartin (CNRS/IPGP, France)

straightforward. By defining a common plane, all the measures can be projected in 2D. Then, an irregular triangulation such as Delaunay or a gridding technique can be applied to the projections on the plane and the third coordinate is used to lift the surface in a 2.5D representation. These mappings can be enhanced by using photomosaics for texture, thus producing a multimodal representation of the area (Campos et al. 2013b; Johnson-Roberson et al. 2009). As a result, the triangulated depth map provides the scientists with a general view of the studied area, while the textured photomosaics allow to reach a high level of detail on the areas of special interest.

Optical and acoustic data, namely maps, should be geometrically registered to align their position and the scale. Given that both types of information are difficult to correlate when interpreted as imagery, the registration mainly relies in the vehicle positioning data. Additionally, manually selected fiducial points can be used to refine the alignment of the two maps. Provided that the resolution between both is significantly different (by some orders of magnitude), small inaccuracies in the registration might be negligible.

On the other hand, although not that extensive, cameras are also used for height-map reconstruction. Regarding full 3D reconstruction, the methods in the literature are more concerned with recovering the point set, obviating the surface reconstruction part. Thus, the focus is usually put on the registration of multiple camera positions, using either SfM systems (Bryson et al. 2012; Nicosevici et al. n.d.) or SLAM approaches (Johnson-Roberson et al. 2010) as well as monocular or stereo cameras (Mahon et al. 2011). The application of these methods in the underwater domain has to face the added complexity of dealing with noisy images, in the sense of the previously commented aberrations introduced by the rapid attenuation of light on the water medium, the nonuniform lighting on the image, and forward/backward scattering. This translates in the methods requiring further pre-processing of the images to alleviate these issues, and having to deal with larger errors in the reconstructions than their less noisier on-land counterparts. Furthermore, as previously stated, the common configuration of downward-looking cameras makes methods tend to represent the shape underlying these points as a height-map in a common reference plane, which may be easily extracted using principal component analysis (PCA) (Nicosevici et al. n.d.; Singh et al. 2007).

7.2.3 3D Mapping

In this section, we deal with the problem of 3D mapping. Recall that in both the 2D and 2.5D cases, we assume that there exists a base plane onto which the images can be projected, that is, once the motion is extracted, building the map mainly consists of warping and deforming the images onto this common plane. However, note that in the 3D case the problem becomes more complex, as this base representation is missing.

This previously mentioned assumption on the area of interest being close to planar has motivated the use of scanning sensors located on the bottom of underwater vehicles, with their optical axis orthogonal to the seafloor. In fact, this configuration is also helpful for the problem of large-area mapping: by using downward-looking cameras/sensors, we attain overview capabilities able to provide an overall notion of the shape of the scene.

As a consequence, there exist very few proposals on underwater mapping, dealing with the 3D reconstruction problem in its more general terms. If we drop both the assumption of the scene being 2D/2.5D and the downward-looking configuration of the sensor, we allow the observation of arbitrary 3D shapes. In both acoustic and optical cases, the trajectory of the vehicle is required in order to be able to reconstruct the shape of the object. On the one hand, for the acoustic case, the individual 2D swath provided by a multibeam sensor can be composed with the motion of the vehicle to obtain a 3D point cloud. On the other hand, for the optical case, once the trajectory of the camera is available, the 3D positions of the points can be triangulated in 3D using the line-of-sight rays emerging from each camera–2D feature pair.

Thus, the mapping problem is closely related to that of trajectory estimation. In the optical domain, those two problems are often formulated as SfM methods, when dealing with pure optical data (Bryson et al. 2012; Nicosevici et al. n.d.), and more generic SLAM approaches, when there is additional information available other than optical (Johnson-Roberson et al. 2010). In both cases, the optical constraint guiding the optimization of the vehicle trajectory and the scene structure is the reprojection error. For a given 3D point, this error is defined as the difference between its corresponding 2D feature in the image, and the back-projection of the 3D point using both the camera pose and its internal geometry. Note that only relevant feature points in the images will be used during the process, which leads to the reconstructed scene being described as a sparse point cloud. In order to get a more faithful representation of the object, dense point set reconstruction methods are commonly used with the estimated trajectory (Furukawa and Ponce 2010; Yang and Pollefeys 2003).

After a smooth recovery of the trajectory of the vehicle, and regardless of the scanning technology used being acoustic or optical, the scene is always retrieved as a point cloud. Note that this also applies to other 3D recovery techniques in land and/or aerial applications (e.g., lidar scans). Regardless of the technology used, the scanning of an object is always in the form of discrete measures (i.e., points) that are supposed to be taken at the surface of the object. Moreover, the resulting point cloud is unstructured, and no assumption on the shape of the object can be made.

It is clear that having the scene represented by a point cloud complicates further interpretation and/or processing of these data. First, it is obvious that these point sets are difficult to visualize. Since the points are infinitesimally small, from any given viewpoint a user cannot tell which part of the object should be visible and which should be occluded, and just expert users are able to interpret the data by moving around the point set with the help of a viewing software. Additionally, working with points alone makes further computations complex to apply to the point set directly. Basically, since the connectivity between those points is unknown, we are not able to compute simple measures on the object (e.g., areas, intersections). Even if some approximations can be extracted directly from the point set, the computations are far simpler when the continuous surface of the object is known.

We can then conclude that a surface representation of the object, derived from the discrete measures in the point cloud, is needed to describe a 3D object. This process is known in the literature as the surface reconstruction problem from a set of unorganized points (in the following referred to as the surface reconstruction problem). A triangle mesh is commonly used as the representation of the surface we aim to obtain, given the ability of modern hardware graphics architectures to efficiently display triangle primitives. In this way, we have a piecewise linear approximation of the surface of the scene that can be used to aid visualization and further calculus. Note that the surface reconstruction problem is inherently ill-posed, since given a set of points one may define several surfaces agreeing with the samples. Additionally, we have the added problem of the points in this set not being perfectly exact measures on the object. In real-world data sets, and regardless of the methodology used to retrieve the point set, these are affected by two main problems: noise and outliers. Noise refers to the repeatability (i.e., the variance) of the measuring sensor, whereas the outliers refer to those badly measured points provided by errors during the point retrieval process. Thus, we might need to reconstruct the surface while attenuating the noise in the input and disregarding outliers.

In the following sections, we overview the state of the art in surface reconstruction, both generic approaches and how the underwater community is starting to gain interest in the topic. Then, we show some additional applications and further processing that can be applied to the resulting triangle meshes.

7.2.3.1 Surface Reconstruction

Due to the above-mentioned common downward-looking configuration of the sensor, there are few approaches tackling the problem of 3D mapping in the underwater community. One of the few examples in this direction can be found in Johnson-Roberson et al. (2010), where they use the surface reconstruction method of Curless and Levoy (1996), originally devised to unrestricted 3D reconstruction. Nevertheless, the added value of applying this method in front of a 2.5D approximation is not clear in this case, since the camera still observes the scene in a downward-looking configuration. Another proposal, this time using a forward-looking camera and working on a more complex structure, is that presented in Garcia et al. (2011), where an underwater hydrothermal vent is reconstructed using dense 3D point cloud retrieval techniques and the Poisson surface reconstruction method (Kazhdan et al. 2006).

For downward-looking configurations, the straightforwardness of changing from depth readings to 2.5D representations makes the reconstruction of the scene as a triangulated terrain model to be just a side result. However, we are now concerned with a more general scenario, where the sensor can be mounted in a less restrictive configuration, that is, located anywhere on the robot and with any orientation. With this new arrangement, objects can be observed from arbitrary viewpoints, so that the retrieved measures are no longer suitable for projection onto a plane (and hence, a 2.5D map cannot be built). Viewing the object from further positions allows a better understanding of the global shape of the object since its features can be observed from angles that are more suitable to their exploration. An example in this direction is depicted in Figure 7.8, where we can find a survey of an underwater hydrothermal vent. It is clear in Figure 7.8b that it is not possible to recover the many details and concavities of this chimney using just a 2.5D representation. The more general configuration of the camera, in this case mounted at the front of the robot oriented approximately at 45° angle with respect to the gravity vector, allowed a more detailed observation of the area, attaining also higher resolution. Consequently, it is obvious that for these new exploration approaches, the problem of surface reconstruction is of utmost importance to complete the 3D mapping pipeline.

Another issue that burdens the development of surface reconstruction techniques is the defect-ridden nature of point sets retrieved on real-world operations. The large levels of noise and the huge number of outliers present in the data clearly complicate

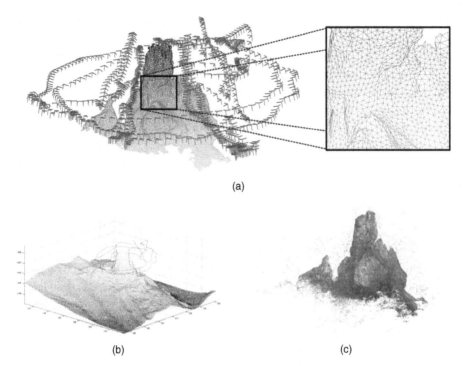

(a)

(b) (c)

Figure 7.8 (a) Trajectory used for mapping an underwater chimney at a depth of about 1700 m in the Mid-Atlantic ridge (pose frames in red/green/blue corresponding to the $X/Y/Z$ axis). We can see the camera pointing always toward the object in a forward-looking configuration. The shape of the object shown was recovered using our approach presented in Campos et al. (2015). Note the difference in the level of detail when compared with a 2.5D representation of the same area obtained using a multibeam sensor in (b). The trajectory followed in (b) was downward-looking, hovering over the object, but for the sake of comparison we show the same trajectory as in (a). Finally, (c) shows the original point cloud, retrieved through optical-based techniques, that was used to generate the surface in (a). Note the large levels of both noise and outliers that this data set contains. Data courtesy of Javier Escartin (CNRS/IPGP, France)

the processing. Thus, the surface reconstruction method to use mainly depends on the quality of the data we are dealing with and the ability of the method to recover faithful surfaces from corrupted input.

Given the ubiquity of point set representations and the generality of the problem itself, surface reconstruction has attracted the attention of many research communities, such as those of computer vision, computer graphics, or computational geometry. In all of them, the different approaches can be mainly classified into two types: those based on point set interpolation, and those approximating the surface with respect to the points. Usually, these methods are applied to range scan data sets because of the spread use of these sensors nowadays. Nevertheless, they tend to be generic enough to be applicable to any point-based data regardless of their origin, consequently including our present case of optical and acoustic point sets retrieved from an underwater scenario.

Another relevant issue is the requirement of some methods to have some additional information associated with the point set. Many methods in the state of the art require available per-point normals to help in disambiguating this ill-posed problem. Moreover, some methods assume even higher level information, such as the pose of the scanning device at the time of capturing the scene, to further restrict the search for a surface that corresponds to that of the real scanned object. The availability of these properties will also guide our selection of the proper algorithm.

In the following sections, we overview both interpolation and approximation-based approaches in the state of the art.

Interpolation-Based Approaches

Mainly studied by the computational geometry community, methods based on interpolating the points commonly rely on space partition techniques such as the Delaunay triangulation, or its equivalent, the Voronoi diagram. Algorithms tackling the problem with a volumetric view try to partition the cells of these structures into those belonging to the *inside* of the object and those from the *outside* of the object. Then, the surface is basically located at the interphase between these two volumes. Widely known methods working with this idea are the Cocone (Amenta et al. 2000) and the Power Crust (Amenta et al. 2001). These algorithms usually rely on some theoretical proofs derived from specific sampling conditions assumed on the point sets. However, fairly often these conditions are not fulfilled in the real-world data, and some heuristics need to be derived to render the methods useful on these cases. We can also distinguish hungry approaches, where the surface is incrementally growing, one triangle at a time, by taking local decisions on which points/triangles to insert next at each iteration (Bernardini et al. 1999; Cohen-Steiner and Da, 2004).

Given the fact that, for the methods trying to interpolate the points, part of the input points will also become vertices of the output surface, the noise is translated to the resulting mesh. Consequently, these kinds of methods cannot deal with noisy inputs. A way to overcome this limitation is to apply a prior noise smoothing step on the point set, which provides considerably better results, as shown in Digne et al. (2011). Nevertheless, some methods have faced the problem of disregarding outliers during reconstruction. The spectral partitioning of Kolluri et al. (2004) or the optical-based graph-cut approach of Labatut et al. (2007) are the clear examples in this direction.

Approximation-Based Approaches

We can find a large variety of procedures based on approximation, which makes them more difficult to classify. Nevertheless, the common feature of most of the methods is to define the surface in implicit form and evaluate it using a discretization of the working volume containing the object. After approximating the surface in this embodiment, the surface triangle mesh can be extracted by means of a surface mesher step (Boissonnat and Oudot 2005; Lorensen and Cline 1987). Thus, we can mainly classify these methods depending on the implicit definition they provide.

One of the most popular approaches is to derive a signed distance function (SDF) from the input points. This SDF can be defined as the distance from a given point to a set of local primitives, such as tangent planes (derived from known normals at input points) (Hoppe et al. 1992; Paulsen et al. 2010), or moving least squares (MLS) approximations (Alexa et al. 2004; Guennebaud and Gross 2007; Kolluri 2008). Alternatively, some methods work with the radial basis function (RBF) interpolation of the SDF. The RBF method, usually used to extrapolate data from samples, is used to derive the SDF from point sets with the associated normals (Carr et al. 2001; Ohtake et al. 2003, 2004).

On the other hand, there are some approximation approaches where the implicit function sought is not a distance function but an indicator function. This simpler definition denotes for a given point whether it is part of the interior of the object or the outside (i.e., it is a pure binary labeling) (Kazhdan et al. 2006; Kazhdan and Hoppe 2013; Manson et al. 2008). Usually, this inside/outside information is derived from the information provided by known per-point normals.

Note that, up to this point, all the reviewed methods require that the surface normal vector is known for each input point. It is clear that the requirement of per-point normals may be a burden in the cases where the scanning methodology does not provide this information. Moreover, estimating the normals at input points to reconstruct a surface is a chicken and egg problem: to compute the normals, we have to infer somehow the surface around each point. Nevertheless, even when working with raw point sets without normals, we can derive some distance function. The only drawback is that the resulting function is bound to be unsigned. When working with unsigned distance functions (UDFs), the main problem resides in the fact that we cannot extract the surface from the zero-level set as is done for SDF or indicator function-based approaches. Thus, methods try to recover the sign of the function using some heuristics (Giraudot et al. 2013; Hornung and Kobbelt 2006; Mullen et al. 2010; Zhao et al. 2001).

In all the above-mentioned cases, both noise attenuation and outlier rejection are problematic, and most of them require per-point normals. Still, there exist other methods proposing unconventional procedures but not requiring any additional information, such as in Campos et al. (2013a, 2015), where they merge a set of local shapes derived from the points into a global surface without resorting to an intermediate implicit formulation. Instead, they modify the surface meshing method in Boissonnat and Oudot (2005) to be able to deal with these local surfaces directly. Thus, in these cases, meshing and surface reconstruction problems are intrinsically related, meaning that the quality of the resulting surface is also a user parameter. Moreover, both methods work with the idea of dealing with noise and outliers in the data, by means of using robust statistics techniques within the different steps of the method, and allow the reconstruction of bounded surfaces, usually appearing when surveying a delimited area of the seafloor. These last two methods are applied specifically to underwater optical mapping data sets, and a sample of the behavior of Campos et al. (2015) can be seen in Figure 7.8a.

7.2.3.2 Further Applications

The ability of modern graphics hardware (i.e., graphics processing units (GPUs)) to display in real-time triangle primitives eases the visualization of the reconstructed scenes. Moreover, the widespread use of triangle meshes has motivated the rapid development of various mesh processing techniques in recent years that may be helpful in further processing (see Botsch et al. (2010) for a broader overview of these methods). Some of these techniques include the following:

- (Re)Meshing: Changes the quality/shape of triangles (see Figure 7.9b). Some computations, such as the finite element method (FEM), require the shape of the triangles to be close to regular, or adaptive to the complexity or curvature of the object. Meshing (or remeshing) methods allow tuning the quality of the

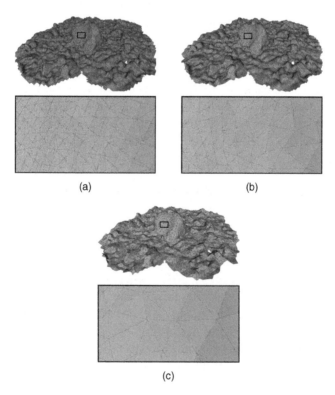

(a)   (b)

(c)

Figure 7.9 A sample of surface processing techniques that can be applied to the reconstructed surface. (a) Original; (b) remeshed; (c) simplified

triangulation according to some user-defined parametrization on the shape of the triangles.

- Simplification: Related to remeshing, we can change the complexity of the mesh (see Figure 7.9c) to attain real-time visualization, or to also simplify further calculus to compute the data.
- Smoothing: Smooths the appearance of the resulting surface. Note that this technique may be specially useful in the case of using an interpolation-based surface reconstruction technique, since in this case a noisy point cloud will result in a rough and spiky approximation of the surface. Smoothing methods try to attenuate small high-frequency components in the mesh, resulting in a more visually pleasant surface.

In contrast to the pure mesh-based approaches, when using optical-based reconstruction we can also benefit from texture mapping. Texture mapping is a post-processing step where the texture of the original images used to reconstruct the scene can also be used to colorize and basically give a texture to each of the triangles of the resulting mesh. Since we have reconstructed the surface from a set of views, both the cameras and the surface are in the same reference frame. Thus, as shown in Figure 7.10, the texture mapping is quite straightforward: we can back-project each triangle to one of its compatible views and use the enclosed texture. The problem then reduces to that of blending, discussed in Section 7.2.1, but in 3D. The different available variants of these methods are mainly concerned with the selection of the best view to extract the texture from a given triangle, and also with alleviating the differences in illumination that may appear when composing the textures obtained from different views. Two representative methods in the literature can be found in Lempitsky and Ivanov (2007) and Gal et al. (2010).

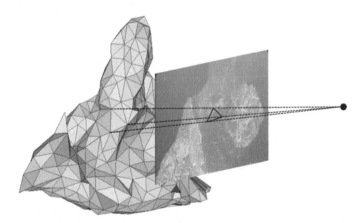

Figure 7.10 Texture mapping process, where the texture filling a triangle in the 3D model is extracted from the original images. Data courtesy of Javier Escartin (CNRS/IPGP, France)

7.2.4   Machine Learning for Seafloor Classification

Underwater image classification is still a relatively new research area compared with the existing large body of work on terrestrial image classification. Apart from the inherent challenges of underwater imagery, there are specific challenges related to image classification in this environment. Significant intraclass and intersite variability in the morphology of seabed organisms or structures of interest, complex spatial borders between classes, variations in viewpoint, distance, and image quality, limits to spatial and spectral resolution, partial occlusion of objects due to the three-dimensional structure of the seabed, gradual changes in the structures of the classes, lighting artifacts due to wave focusing, and variable optical properties of the water column can be considered some of the major challenges in this field.

Seafloor imagery collected by AUVs and ROVs is usually manually classified by marine biologists and geologists. Due to the involved hard manual labor, several methods have been developed toward the automatic segmentation and classification of benthic structures and elements. Although the results of these methods have proved to be less accurate than manual classification, this automated classification is nonetheless very valuable as a starting point for further analysis.

A general supervised approach for object classification in the computer vision community contains several standard steps such as image collection, pre-processing, invariant feature extraction (texture, color, shape), feature modification (kernel mapping, dimension reduction, normalization), classifier training, and, finally, accuracy testing. There are many different computer vision techniques available for each of these steps in the framework to be used in the case of seafloor object classification.

In one of the initial efforts in automated seabed classification using optical imagery, Pican et al. (1998) used gray-level co-occurrence matrix (GLCM). Haralick et al. (1973) and Kohonen maps (Heskes 1999) are used as texture descriptors. In Shiela et al. (2008) and Soriano et al. (2001), the authors use a feed-forward back-propagation neural network to classify underwater images. They use local binary patterns (LBP) (Ojala et al. 1996) as texture descriptors and normalized chromaticity coordinates (NCC) and mean hue saturation value (HSV) as color descriptors. The works by Johnson-Roberson et al. (2006a, b) employ both acoustic and optical imagery for benthic classification. Acoustic and visual features are classified separately using a support vector machine (SVM) by Cortes and Vapnik (1995), with assigned weights which are determined empirically. A similar approach is proposed in Mehta et al. (2007), where SVM are used to classify each pixel in the images.

Alternatively, one of the most common strategies for general object classification for image characterization is the use of Bag of Words (Csurka et al. 2004), such as in the work of Pizarro et al. (2008). This method yields a good level of accuracy and can be considered as one of the main references in the state of the art.

Color and texture features have been used by Gleason et al. (2007b) in a two-step algorithm to classify three broad cover types. This system requires expensive acquisition hardware, capable of acquiring narrow spectral band images. The work by Marcos et al. (2005) uses LBP and NCC histograms as feature descriptors and a linear discriminant analysis (LDA) (Mika et al. 1999) as the classifier. The work of Stokes and Deane (2009) uses normalized color space and discrete cosine transforms (DCT) to classify benthic images. The final classification is done using their proposed probability density weighted mean distance (PDWMD) classifier from the tail of the distribution. This method is time efficient with good accuracy but requires accurate color correction, which may be difficult to achieve on underwater images without controlled lighting.

The work by Diaz and Torres (2006) uses the local homogeneity coefficient (LHC) by Francisco et al. (2003) for segmentation and pixel-by-pixel distance of texture features such as energy, entropy, and homogeneity to classify. This method can only deal with classes that are highly discriminative by nature and, therefore, has limited underwater applications. Beijbom et al. (2012) proposed a novel framework for seabed classification, which consists of feature vector generation using a maximum response (MR) filter bank (Varma and Zisserman 2005), and an SVM classifier with a RBF kernel. In this method, multiple patch sizes were used, providing a significant improvement relative to classification accuracy. Bender et al. (2012) in their recent work used a novel approach of probabilistic targets least square classifier to cluster the similar types of areas on the seabed. This method shows promising results and is likely to evolve in future research.

For the cases where the survey images contain enough overlap to allow the extraction of depth information, then 2.5D- or even 3D-based features can provide significant additional information. The work by Friedman et al. (2012) presented a new method for calculating the rugosity, slope, and aspect features of the Delaunay triangulated surface mesh of the seabed terrain by projecting areas onto a plane using PCA. They used these features to define the characteristics of the seabed terrain for scientific communities. Geographic information system (GIS) tools such as St John BIOMapper use statistics such as curvature, plan curvature, profile curvature, mean depth, variance of depth, surface rugosity, steepness and direction of slope to characterize the complexity of the seafloor. Some of these features can be considered as potential 3D or 2.5D features for underwater object description.

Shihavuddin et al. (2013) presented an adaptive scheme for seafloor classification, which uses a novel image classification framework that is applicable to both single images and composite mosaic data sets, as illustrated in Figure 7.11. This method can be configured to the characteristics of individual data sets such as the size, number of classes, resolution of the samples, color information availability, and class types. In another work Shihavuddin et al. (2014), 2D and 2.5D features were fused to obtain a better classification accuracy, focusing on munition detection. They used several 2.5D features such as symmetry, rugosity, curvature, and so on, on the highest resolution map of the terrain together with the 2D features.

Schoening (2015) proposed a combined feature method for automated detection and classification of benthic megafauna and finally quantity estimation of benthic mineral

(a)

(b)

Figure 7.11   Seafloor classification example on a mosaic image of a reef patch in the Red Sea, near Eilat, covering approximately 3×6 m. (a) Original mosaic. (b) Classification image using five classes: Brain Coral (green), Favid Coral (purple), Branching Coral (yellow), Sea Urchin (pink), and Sand (gray). Data courtesy of Assaf Zvuloni and Yossi Loya (Tel Aviv University)

resources for deep sea mining. This method was designed for special types of seafloor object detection.

Regardless of the particularities of the employed methods, automated classification of the seafloor will only achieve accurate results when the imagery is acquired under adequately good conditions. In this aspect, autonomous vehicles play an important, if not crucial, role as optimum classification results are obtained using visual data acquired at high resolution under clear visibility conditions, uniform illumination, consistent view angles and altitude, and sufficient image overlap.

7.3   Acoustic Mapping Techniques

Several researchers have drawn attention to the use of FLS either as a substitute or as a complementary device for optical cameras in mapping purposes. The sensor parallelism becomes straightforward: FLS can be exploited to mosaic the seafloor through the registration of FLS images, following the same concept of 2D photomosaicing. Even though the range of FLS is greater than that of optical cameras, their field of view is also limited. Thus, it is often not possible to image a given area within a single frame or at least to do so without sacrificing a great deal of resolution by pushing the device's range to the limit. In such circumstances, mosaicing of FLS images allows to obtain an extended overview of an area of interest regardless of the visibility conditions and without compromising the resolution.

Similar to the optical mosaicing, the workflow to create an acoustic image mosaic follows three main steps:

Image registration: First, frame-to-frame transformations are computed using an image registration method. The particularities of FLS imagery pose a significant challenge to the registration techniques typically used in photomosaicing. In this sense, area-based approaches (Hurtós et al. 2014b) that use all the image content become more suitable than feature-based approaches (Kim et al. 2005, 2006; Negahdaripour et al. 2005) that have a more unstable behavior on low signal-to-noise ratio (SNR) images. In addition, by avoiding the extraction of explicit features, the registration technique remains independent of the type and number of features present in the environment, and it can be robustly applied to a wide variety of environments ranging from more featureless natural terrains to man-made scenarios.

Global alignment: Consecutive images are aligned by transforming them to a common reference frame through compounding of the different transformations. Errors that accumulate along the trajectory can be corrected by means of global optimization techniques that make use of the transformations between nonconsecutive images. In Hurtós et al. (2014b), the problem of obtaining a globally consistent acoustic mosaic is set down as a pose-based graph optimization. A least squares minimization is formulated to estimate the maximum-likelihood configuration for the sonar images based on the pairwise constraints between consecutive and nonconsecutive frame registrations. In order to integrate the sonar constraints into the optimization framework, a method is established to quantify the uncertainty of the registration results. Apart from the sonar motion constraints, the same framework can integrate constraints coming from dead-reckoning navigation sensors or absolute positioning sensors. In addition, a strategy needs to be established to identify putative loop closures according to the spatial arrangement of the image's positions, so that registration is attempted only between those pairs of frames that overlap (Hurtós et al. 2014a). Once the graph is constructed, different back-ends developed to efficiently optimize pose graphs (e.g., g2o (Kummerle et al. 2011), iSAM (Kaess et al. 2012)) can be used to obtain the final set of absolute positions in which to render the individual images.

Mosaic rendering: Finally, in order to achieve an informative and smooth mosaic, the individual sonar frames are fused. Unlike the blending in optical mosaics, this implies dealing with a high number of overlapping images as well as with sonar-specific artifacts arising from its image formation geometry. Different strategies can be enabled according to the photometric irregularities present in the data both at frame level (i.e., inhomogeneous insonification patterns due to different sensitivity of the sonar transducer elements, nonuniform illumination across frames, blind areas due to improper imaging configuration) and at mosaic level (i.e., seams along different tracklines due to a different number of overlapping images and different resolution) (Hurtós et al. 2013a).

A mosaicing system as such is of great interest in many mapping tasks that are carried out in turbid waters and murky environments. A clear example is the mapping of ship hulls, which are routinely inspected for security reasons using divers, being a hazardous and time consuming task. Given that these inspections are carried out inside harbor, where water visibility is often limited, they are a good example of target application for the described mapping methodology. Figure 7.12 shows an example of a mosaic obtained from King Triton vessel in Boston Harbor using the HAUV (Vaganay et al. 2005) equipped with a DIDSON FLS (Sou 2015) (data courtesy of Bluefin Robotics (Blu 2015b)). The mosaic, consisting of 518 frames, presents a consistent overall appearance and allows the identification of the various features on the hull.

Another significant application is the mapping of harbors, bays, and estuaries, which typically suffer from poor visibility conditions. Figure 7.13 shows an example of a mosaic generated in a marina environment using an Autonomous Surface Craft from the Center of Maritime Research and Experimentation (CMRE). In this case,

Figure 7.12 Ship hull inspection mosaic. Data gathered with HAUV using DIDSON FLS. Data courtesy of Bluefin Robotics

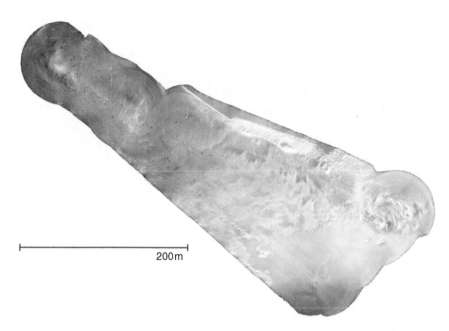

200 m

Figure 7.13 Harbor inspection mosaic. Data gathered from an Autonomous Surface Craft with BlueView P900-130 FLS. Data courtesy of Center for Maritime Research and Experimentation

a BlueView P900-130 FLS was used (Blu 2015a), providing individual images with a wide field of view, long range, and low resolution. The mosaic exhibits consistency, thanks to the detection of several loop closures across the different tracks, even though consecutive ones have reciprocal headings and the image appearance is highly distinct.

A final example of acoustic mapping with FLS can be seen in Figure 7.14. A mosaic composed of four different tracks and more than 1500 FLS frames shows the remains of the *Cap de Vol* Iberian shipwreck. The mosaic was created in real time, thanks to a restrictive criterion on the frame candidate selection to attempt registrations. A mosaic of the same area built from optical data is shown for comparison purposes.

7.4 Concluding Remarks

In this chapter, we discuss the most relevant underwater mapping and classification techniques. The use of the presented mapping techniques allows large-scale, yet detailed, visual representations of the environment surveyed by the underwater vehicle. Choosing which mapping approach to employ has to be done depending on various factors: (i) the mapping application, (ii) the type of survey and the acquisition sensors, and (iii) the characteristics of the environment. Specifically, when only visual information (i.e., color, texture, shape) is required for a specific study and

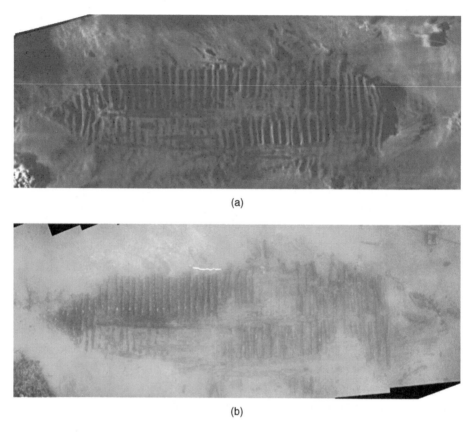

(a)

(b)

Figure 7.14   *Cap de Vol* shipwreck mosaic: (a) acoustic mosaic and (b) optical mosaic

the surveyed area is relatively flat, 2D mapping techniques are the most suitable. In contrast, when structural information is important or when the surveyed area is characterized by significant relief variations, 2.5D and 3D mapping techniques are the most adequate.

Additionally, for applications/studies that require semantic information, we present machine learning techniques that enable automatic classification of visual data. These techniques use supervised learning approaches, allowing the transfer of knowledge from an expert to the system. The system then uses this knowledge to classify new visual data and provide the user with meaningful semantic interpretations.

8

Closing Notes

Antonio M. López

ADAS Group, Computer Vision Center (CVC) and Computer Science Department, Universitat Autònoma de Barcelona (UAB), Barcelona, Spain

With more than 20 years of experience in computer vision so far and after going through the different chapters of this book, one feels astonished about the progress made in this field. The contribution of computer vision for vehicular technologies is beyond doubt, in land, sea, and air. The current level of maturity has been possible thanks to advances in different axes, namely, in a continuous improvement of cameras (cost, resolution, frame rate, size, weight), more powerful processing units ready for on-board embedding (CPUs, GPUs, FPGAs), more publicly available data sets and evaluation protocols (e.g., the KITTI Vision Benchmark Suite), and of course more and more consolidated computer vision and machine learning algorithms for discriminative feature extraction, matching, stereo and optical flow computation, object detection and tracking, localization and mapping, spatiotemporal reasoning, semantic segmentation, and so on.

Overall, we can find different vision-based commercial solutions for real-live problems related to vehicles (especially for driver assistance). However, despite this great progress, if we compare the state of the art of computer vision for vehicles with the visual capabilities of humans, one can safely say that still there is a large room for improvement. Just taking the driver task as an example, we can see that high-level reasoning must be much improved (i.e., the AI for real-time risk analysis and decision making), which may even involve ethical and legislative considerations (e.g., when a crash involving third parties may be unavoidable). In the other extreme, that is, low-level vision, even feature extraction must be improved for increasing robustness under adverse conditions and to cope with the fact that the world is a changing

Computer Vision in Vehicle Technology: Land, Sea, and Air, First Edition.
Edited by Antonio M. López, Atsushi Imiya, Tomas Pajdla and Jose M. Álvarez.
© 2017 John Wiley & Sons Ltd. Published 2017 by John Wiley & Sons Ltd.

entity (e.g., if we navigate by relying on maps and vision-based localization, we must be robust to even severe seasonal changes of the world's visual appearance).

It is worth mentioning the recent astonishing performance of *deep* convolutional neural networks (DCNNs) in difficult visual tasks such as image classification (Krizhevsky et al. 2012), object recognition/localization/detection (Girshick et al. 2016; Sermanet et al. 2014), and semantic segmentation (Long et al. 2015; Noh et al. 2015). Note that the layers of a given DCNN architecture can even be used for tasks different from those assumed during the original end-to-end training of the DCNN (Hariharan et al. 2015). In fact, different DCNN architectures are already being explored for low-level tasks such as optical flow and disparity computation (Dosovitskiy et al. 2015; Mayer et al. 2015), and higher level ones such as place recognition (Chena et al. 2015; Sunderhauf et al. 2015). This opens a new avenue of methods based on deep learning that will boost computer vision performance in vehicle technology (e.g., see Huval et al. (2015) in the context of autonomous driving). In fact, major hardware-oriented companies are gambling on the use of computer vision and deep learning to develop vehicle perception, an example is the embedded GPU-based supercomputer known as NVIDIA Drive PX 2 (see (NVIDIA at CES 2016)). Moreover, we have to add the recent announcement at the GTC 2016 of the new supercomputer especially designed to train DCNNs, the so-called NVIDIA DGX-1. Deep models trained in DGX-1 will be directly transferable to Drive PX 2.

Despite the advances that we can foresee, thanks to all these new scientific and technological tools, still there are different challenges to address. For instance, computer vision methods tend to fail in adverse weather conditions and under poor illumination. Thus, improvements from cameras operating either the visual spectrum or the far infrared are necessary. Otherwise, complementing vision with other sensors will be mandatory not only in the short midterm but also in the long term. In fact, whenever it is possible taking into account system cost, complementing vision with other types of sensors (light detection and ranging (lidar), radar, etc.) is a good practice to ensure redundancy and, thus, overall system reliability. Accordingly, multimodal perception is and is going to be a very relevant topic too. An interesting type of sensor announced by the end of 2016 is the solid-state lidar, which promises a low-cost array of depth information that can complement the visual spectrum.

Another important consideration for training and testing of the algorithms under development, especially relevant for using deep learning techniques, is to increase drastically the size and annotation quality of the publicly available data sets. A recent and notable example is Cityscapes (Cordts et al. 2015), a large data set with manually collected, pixel-level annotations of driving scenarios. A different approach consists of using realistic computer graphics to generate training images with automatically generated ground-truth. For instance, this is the case of SYNTHIA (Ros et al. 2016), which contains pixel-level information of RGB, depth, and semantic class. In fact, object detectors trained on virtual worlds and domain adapted to real scenarios already have demonstrated their usefulness in the context of driving assistance (Marín et al. 2010; Vazquez et al. 2014; Xu et al. 2014a,b, 2016). In addition, incremental self-learning methods able to use not only annotated data but also nonannotated data could be a key to improve the robustness of vision-based perception.

Finally, a core problem to address is overall vehicle validation. If we take an autonomous vehicle as an example, we can easily imagine the many situations it must be able to handle. How to measure the reliability of such a system for its massive production is an open question. In fact, the use of realistic virtual environments that allow use-case-driven testing can be a line to pursue for drastically reducing validation cost. An example is the Virtual KITTI (Gaidon et al. 2016) designed for testing vision-based vehicle detection algorithms under adverse weather conditions. Of course, once these systems are comprehensively evaluated in such simulated environments, still it is necessary to validate them in real-world scenarios both in dedicated infrastructures and regular conditions.

In summary, the academic and industry communities working on computer vision for vehicles are facing a really exciting revolution which, undoubtedly, will bring enormous social benefits and unbelievable technological advances. For instance, autonomous vehicles and UAVs are among the *ten technologies which could change our lives* according to the European parliament (Van Woensel et al. 2015).

References

Achtelik M, Bachrach A, He R, Prentice S and Roy N. 2009. Stereo vision and laser odometry for autonomous helicopters in GPS-denied indoor environments. *SPIE Conference on Unmanned Systems Technology*, Orlando, FL, USA.

Achtelik MC, Doth KM, Gurdan D and Stumpf J. 2012. Design of a multi rotor MAV with regard to efficiency, dynamics and redundancy. *AIAA Guidance, Navigation, and Control Conference*.

Achtelik M, Weiss S and Siegwart R. 2011. Onboard IMU and monocular vision based control for MAVs in unknown in and outdoor environments. *Proceedings of the IEEE International Conference on Robotics and Automation*.

Adnriluka M, Roth S and Schiele B. 2008. People-tracking-by-detection and people-detection-by-tracking. *Proceedings of the conference on Computer Vision and Pattern Recognition*, Anchorage, AK, USA.

Agarwala A, Dontcheva M, Agrawala M, Drucker S, Colburn A, Curless B, Salesin D and Cohen M. 2004. Interactive digital photomontage. *Proceedings of the SIGGRAPH*.

Ahrens S, Levine D, Andrews G and How J. 2009. Vision-based guidance and control of a hovering vehicle in unknown, GPS-denied environments. *Proceedings of the IEEE International Conference on Robotics and Automation*.

Alexa M, Rusinkiewicz S, Alexa M and Adamson A. 2004. On normals and projection operators for surfaces defined by point sets. *Proceedings of the Eurographics Symposium on Point-Based Graphics*.

Alon Y, Ferencz A and Shashua A. 2006. Off-road path following using region classification and geometric projection constraints. *Proceedings of the conference on Computer Vision and Pattern Recognition*, San Francisco, CA.

Alvarez J, Lopez A and Baldrich R. 2007. Shadow resistant road segmentation from a mobile monocular system. *Proceedings of the Iberian Conference on Pattern Recognition and Image Analysis*, Girona, Spain.

Amenta N, Choi S, Dey TK and Leekha N. 2000. A simple algorithm for homeomorphic surface reconstruction. *Proceedings of the Annual Symposium on Computational Geometry*.

Amenta N, Choi S and Kolluri R. 2001. The power crust. *Proceedings of the ACM Symposium on Solid Modeling and Applications*.

Computer Vision in Vehicle Technology: Land, Sea, and Air, First Edition.
Edited by Antonio M. López, Atsushi Imiya, Tomas Pajdla and Jose M. Álvarez.
© 2017 John Wiley & Sons Ltd. Published 2017 by John Wiley & Sons Ltd.

Ancuti C, Ancuti CO, Haber T and Bekaert P. 2012. Enhancing underwater images and videos by fusion. *Proceedings of the conference on Computer Vision and Pattern Recognition.*

Ancuti CO, Ancuti C, Hermans C and Bekaert P. 2011. A fast semi-inverse approach to detect and remove the haze from a single image. *Proceedings of the Asian Conference on Computer Vision.*

Andreone L, Bellotti F, Gloria A and Laulett R. 2005. SVM based pedestrian recognition on near infrared images. *Proceedings of the International Symposium on Image and Signal Processing and Analysis*, Zagreb, Croatia.

Angeli A, Doncieux S, Meyer JA and Filliat D. 2008a. Incremental vision-based topological SLAM. *Proceedings of the IEEE/RSJ International Conference on Intelligent Robots and Systems.*

Angeli A, Doncieux S, Meyer JA and Filliat D. 2008b. Real-time visual loop-closure detection. *Proceedings of the IEEE International Conference on Robotics and Automation.*

Anuradha and Kaur H. 2015. Improved underwater image enhancement using L*A*B on CLAHE and gradient based smoothing. *International Journal of Computer Applications* **114**, 45–52.

Arndt R, Schweiger R, Ritter W, Paulus D and Löhlein O. 2007. Detection and tracking of multiple pedestrians in automotive applications. *Proceedings of the IEEE Intelligent Vehicles Symposium*, Istanbul, Turkey.

Aulinas J, Lladó X, Salvi J and Petillot YR. 2010. Feature based SLAM using side-scan salient objects. *Proceedings of the IEEE/MTS OCEANS Conference.*

Aykin MD and Negahdaripour S. 2013. On feature matching and image registration for two-dimensional forward-scan sonar imaging. *Journal of Field Robotics* **30**, 602–623.

Bachrach A. 2009. *Autonomous Flight in Unstructured and Unknown Indoor Environments.* Master's thesis, Massachusetts Institute of Technology.

Bachrach A, He R and Roy N. 2009. Autonomous flight in unstructured and unknown indoor environments. *Proceedings of the European Conference on Micro Air Vehicles.*

Badino H. 2004. A robust approach for ego-motion estimation using a mobile stereo platform. *Proceedings of the IWCM Workshop on Complex Motion*, Günzburg, Germany.

Badino H, Franke W and Mester R. 2007. Free space computation using stochastic occupancy grids and dynamic programming. *Proceedings of the International Conference on Computer Vision, Workshop on Dynamical Vision*, Rio de Janeiro, Brazil.

Badino H, Franke U and Pfeiffer D. 2009. The stixel world - a compact medium level representation of the 3D-world. *Proceedings of the German Conference on Pattern Recognition*, Jena, Germany.

Barkby S, Williams S, Pizarro O and Jakuba M. 2012. Bathymetric particle filter SLAM using trajectory maps. *International Journal of Robotics Research* **31**, 1409–1430.

Barnes N, Zelinsky A and Fletcher L. 2008. Real-time speed sign detection using the radial symmetry detector. *IEEE Transactions on Intelligent Transportation Systems* **9**, 322–332.

Barth A, Pfeiffer D and Franke U. 2009. Vehicle tracking at urban intersections using dense stereo. *Proceedings of the BMI, Workshop on Behaviour Monitoring and Interpretation*, Ghent, Belgium.

Barth A, Siegmund J, Meissner A, Franke U and Förstner W. 2010. Probabilistic multi-class scene flow segmentation for traffic scenes. *Proceedings of the German Conference on Pattern Recognition.*

Bay H, Tuytelaars T and Gool LV. 2006. SURF: speeded up robust features. *Proceedings of the European Conference on Computer Vision.*

Beardsley PA, Zisserman A and Murray DW. 1994. Navigation using affine structure from motion. *Proceedings of the European Conference on Computer Vision*, vol. 801.

Beaudet PR. 1978. Rotationally invariant image operators. *Proceedings of the International Conference in Pattern Recognition*, Kyoto, Japan.

Beijbom O, Edmunds P, Kline D, Mitchell B and Kriegman D. 2012. Automated annotation of coral reef survey images. *Proceedings of the Conference on Computer Vision and Pattern Recognition*, Providence, RI, USA.

Beirness D, Simpson H and Pak A. 2002. The road safety monitor: driver distraction. Technical report, Traffic Injury Research Foundation, Ontario, Canada, http://www.tirf.ca/publications/PDF_publications/RSM_Driver_Distraction.pdf.

Bellman R. 1957. *Dynamic Programming.* Princeton University Press, Princeton, NJ, USA.

Bender A, Williams S and Pizarro O. 2012. Classification with probabilistic targets. *Proceedings of the IEEE/RSJ International Conference on Intelligent Robots and Systems.*

Benenson R, Mathias M, Timofte R and van Gool L. 2012. Fast stixel computation for fast pedestrian detection. *Proceedings of the European Conference on Computer Vision, Workshop on Computer Vision in Vehicle Technology*, Firenze, Italy.

Benenson R, Timofte R and van Gool L. 2011. Stixels estimation without depth map computation. *Proceedings of the International Conference on Computer Vision, Workshop on Computer Vision in Vehicular Technology.*

Bergasa L, Nuevo J, Sotelo M and Vazquez M. 2004. Real time system for monitoring driver vigilance. *Proceedings of the IEEE Intelligent Vehicles Symposium.*

Bernardini F, Mittleman J, Rushmeier H, Silva C and Taubin G. 1999. The ball-pivoting algorithm for surface reconstruction. *IEEE Transactions on Visualization and Computer Graphics* **5**, 349–359.

Bertozzi M, Broggi A, Chapuis R, Chausse F, Fascioli A and Tibaldi A. 2003. Shapebased pedestrian detection and localization. *Proceedings of the IEEE International Conference on Intelligent Transportation Systems*, Shanghai, China.

Biber P and Straßer W. 2003. The normal distributions transform: a new approach to laser scan matching. *Proceedings of the IEEE/RSJ International Conference on Intelligent Robots and Systems.*

Bills C, Chen J and Saxena A. 2011a. Autonomous MAV flight in indoor environments using single image perspective cues. *Proceedings of the IEEE International Conference on Robotics and Automation.*

Bills C, Chen J and Saxena A. 2011b. Autonomous MAV flight in indoor environments using single image perspective cues. *Proceedings of the IEEE International Conference on Robotics and Automation.*

Bingham B, Foley B, Singh H, Camilli R, Delaporta K, Eustice R, Mallios A, Mindell D, Roman CN and Sakellariou D. 2010. Robotic tools for deep water archaeology: surveying an ancient shipwreck with an autonomous underwater vehicle. *Journal of Field Robotics* **27**, 702–717.

Bleyer M and Chambon S. 2010. Does color really help in dense stereo matching. *3DPVT*, Paris, France.

Bloesch M, Weiss S, Scaramuzza D and Siegwart R. 2010. Vision based MAV navigation in unknown and unstructured environments. *Proceedings of the IEEE International Conference on Robotics and Automation.*

Blu. 2015a. Retrieved February 26, 2015, from www.blueview.com.

Blu. 2015b. Retrieved February 26, 2015, from www.bluefinrobotics.com.

Bohren CF and Clothiaux EE. 2006. *Fundamentals of Atmospheric Radiation: An Introduction with 400 Problems*. Wiley-VCH Verlag GmbH & Co. KGaA, Weinheim.

Boissonnat JD and Oudot S. 2005. Provably good sampling and meshing of surfaces. *Graphical Models* **67**, 405–451.

Bosch S, Lacroix S and Caballero F. 2006. Autonomous detection of safe landing areas for an UAV from monocular images. *Proceedings of the IEEE/RSJ International Conference on Intelligent Robots and Systems*.

Botsch M, Kobbelt L, Pauly M, Alliez P and Lévy B. 2010. *Polygon Mesh Processing*. AK Peters / CRC Press.

Bouabdallah S, Murrieri P and Siegwart R. 2004. Design and control of an indoor micro quadrotor. *Proceedings of the IEEE International Conference on Robotics and Automation*.

Bowling M, Wilkinson D, Ghodsi A and Milstein A. 2005. Subjective localization with action respecting embedding. *Proceedings of the International Symposium of Robotics Research*.

Boykov Y, Veksler O and Zabih R. 1999. Fast approximate energy minimization via graph cuts. *Proceedings of the International Conference on Computer Vision*, Kerkyra, Corfu, Greece.

Briassouli A and Kompatsiaris I. 2010. Change detection for temporal texture in the Fourier domain. *Proceedings of the Asian Conference on Computer Vision*.

Bristeau PJ, Callou F, Vissière D and Petit N. 2011. The navigation and control technology inside the ar.drone micro UAV. *IFAC Proceedings Volumes (IFAC-PapersOnline)*, vol. **18**, pp. 1477–1484.

Brockers R, Hummenberger M, Weiss S and Matthies L. 2014. Towards autonomous navigation of miniature UAV. *Proceedings of the conference on Computer Vision and Pattern Recognition Workshops*.

Broggi A, Bertozzi M, Fascioli A and Sechi M. 2000. Shape–based pedestrian detection. *Proceedings of the IEEE Intelligent Vehicles Symposium*, Dearborn, MI, USA.

Broggi A, Cerri P, Medici P, Porta P and Ghisio G. 2007. Real time road signs recognition. *Proceedings of the IEEE Intelligent Vehicles Symposium*, Istanbul, Turkey.

Brown M, Hartley R and Nister D. 2007. Minimal solutions for panoramic stitching. *Proceedings of the Conference on Computer Vision and Pattern Recognition*.

Brox T, Bruhn A, Papenberg N and Weickert J. 2004. High accuracy optical flow estimation based on a theory for warping. *Proceedings of the European Conference on Computer Vision*.

Bryson M, Johnson-Roberson M, Pizarro O and Williams S. 2012. Colour-consistent structure-from-motion models using underwater imagery. *Robotics: Science and Systems*.

Caballero F, Merino L, Ferruz J and Ollero A. 2007. Homography based Kalman filter for mosaic building. applications to UAV position estimation. *Proceedings of the IEEE International Conference on Robotics and Automation*.

Caimi F, Kocak D, Dalgleish F and Watson J. 2008. Underwater imaging and optics: recent advances. *Proceedings of the IEEE/MTS OCEANS Conference*.

Campos R, Garcia R, Alliez P and Yvinec M. 2013a. Splat-based surface reconstruction from defect-laden point sets. *Graphical Models* **75**, 346–361.

Campos R, Gracias N, Prados R and Garcia R. 2013b. Merging bathymetric and optical cues for in-detail inspection of an underwater shipwreck. *Instrumentation Viewpoint*, pp. 67–68.

Campos R, Garcia R, Alliez P and Yvinec M. 2015. A surface reconstruction method for in-detail underwater 3D optical mapping. *International Journal of Robotics Research* **34**, 64–89.

Can A, Stewart C, Roysam B and Tanenbaum H. 2002. A feature-based technique for joint, linear estimation of high-order image-to-mosaic transformations: mosaicing the curved human retina. *IEEE Transactions on Pattern Analysis and Machine Intelligence* **24**, 412–419.

Capel DP. 2001. *Image Mosaicing and Super-resolution*. PhD thesis, University of Oxford, Oxford, UK.

Capel DP. 2004. *Image Mosaicing and Super-resolution*. Springer Verlag.

Carlevaris-Bianco N, Mohan A and Eustice RM. 2010. Initial results in underwater single image dehazing. *Proceedings of the IEEE/MTS OCEANS Conference*.

Carr JC, Beatson RK, Cherrie JB, Mitchell TJ, Fright WR, McCallum BC and Evans TR. 2001. Reconstruction and representation of 3D objects with radial basis functions. *Proceedings of the Annual Conference on Computer Graphics and Interactive Techniques*.

Chena Z, Lowrya S, Jacobsona A, Hasselmoc ME and Milford M. 2015. Bio-inspired homogeneous multi-scale place recognition. *Neural Networks* **38**, 142–158.

Chiang JY and Chen YC. 2012. Underwater image enhancement by wavelength compensation and dehazing. *IEEE Transactions on Image Processing* **21**, 1756–1769.

Chiuso A, Favaro P, Jin H and Soatto S. 2002. Structure from motion causally integrated over time. *IEEE Transactions on Pattern Analysis and Machine Intelligence* **24**, 523–535.

Choi K, Park S, Kim S, Lee K, Park J and Cho S. 2010. Methods to detect road features for video-based in-vehicle navigation systems. *Journal of Intelligent Transportation Systems: Technology Planning Operations* **14**, 13–26.

CIPA. 2009. Camera & imaging products association 2009 multi-picture format, dc-007-2009.

Cohen-Steiner D and Da F. 2004. A greedy Delaunay-based surface reconstruction algorithm. *The Visual Computer* **20**, 4–16.

Cordts M, Omran M, Ramos S, Scharwächter T, Enzweiler M, Benenson R, Franke U, Roth S and Schiele B. 2015. The cityscapes dataset. *Proceedings of the conference on Computer Vision and Pattern Recognition, Workshop on The Future of Datasets in Vision*.

Cortes C and Vapnik V. 1995. Support-vector networks. *Machine Learning* **20**, 273–297.

Crisman J and orpe CT. 1993. Scarf: a colour vision system that tracks roads and intersections. *IEEE Transactions on Robotics and Automation* **9**, 49–58.

Crowley J and Sanderson A. 1987. Multiple resolution representation and probabilistic matching of 2-d gray-scale shape. *IEEE Transactions on Pattern Analysis and Machine Intelligence* **9**, 113–121.

Csurka G, Dance C, Fan L, Willamowski J and Bray C. 2004. Visual categorization with bags of keypoints. *Proceedings of the European Conference on Computer Vision, Workshop on statistical learning in computer vision*, vol. 1, p. 22.

Cummins M and Newman P. 2007. Probabilistic appearance based navigation and loop closing. *Proceedings of the IEEE International Conference on Robotics and Automation*, Rome, Italy.

Cummins M and Newman P. 2008. FAB-MAP: probabilistic localization and mapping in the space of appearance. *International Journal of Robotics Research* **27**, 647–665.

Cummins M and Newman P. 2009. Highly scalable appearance-only SLAM FAB-MAP 2.0. *Robotics: Science and Systems*.

Curless B and Levoy M. 1996. A volumetric method for building complex models from range images. *Proceedings of the Annual Conference on Computer Graphics and Interactive Techniques.*

Dalal N and Triggs B. 2005. Histograms of oriented gradients for human detection. *Proceedings of the conference on Computer Vision and Pattern Recognition*, San Diego, CA, USA.

Danescu R and Nedevschi S. 2009. Probabilistic lane tracking in difficult road scenarios using stereovision. *IEEE Transactions on Intelligent Transportation Systems* **10**, 272–282.

Danescu R and Nedevschi S. 2011. New results in stereovision based lane tracking. *Proceedings of the IEEE Intelligent Vehicles Symposium*, Baden-Baden, Germany.

Dang T, Desens J, Franke U, Gavrila D, Schäfers L and Ziegler W. 2004. Steering and evasion assist, In *Handbook of Intelligent Vehicles* (ed. Eskandarian A), Springer, London.

Dang T, Hoffmann C and Stiller C. 2009. Continuous stereo self-calibration by camera parameter tracking. *IEEE Transactions on Image Processing* **18**, 1536–1550.

Davis J. 1998. Mosaics of scenes with moving objects. *Proceedings of the Conference on Computer Vision and Pattern Recognition*, Santa Barbara, CA, USA.

Davison A, Reid I, Molton N and Stasse O. 2007. MonoSLAM: real-time single camera SLAM. *IEEE Transactions on Pattern Analysis and Machine Intelligence* **29**, 1052–1067.

Delaunoy O, Gracias N and Garcia R. 2008. Towards detecting changes in underwater image sequences. *Proceedings of the IEEE/MTS OCEANS Conference.*

DePiero FW and Trivedi MM. 1996. 3D computer vision using structured light: design, calibration and implementation issues. *Advances in Computers* **43**, 243–278.

Desaraju V, Michael N, Humenberger M, Brockers R, Weiss S and Matthies L. 2014. Vision-based landing site evaluation and trajectory generation toward rooftop landing. *Robotics: Science and Systems.*

Diaz J and Torres R. 2006. Classification of underwater color images with applications in the study of deep coral reefs. *Proceedings of the International Midwest Symposium on Circuits and Systems.*

Dickmanns E. 1988. An integrated approach to feature based dynamic vision. *Proceedings of the Conference on Computer Vision and Pattern Recognition.*

Dickmanns E. 2007. *Dynamic Vision for Perception and Control of Motion.* Springer-Verlag, Berlin.

Digne J, Morel JM, Souzani CM and Lartigue C. 2011. Scale space meshing of raw data point sets. *Computer Graphics Forum (Proceedings of the Symposium on Geometry Processing)* **30**, 1630–1642.

Dinges D and Grace R. 1998. PERCLOS: a valid psychophysiological measure of alertness as assessed by psychomotor vigilance. Technical report FHWA-MCRT-98-006, Federal Highway Administration, https://trid.trb.org/view.aspx?id=498744.

Doitsidis L, Weiss S, Renzaglia A, Achtelik MW, Kosmatopoulos E, Siegwart R and Scaramuzza D. 2012. Optimal surveillance coverage for teams of micro aerial vehicles in GPS-denied environments using onboard vision. *Autonomous Robots* **33**, 173–188.

Dollár P, Tu Z, Perona P and Belongie S. 2009. Integral channel features. *Proceedings of the British Machine Vision Conference*, London, UK.

Dollár P, Wojek C, Schiele B and Perona P. 2012. Pedestrian detection: an evaluation of the state of the art. *IEEE Transactions on Pattern Analysis and Machine Intelligence* **34**, 743–761.

Dosovitskiy A, Fischer P, Ilg E, Häusser P, Hazrbas C, Golkov V, Smagt P, Cremers D and Brox T. 2015. FlowNet: learning optical flow with convolutional networks. *Proceedings of the International Conference on Computer Vision.*

Drap P, Scaradozzi D, Gambogi P and Gauch F. 2008. Underwater photogrammetry for archaeology–the venus project framework. *Proceedings of the International Conference on Computer Graphics Theory and Applications.*

Eberli D, Scaramuzza D, Weiss S and Siegwart R. 2011. Vision based position control for MAVs using one single circular landmark. *Journal of Intelligent Robotic Systems* **61**, 495–512.

Efros A and Freeman W. 2001. Image quilting for texture synthesis and transfer. *Proceedings of the Conference on Computer Graphics and Interactive Techniques.*

Elibol A, Garcia R, Delaunoy O and Gracias N. 2008. A new global alignment method for feature based image mosaicing. *Proceedings of the International Symposium on Advances in Visual Computing*, Las Vegas, NV, USA.

Elibol A, Gracias N and Garcia R. 2010. Augmented state–extended Kalman filter combined framework for topology estimation in large-area underwater mapping. *Journal of Field Robotics* **27**, 656–674.

Elibol A, Garcia R and Gracias N. 2011a. A new global alignment approach for underwater optical mapping. *Ocean Engineering* **38**, 1207–1219.

Elibol A, Gracias N, Garcia R, Gleason A, Gintert B, Lirman D and Reid PR. 2011b. Efficient autonomous image mosaicing with applications to coral reef monitoring. *Proceedings of the IEEE/RSJ International Conference on Intelligent Robots and Systems, Workshop on Robotics for Environmental Monitoring.*

Elibol A, Gracias N and Garcia R. 2013. Fast topology estimation for image mosaicing using adaptive information thresholding. *Robotics and Autonomous Systems* **61**, 125–136.

Engel J, Sturm J and Cremers D. 2014. Scale-aware navigation of a low-cost quadrocopter with a monocular camera. *Robotics and Autonomous Systems* **62**, 1646–1656.

Enzweiler M et al. 2010. Multi-cue pedestrian classification with partial occlusion handling. *Proceedings of the conference on Computer Vision and Pattern Recognition.*

Enzweiler M et al. 2013. Towards multi-cue urban curb recognition. *Proceedings of the IEEE Intelligent Vehicles Symposium.*

Enzweiler M and Gavrila D. 2009. Monocular pedestrian detection: survey and experiments. *IEEE Transactions on Pattern Analysis and Machine Intelligence* **31**, 2179–2195.

Enzweiler M and Gavrila DM. 2011. A multi-level Mixture-of-Experts framework for pedestrian classification. *IEEE Transactions on Image Processing* **20**, 2967–2979.

Enzweiler M, Hummel M, Pfeiffer D and Franke U. 2012. Efficient stixel-based object recognition. *Proceedings of the IEEE Intelligent Vehicles Symposium.*

Erbs F and Franke U. 2012. Stixmentation - probabilistic stixel based traffic scene labeling. *Proceedings of the British Machine Vision Conference*, Guildford, UK.

Escartin J, Garcia R, Delaunoy O, Ferrer J, Gracias N, Elibol A, Cufi X, Neumann L, Fornari D and Humphris S. 2009. Globally-aligned photo mosaic of the lucky strike hydrothermal vent field (mid-Atlantic ridge, 37 18.5N): release of georeferenced data and interactive viewer software. *Geochemistry, Geophysics, Geosystems* **9**, http://onlinelibrary.wiley.com/doi/10 .1029/2008GC002204/abstract.

EURO NCAP. 2014. Advanced safety systems award. Technical report.

Eustice RM. 2005. *Large-Area Visually Augmented Navigation for Autonomous Underwater Vehicles*. PhD thesis, Massachusetts Institute of Technology and Woods Hole Oceanographic Institution.

Eustice R, Pizarro O and Singh H. 2004. Visually augmented navigation in an unstructured environment using a delayed state history. *Proceedings of the IEEE International Conference on Robotics and Automation*.

Eustice R, Singh H, Leonard J and Walter M. 2006a. Visually mapping the RMS Titanic: conservative covariance estimates for SLAM information filters. *International Journal of Robotics Research* **25**, 1223–1242.

Eustice R, Singh H, Leonard J, Walter M and Ballard R. 2005. Visually navigating the RMS Titanic with SLAM information filters. *Robotics: Science and Systems*.

Eustice RM, Singh H and Leonard JJ. 2006b. Exactly sparse delayed-state filters for view-based SLAM. *IEEE Transactions on Robotics* **22**, 1100–1114.

Faessler M, Fontana F, Forster C and Scaramuzza D. 2015a. Automatic re-initialization and failure recovery for aggressive flight with a monocular vision-based quadrotor. *Proceedings of the IEEE International Conference on Robotics and Automation*.

Faessler M, Fontana F, Forster C, Mueggler E, Pizzoli M and Scaramuzza D. 2015b. Autonomous, vision-based flight and live dense 3D mapping with a quadrotor MAV. *Journal of Field Robotics* **33**, 431–450.

Fairfield N, Jonak D, Kantor GA and Wettergreen D. 2007. Field results of the control, navigation, and mapping systems of a hovering AUV. *Proceedings of the International Symposium on Unmanned Untethered Submersible Technology*, Durham, NH, USA.

Fattal R. 2008. Single image dehazing. *ACM Transactions on Graphics* **27**, 1–8.

Felzenszwalb P, McAllester D and Ramanan D. 2008. A discriminatively trained, multiscale, deformable part model. *Proceedings of the Conference on Computer Vision and Pattern Recognition*, Anchorage, AK, USA.

Ferrer J and Garcia R. 2010. Bias reduction for stereo triangulation. *Electronic Letters* **46**, 1665–1666.

Ferrer J, Elibol A, Delaunoy O, Gracias N and Garcia R. 2007. Large-area photo-mosaics using global alignment and navigation data. *Proceedings of the IEEE/MTS OCEANS Conference*, Vancouver, Canada.

Filippo FD, Gracias N, Garcia R, Ferrer J and Bruno F. 2013. Incremental underwater mapping in 6DOF with stereo tracking. *Electronic Letters* **15**, 20–21.

Filliat D. 2007. A visual bag of words method for interactive qualitative localization and mapping. *Proceedings of the IEEE International Conference on Robotics and Automation*.

Fischler M and Bolles R. 1981. Random sample consensus: a paradigm for model fitting with applications to image analysis and automated cartography. *Communications of the ACM* **24**, 381–395.

Fitzgibbon AW and Zisserman A. 1998. Automatic camera recovery for closed or open image sequences. *Proceedings of the European Conference on Computer Vision*.

Fleischer SD. 2000. *Bounded-Error Vision-Based Navigation of Autonomous Underwater Vehicles*. PhD thesis, Department of Aeronautics and Astronautics, Stanford University.

Flohr F, Dumitru-Guzu M, Kooij JFP and Gavrila DM. 2014. Joint probabilistic pedestrian head and body orientation estimation. *Proceedings of the IEEE Intelligent Vehicles Symposium*.

Floreano D, Zufferey J, Srinivasan M and Ellington C. 2009. *Flying Insects and Robots*. Springer.

Floros G and Leibe B. 2012. Joint 2D-3D temporally consistent semantic segmentation of street scenes. *Proceedings of the Conference on Computer Vision and Pattern Recognition*.

Forster C, Fässler M, Fontana F, Werlberger M and Scaramuzza D. 2015. Continuous on-board monocular-vision–based aerial elevation mapping for quadrotor landing. *Proceedings of the IEEE International Conference on Robotics and Automation*.

Forster C, Lynen S, Kneip L and Scaramuzza D. 2013. Collaborative monocular SLAM with multiple micro aerial vehicles. *Proceedings of the IEEE/RSJ International Conference on Intelligent Robots and Systems*.

Forster C, Pizzoli M and Scaramuzza D. 2014a. Appearance-based active, monocular, dense depth estimation for micro aerial vehicles. *Robotics: Science and Systems*.

Forster C, Pizzoli M and Scaramuzza D. 2014b. SVO: fast semi-direct monocular visual odometry. *Proceedings of the IEEE International Conference on Robotics and Automation*.

Fournier G, Bonnier D, Forand JL and Pace P. 1993. Range-gated underwater laser imaging system. *Optical Engineering* **32**, 2185–2190.

Fournier G, Bonnier D, Forand JL and Pace P. 1995. Short-pulse range-gated optical imaging in turbid water. *Applied Optics* **34**, 4343–4351.

Francisco J, Raul E and Luis O. 2003. Hough transform for robust segmentation of underwater multispectral images. *Proceedings of the conference on Algorithms and Technologies for Multispectral, Hyperspectral, and Ultraspectral Imagery*.

Franke U et al. 1995. Autonomous driving goes downtown. *IEEE Intelligent Systems* **13**, 40–48.

Franke U and Joos A. 2000. Real-time stereo vision for urban traffic scene understanding. *Proceedings of the IEEE Intelligent Vehicles Symposium*, Dearborn, MI, USA.

Franke U, Rabe C, Badino H and Gehrig S. 2005. 6d-vision: fusion of stereo and motion for robust environment perception. *Proceedings of the German Conference on Pattern Recognition*, Vienna, Austria.

Fraundorfer F, Heng L, Honegger D, Lee GH, Meier L, Tanskanen P and Pollefeys M. 2012. Vision-based autonomous mapping and exploration using a quadrotor MAV. *Proceedings of the IEEE/RSJ International Conference on Intelligent Robots and Systems*.

Friedman A, Pizarro O, Williams S and Johnson-Roberson M. 2012. Multi-scale measures of rugosity, slope and aspect from benthic stereo image reconstructions. *PLoS ONE* **7**, e50440.

Furgale P et al. 2013. Toward automated driving in cities using close-to-market sensors, an overview of the V-Charge Project. *Proceedings of the IEEE Intelligent Vehicles Symposium*.

Furukawa Y and Ponce J. 2010. Accurate, dense, and robust multiview stereopsis. *IEEE Transactions on Pattern Analysis and Machine Intelligence* **32**, 1362–1376.

Gaidon A, Wang Q, Cabon Y and Vig E. 2016. Virtual worlds as proxy for multi-object tracking analysis. *Proceedings of the Conference on Computer Vision and Pattern Recognition*.

Gal R, Wexler Y, Ofek E, Hoppe H and Cohen-Or D. 2010. Seamless montage for texturing models. *Computer Graphics Forum (Proceedings of the Symposium on Geometry Processing)* **29**, 479–486.

Galvez-Lopez D and Tardos J. 2011. Real-time loop detection with bags of binary words. *Intelligent Robots and Systems*, pp. 51–58.

Gao X, Podladchikova L, Shaposhnikov D, Hong K and Shevtsova N. 2006. Recognition of traffic signs based on their colour and shape features extracted using human vision models. *Journal of Visual Communication and Image Representation* **17**, 675–685.

Garcia-Garrido MA, Ocana M, Llorca DF, Sotelo MA, Arroyo E and Llamazares A. 2011. Robust traffic signs detection by means of vision and v2i communications. *Proceedings of the IEEE International Conference on Intelligent Transportation Systems*, Washington DC, USA.

Garcia-Pardo PJ, Sukhatme GS and Montgomery JF. 2002. Towards vision-based safe landing for an autonomous helicopter. *Robotics and Autonomous Systems* **38**, 19–29.

Garcia R and Gracias N. 2011. Detection of interest points in turbid underwater images. *Proceedings of the IEEE/MTS OCEANS Conference*, pp. 1–9.

Garcia R, Campos R and Escartín J. 2011. High-resolution 3D reconstruction of the seafloor for environmental monitoring and modelling. *Proceedings of the IEEE/RSJ International Conference on Intelligent Robots and Systems, Workshop on Robotics for Environmental Monitoring*, San Francisco, CA, USA.

Garcia R, Cufi X and Batlle J. 2001. Detection of matchings in a sequence of underwater images through texture analysis. *Proceedings of the IEEE International Conference on Image Processing*.

Garcia R, Cufí X and Ila V. 2003a. Recovering camera motion in a sequence of underwater images through mosaicking. *Proceedings of the Iberian Conference on Pattern Recognition and Image Analysis*.

Garcia R, Nicosevici T, Ridao P and Ribas D. 2003b. Towards a real-time vision-based navigation system for a small-class UUV. *Proceedings of the IEEE/RSJ International Conference on Intelligent Robots and Systems*, Las Vegas, NV, USA.

Garcia R, Cufí X, Prados R, Elibol A, Ferrer J, Villanueva M and Nicosevici T. 2005. Georeferenced photo-mosaicing of the seafloor. *Instrumentation ViewPoint Journal* **4**, 45–46.

Garcia R, Puig J, Ridao P and Cufi X. 2002. Augmented state Kalman filtering for AUV navigation. *Proceedings of the IEEE International Conference on Robotics and Automation*, Washington, DC, USA.

Gavrila D. 2001. Sensor–based pedestrian protection. *IEEE Intelligent Systems* **16**, 77–81.

Gavrila D, Giebel J and Munder S. 2004. Vision–based pedestrian detection: the PROTECTOR system. *Proceedings of the IEEE Intelligent Vehicles Symposium*, Parma, Italy.

Ge J, Luo Y and Tei G. 2009. Real-time pedestrian detection and tracking at nighttime for driver assistance systems. *IEEE Transactions on Intelligent Transportation Systems* **10**, 283–298.

Gehrig S, Eberli F and Meyer T. 2009. A real-time low-power stereo vision engine using semi-global matching. *Proceedings of the International Conference on Computer Vision Systems*.

Gehrig S, Reznitskii M, Schneider N, Franke U and Weickert J. 2013. Priors for stereo vision under adverse weather conditions. *Proceedings of the International Conference on Computer Vision*, Sydney, Australia.

Gehrig S, Schneider N and Franke U. 2014. Exploiting traffic scene disparity statistics for stereo vision. *Proceedings of the conference on Computer Vision and Pattern Recognition, Workshop on Embedded Computer Vision*.

Geiger A n.d. www.cvlibs.net/datasets/kitti/.

Geiger A, Lenz P and Urtasun R. 2012. Are we ready for autonomous driving? The KITTI vision benchmark suite. *Proceedings of the Conference on Computer Vision and Pattern Recognition*, Providence, RI, USA.

Geng H, Chien J, Nicolescu R and Klette R. 2015. Egomotion estimation and reconstruction with Kalman filters and GPS integration. *Proceedings of the Conference on Computer Analysis of Images and Patterns*.

Gerónimo D and López A. 2014. *Vision-based Pedestrian Protection Systems for Intelligent Vehicles*. SpringerBriefs in Computer Science.

Gerónimo D, López A, Sappa A and Graf T. 2010. Survey of pedestrian detection for advanced driver assistance systems. *IEEE Transactions on Pattern Analysis and Machine Intelligence* **32**, 1239–1258.

Giraudot S, Cohen-Steiner D and Alliez P. 2013. Noise-adaptive shape reconstruction from raw point sets. *Computer Graphics Forum (Proceedings of the Symposium on Geometry Processing)* **32**, 229–238.

Girshick R, Donahue J, Darrell T and Malik J. 2016. Region-based convolutional networks for accurate object detection and segmentation. *IEEE Transactions on Pattern Analysis and Machine Intelligence* **72**, 48–61.

Gleason A, Lirman D, Williams D, Gracias N, Gintert B, Madjidi H, Reid R, Boynton G, Negahdaripour S, Miller M and Kramer P. 2007a. Documenting hurricane impacts on coral reefs using two–dimensional video–mosaic technology. *Marine Ecology* **28**, 254–258.

Gleason A, Reid R and Voss K. 2007b. Automated classification of underwater multispectral imagery for coral reef monitoring. *Proceedings of the IEEE/MTS OCEANS Conference*.

Glover A, Maddern W, Milford M and Wyeth G. 2011. FAB-MAP + RatSLAM: appearance-based slam for multiple times of day. *Proceedings of the IEEE International Conference on Robotics and Automation*.

Goedeme T, Tuytelaars T and Gool LV. 2006. Visual topological map building in self-similar environments. *International Conference on Informatics in Control, Automation and Robotics*.

Golz M, Sommer D, Trutschel U, Sirois B and Edwards D. 2010. Evaluation of fatigue monitoring technologies. *Somnologie* **14**, 187–199.

Gracias N. 2002. *Mosaic-based Visual Navigation for Autonomous Underwater Vehicles*. PhD thesis. Instituto Superior Técnico, Universidade Técnica de Lisboa Lisbon, Portugal.

Gracias N and Santos-Victor J. 2000. Underwater video mosaics as visual navigation maps. *Computer Vision and Image Understanding* **79**, 66–91.

Gracias N, Costeira J and Santos-Victor J. 2004. Linear global mosaics for underwater surveying. *Proceedings of the IFAC/EURON Symposium on Autonomous Vehicles*, Lisbon, Portugal.

Gracias N, Negahdaripour S, Neumann L, Prados R and Garcia R. 2008. A motion compensated filtering approach to remove sunlight flicker in shallow water images. *Proceedings of the IEEE/MTS OCEANS Conference*, Quebec City, Canada.

Gracias N, Zwaan S, Bernardino A and Santos-Victor J. 2003. Mosaic based navigation for autonomous underwater vehicles. *Journal of Oceanic Engineering* **28**, 609–624.

Grubb G, Zelinsky A, Nilsson L and Rilbe M. 2004. 3D vision sensing for improved pedestrian safety. *Proceedings of the IEEE Intelligent Vehicles Symposium*, Parma, Italy.

Grzonka S, Grisetti G and Burgard W. 2012. A fully autonomous indoor quadrotor. *IEEE Transactions on Robotics* **28**, 90–100.

Guennebaud G and Gross M. 2007. Algebraic point set surfaces. *ACM Transactions on Graphics* **26**, 23.1–23.9.

Haeusler R and Klette R. 2010. Benchmarking stereo data (not the matching algorithms). *Proceedings of the German Conference on Pattern Recognition.*

Haeusler R and Klette R. 2012. Analysis of KITTI data for stereo analysis with stereo confidence measures. *Proceedings of the European Conference on Computer Vision, Workshops and Demonstrations.*

Haralick R, Shanmugam K and Dinstein I. 1973. Textural features for image classification. *IEEE Transactions on Systems, Man, and Cybernetics* **SMC-3**, 610–621.

Hariharan B, Arbelaez P, Girshick R and Malik J. 2015. Hypercolumns for object segmentation and fine-grained localization. *Proceedings of the conference on Computer Vision and Pattern Recognition.*

Harris C and Stephens M. 1988. A combined corner and edge detector. *Proceedings of the Alvey Vision Conference*, Manchester, UK.

Hartley R and Zisserman A. 2003. *Multiple View Geometry in Computer Vision*, 2nd edition. Cambridge University Press.

He K, Su J and Tang X. 2010. Guided image filtering. *Proceedings of the European Conference on Computer Vision.*

He K, Sun J and Tang X. 2009. Single image haze removal using dark channel prior. *Proceedings of the Conference on Computer Vision and Pattern Recognition.*

Heng L, Honegger D, Lee GH, Meier L, Tanskanen P, Fraundorfer F and Pollefeys M. 2014. Autonomous visual mapping and exploration with a micro aerial vehicle. *Journal of Field Robotics* **31**, 654–675.

Herisse B, Russotto FX, Hamel T and Mahony R. 2008. Hovering flight and vertical landing control of a vtol unmanned aerial vehicle using optical flow. *Proceedings of the IEEE/RSJ International Conference on Intelligent Robots and Systems.*

Hermann S and Klette R. 2009. The naked truth about cost functions for stereo matching. Technical Report MItech-TR-33, Multimedia Imaging, Auckland.

Hermann S and Klette R. 2012. Iterative semi-global matching for robust driver assistance systems. *Proceedings of the Asian Conference on Computer Vision.*

Hermann S and Werner R. 2013. High accuracy optical flow for 3D medical image registration using the census cost function. *Proceedings of the Pacific Rim Symposium on Image and Video Technology.*

Hermann S, Boerner A and Klette R. 2011. Mid-level segmentation and segment tracking for long-range stereo analysis. *Proceedings of the Pacific Rim Symposium on Image and Video Technology.*

Heskes T. 1999. Energy functions for self-organizing maps, In *Kohonen Maps* (ed. Oja E and Kaski S) Elsevier Science Inc., Amsterdam, pp. 303–315.

Hillel AB, Lerner R, Levi D and Raz G. 2014. Recent progress in road and lane detection: a survey. *Machine Vision and Applications* **25**, 727–745.

Hirschmüller H. 2005. Accurate and efficient stereo processing by semi-global matching and mutual information. *Proceedings of the conference on Computer Vision and Pattern Recognition.*

Hirschmüller H and Scharstein D. 2009. Evaluation of stereo matching costs on images with radiometric differences. *IEEE Transactions on Pattern Analysis and Machine Intelligence* **31**, 1582–1599.

Hitam MS and Awalludin EA. 2013. Mixture contrast limited adaptive histogram equalization for underwater image enhancement. *Proceedings of the International Conference on Computer Applications Technology.*

Honegger D, Meier L, Tanskanen P and Pollefeys M. 2013. An open source and open hardware embedded metric optical flow CMOS camera for indoor and outdoor applications. *Proceedings of the IEEE International Conference on Robotics and Automation.*

Hoppe H, DeRose T, Duchamp T, McDonald J and Stuetzle W. 1992. Surface reconstruction from unorganized points. *SIGGRAPH Computer Graphics* **26**, 71–78.

Horn B. 1986. *Robot Vision.* MIT Press.

Horn B and Schunck B. 1981. Determining optic flow. *Artificial Intelligence* **17**, 185–203.

Hornung A and Kobbelt L. 2006. Robust reconstruction of watertight 3D models from non-uniformly sampled point clouds without normal information. *Proceedings of the Eurographics/ACM SIGGRAPH Symposium on Geometry Processing*, Cagliari, Sardinia, Italy.

Hrabar S and Sukhatme G. 2009. Vision-based navigation through urban canyons. *Journal of Field Robotics* **26**, 431–452.

Hrabar S, Sukhatme GS, Corke P, Usher K and Roberts J. 2005. Combined optic-flow and stereo-based navigation of urban canyons for a UAV. *Proceedings of the IEEE/RSJ International Conference on Intelligent Robots and Systems.*

Huang A, Moore D, Antone M, Olson E and Teller S. 2009. Finding multiple lanes in urban road networks with vision and lidar. *Autonomous Robots* **26**, 103–122.

Huang JF, Lai SH and Cheng CM. 2007. Robust fundamental matrix estimation with accurate outlier detection. *Journal of Information Science and Engineering* **23**, 1213–1225.

Hurtós N, Cufí X and Salvi J. 2013a. A novel blending technique for two dimensional forward looking sonar mosaicking. *Proceedings of the IEEE/MTS OCEANS Conference*, San Diego, CA, USA.

Hurtós N, Nagappa S, Cufí X, Petillot Y and Salvi J. 2013b. Evaluation of registration methods on two-dimensional forward-looking sonar imagery. *Proceedings of the IEEE/MTS OCEANS Conference*, Bergen, Norway.

Hurtós N, Nagappa S, Palomeras N and Salvi J. 2014a. Real-time mosaicing with two-dimensional forward-looking sonar. *Proceedings of the IEEE International Conference on Robotics and Automation*, Hong-Kong.

Hurtós N, Ribas D, Cufi X, Petillot Y and Salvi J. 2014b. Fourier-based registration for robust forward-looking sonar mosaicing in low-visibility underwater environments. *Journal of Field Robotics* **32**, 123–151.

Huval B, Wang T, Tandon S, Kiske J, Song W, Pazhayampallil J, Andriluka M, Rajpurkar P, Migimatsu T, Cheng-Yue R, Mujica F, Coates A and Ng AY. 2015. An empirical evaluation of deep learning on highway driving. *arXiv:1504.01716.*

Ila V, Andrade-Cetto J, Valencia R and Sanfeliu A. 2007. Vision-based loop closing for delayed state robot mapping. *Proceedings of the IEEE/RSJ International Conference on Intelligent Robots and Systems.*

Jaffe JS, Moore KD, McLean J and Strand MP. 2002. Underwater optical imaging: status and prospects. *Oceanography* **14**, 66–76.

Jerosch K, Lüdtke A, Schlüter M and Ioannidis GT. 2007. Automatic content-based analysis of georeferenced image data: detection of beggiatoa mats in seafloor video mosaics from the hakon mosbymud volcano. *Computers and Geotechnics* **33**, 202–218.

Ji Q and Yang X. 2002. Real-time eye, gaze, and face pose tracking for monitoring driver vigilance. *Real-Time Imaging* **8**, 357–377.

Jiménez P, Bergasa L, Nuevo J and Alcantarilla P. 2012a. Face pose estimation with automatic 3D model creation in challenging scenarios. *Image and Vision Computing* **30**, 589–602.

Jiménez P, Bergasa L, Nuevo J, Hernández N and Daza I. 2012b. Gaze fixation system for the evaluation of driver distractions induced by ivis. *IEEE Transactions on Intelligent Transportation Systems* **13**, 1167–1178.

Jiménez P, Nuevo J, Bergasa L and Sotelo M. 2009. Face tracking and pose estimation with automatic three-dimensional model construction. *IET Computer Vision* **3**, 93–102.

Johannsson H, Kaess M, Englot B, Hover F and Leonard J. 2010. Imaging sonar-aided navigation for autonomous underwater harbor surveillance. *Proceedings of the IEEE/RSJ International Conference on Intelligent Robots and Systems*.

Johnson A, Montgomery J and Matthies L. 2005. Vision guided landing of an autonomous helicopter in hazardous terrain. *Proceedings of the IEEE International Conference on Robotics and Automation*.

Johnson-Roberson M, Kumar S and Willams S. 2006a. Segmentation and classification of coral for oceanographic surveys: a semi-supervised machine learning approach. *Proceedings of the IEEE/MTS OCEANS Conference*.

Johnson-Roberson M, Kumar S, Pizarro O and Willams S. 2006b. Stereoscopic imaging for coral segmentation and classification. *Proceedings of the IEEE/MTS OCEANS Conference*.

Johnson-Roberson M, Pizarro O and Willams S. 2009. Towards large scale optical and acoustic sensor integration for visualization. *Proceedings of the IEEE/MTS OCEANS Conference*.

Johnson-Roberson M, Pizarro O, Williams SB and Mahon I. 2010. Generation and visualization of large-scale three-dimensional reconstructions from underwater robotic surveys. *Journal of Field Robotics* **27**, 21–51.

Juliussen E and Robinson R. 2010. Is Europe in the driver's seat? The competitiveness of the European automotive embedded systems industry. Technical report 61541, European Commission Joint Research Centre Institute for Prospective Technological Studies.

Jung I and Lacroix S. 2003. Simultaneous localization and mapping with stereovision. *Proceedings of the International Symposium of Robotics Research*.

Kaess M, Johannsson H, Roberts R, Ila V, Leonard JJ and Dellaert F. 2012. iSAM2: incremental smoothing and mapping using the Bayes tree. *International Journal of Robotics Research* **31**, 216–235.

Kang E, Cohen I and Medioni G. 2000. A graph–based global registration for 2D mosaics. *Proceedings of the International Conference in Pattern Recognition*, Barcelona, Spain.

Kazhdan M and Hoppe H. 2013. Screened Poisson surface reconstruction. *ACM Transactions on Graphics* **32**, 29:1–29:13.

Kazhdan M, Bolitho M and Hoppe H. 2006. Poisson surface reconstruction. *Eurographics/ACM SIGGRAPH Symposium on Geometry Processing*, Cagliari, Sardinia, Italy.

Keller C and Gavrila D. 2014. Will the pedestrian cross? A study on pedestrian path prediction. *IEEE Transactions on Intelligent Transportation Systems* **15**, 494–506.

Keller C et al. 2011. The benefits of dense stereo for pedestrian recognition. *IEEE Transactions on Intelligent Transportation Systems* **12**, 1096–1106.

Khan W, Suaste V, Caudillo D and Klette R. 2013. Belief propagation stereo matching compared to iSGM on binocular or trinocular video data. *Proceedings of the IEEE Intelligent Vehicles Symposium*.

Kim K, Neretti N and Intrator N. 2005. Mosaicing of acoustic camera images. *IEE Proceedings Radar, Sonar and Navigation* **152**, 263–270.

Kim K, Neretti N and Intrator N. 2006. Video enhancement for underwater exploration using forward looking sonar. *Proceedings of the Conference on Advanced Concepts for Intelligent Vision Systems*.

Kim K, Neretti N and Intrator N. 2008. MAP fusion method for superresolution of images with locally varying pixel quality. *International Journal of Imaging Systems and Technology* **18**, 242–250.

Kinsey J, Eustice R and Whitcomb L. 2006. A survey of underwater vehicle navigation: recent advances and new challenges. *Proceedings of the IFAC Conference on Manoeuvring and Control of Marine Crafts*, Lisbon, Portugal.

Klein G and Murray D. 2007. Parallel tracking and mapping for small AR workspaces. *IEEE and ACM International Symposium on Mixed and Augmented Reality*, Nara, Japan.

Klette R. 2014. *Concise Computer Vision: An Introduction into Theory and Algorithms.* Springer.

Klette R, Krüger N, Vaudrey T, van Hulle KPM, Morales S, Kandil F, Haeusler R, Pugeault N, Rabe C and Lappe M. 2011. Performance of correspondence algorithms in vision-based driver assistance using an online image sequence database. *IEEE Transactions on Vehicular Technology* **60**, 2012–2026.

Klose S, Wang J, Achtelik MC, Panin G, Holzapfel F and Knoll A. 2010. Markerless, vision-assisted flight control of a quadrocopter. *Proceedings of the IEEE/RSJ International Conference on Intelligent Robots and Systems.*

Kolluri R. 2008. Provably good moving least squares. *ACM Transactions on Algorithms* **4**, 18:1–18:25.

Kolluri R, Shewchuk JR and O'Brien JF. 2004. Spectral surface reconstruction from noisy point clouds. *Eurographics/ACM SIGGRAPH Symposium on Geometry Processing*, Nice, France.

Kolmogorov V and Rother C. 2007. Minimizing nonsubmodular functions with graph cuts—a review. *IEEE Transactions on Pattern Analysis and Machine Intelligence* **29**, 1274–1279.

Konolige K, Bowman J, Chen J, Mihelich P, Calonder M, Lepetit V and Fua P. 2010. View-based maps. *International Journal of Robotics Research* **29**, 941.

Kopf J, Neubert B, Chen B, Cohen M, Cohen-Or D, Deussen O, Uyttendaele M and Lischinski D. 2008. Deep photo: model-based photograph enhancement and viewing. *ACM SIGGRAPH Asia.*

Kovesi P. 1993. A dimensionless measure of edge significance from phase congruency calculated via wavelets. *Proceedings of the New Zealand Conference on Image Vision Computing.*

Kratz L and Nishino K. 2009. Factorizing scene albedo and depth from a single foggy image. *ICCV'09*, pp. 1071–1078.

Krizhevsky A, Sutskever I and Hinton GE. 2012. Imagenet classification with deep convolutional neural networks. *Proceedings of the Conference on Advances in Neural Information Processing Systems.*

Kroese BJA, Vlassis NA, Bunschoten R and Motomura Y. 2001. A probabilistic model for appearance-based robot localization. *Image and Vision Computing* **19**, 381–391.

Krotosky S and Trivedi MM. 2007. On color-, infrared-, and multimodal-stereo approaches to pedestrian detection. *IEEE Transactions on Intelligent Transportation Systems* **8**, 619–629.

Kumar V and Michael N. 2012. Opportunities and challenges with autonomous micro aerial vehicles. *International Journal of Robotics Research* **31**, 1279–1291.

Kummerle R, Grisetti G, Strasdat H, Konolige K and Burgard W. 2011. g2o: a general framework for graph optimization. *Proceedings of the IEEE International Conference on Robotics and Automation.*

Labatut P, Pons JP and Keriven R. 2007. Efficient multi-view reconstruction of large-scale scenes using interest points, Delaunay triangulation and graph cuts. *Proceedings of the International Conference on Computer Vision.*

Labayrade R, Aubert D and Tarel J. 2002. Real time obstacle detection in stereovision on non flat road geometry through "v–disparity" representation. *Proceedings of the IEEE Intelligent Vehicles Symposium*, Versailles, France.

Lal S and Craig A. 2002. Driver fatigue: electroencephalography and psychological assessment. *Psychophysiology* **39**, 313–321.

Lamon P, Nourbakhsh I, Jensen B and Siegwart R. 2001. Deriving and matching image fingerprint sequences for mobile robot localization. *Proceedings of the IEEE International Conference on Robotics and Automation.*

Lategahn H. 2013. *Mapping and Localization in Urban Environments Using Cameras.* KIT Scientific Publishing.

Leibe B, Cornelis N, Cornelis K and Van Gool L. 2007. Dynamic 3D scene analysis from a moving vehicle. *Proceedings of the conference on Computer Vision and Pattern Recognition*, Minneapolis, MN, USA.

Leibe B, Leonardis A and Schiele B. 2008. Robust object detection with interleaved categorization and segmentation. *International Journal of Computer Vision* **77**, 259–289.

Lempitsky V and Ivanov D. 2007. Seamless mosaicing of image-based texture maps. *Proceedings of the conference on Computer Vision and Pattern Recognition.*

Leonard J, Bennett A, Smith C and Feder H. 1998. *Autonomous Underwater Vehicle Navigation.* Technical memorandum 98-1. MIT Marine Robotics Laboratory.

Levin A, Zomet A, Peleg S and Weiss Y. 2004. Seamless image stitching in the gradient domain. *Proceedings of the European Conference on Computer Vision*, Prague, Czech Republic.

Li X and Hu Z. 2010. Rejecting mismatches by correspondence function. *International Journal of Computer Vision* **89**, 1–17.

Lim K, Ang L and Seng K. 2009. New hybrid technique for traffic sign recognition. *Proceedings of the International Symposium on Intelligent Signal Processing and Communications Systems*, Kanazawa, Japan.

Linarth A and Angelopoulou E. 2011. On feature templates for particle filter based lane detection. *Proceedings of the IEEE International Conference on Intelligent Transportation Systems*, Washington, DC, USA.

Lindeberg T. 1994. *Scale-Space Theory in Computer Vision.* Kluwer Academic Publishers.

Lindeberg T. 1998. Feature detection with automatic scale selection. *International Journal of Computer Vision* **30**, 79–116.

Lindner F, Kressel U and Kälberer S. 2004. Robust recognition of traffic signals. *Proceedings of the IEEE Intelligent Vehicles Symposium.*

Lirman D, Gracias N, Gintert B, Gleason A, Deangelo G, Dick M, Martinez E and Reid RP. 2010. Damage and recovery assessment of vessel grounding injuries on coral reef habitats using georeferenced landscape video mosaics. *Limnology and Oceanography: Methods* **8**, 88–97.

Lirman D, Gracias N, Gintert B, Gleason A, Reid RP, Negahdaripour S and Kramer P. 2007. Development and application of a video–mosaic survey technology to document the status of coral reef communities. *Environmental Monitoring and Assessment* **159**, 59–73.

Liu H, Liu D and Xin J. 2002. Real-time recognition of road traffic sign in motion image based on genetic algorithm. *Proceedings of the International Conference on Machine Learning and Cybernetics*, Beijing, China.

Liu G, Worgotter F and Markeli I. 2011. Lane shape estimation using a partitioned particle filter for autonomous driving. *Proceedings of the IEEE International Conference on Robotics and Automation*, Shanghai, China.

Liu L, Xing J, Ai H and Lao S. 2012. Semantic superpixel based vehicle tracking. *Proceedings of the International Conference in Pattern Recognition*.

Loianno G and Kumar V. 2014. Smart phones power flying robots. *RSS Robotics Science and Systems, Workshop on Resource-efficient Integration of Planning and Perception for True Autonomous Operation of Micro Air Vehicles (MAVs)*.

Long J, Shelhamer E and Darrell T. 2015. Fully convolutional networks for semantic segmentation. *Proceedings of the conference on Computer Vision and Pattern Recognition*.

Longuet-Higgins HC. 1981. A computer algorithm for reconstructing a scene from two projections. *Nature* **293**, 122–135.

Loose H and Franke U. 2009. Kalman particle filter for lane recognition on rural roads. *Proceedings of the IEEE Intelligent Vehicles Symposium*, Xian, China.

Lopez A, Hilgenstock J, Busse A, Baldrich R, Lumbreras F and Serrat J. 2008a. Nighttime vehicle detection for intelligent headlight control. *Proceedings of the Conference on Advanced Concepts for Intelligent Vision Systems*, Juan-les-Pins, France.

Lopez A, Hilgenstock J, Busse A, Baldrich R, Lumbreras F and Serrat J. 2008b. Temporal coherence analysis for intelligent headlight control. *Proceedings of the IEEE/RSJ International Conference on Intelligent Robots and Systems, Workshop on Planning, Perception and Navigation for Intelligent Vehicles*, Nice, France.

Lorensen WE and Cline HE. 1987. Marching cubes: a high resolution 3D surface construction algorithm. *SIGGRAPH Computer Graphics* **21**, 163–169.

Lowe D. 1999. Object recognition from local scale-invariant features. *Proceedings of the International Conference on Computer Vision*, p. 1150.

Lowe D. 2004. Distinctive image features from scale-invariant keypoints. *International Journal of Computer Vision* **60**, 90–110.

Lupashin S, Hehn M, Mueller MW, Schoellig AP, Sherback M and D'Andrea R. 2014. A platform for aerial robotics research and demonstration: the Flying Machine Arena. *Mechatronics* **24**, 41–54.

Lupashin S, Schollig A, Hehn M and D'Andrea R. 2011. The flying machine arena as of 2010. *Proceedings of the IEEE International Conference on Robotics and Automation*.

Luzon-Gonzalez R, Nieves JL and Romero J. 2015. Recovering of weather degraded images based on RGB response ratio constancy. *Applied Optics* **54**, B222–B231.

Ma KY, Chirarattananon P, Fuller SB and Wood RJ. 2013. Controlled flight of a biologically inspired, insect-scale robot. *Science* **340**, 603–607.

Ma Y, Soatto S, Kosecka J and Sastry S. 2003. *An Invitation to 3-D Vision: From Images to Geometric Models*. Springer-Verlag.

Madjidi H and Negahdaripour S. 2005. Global alignment of sensor positions with noisy motion measurements. *IEEE Transactions on Robotics* **21**, 1092–1104.

Madjidi H and Negahdaripour S. 2006. On robustness and localization accuracy of optical flow computation for underwater color images. *Photogrammetric Engineering* **104**, 61–76.

Mahieu Y. 2009. Highlights of the panorama of transport. Technical report, Eurostats, http://ec.europa.eu/eurostat/documents/3217494/5711595/KS-DA-09-001-EN.PDF/9c90d489-5009-4acc-9810-ae39612897d3.

Mahon I, Pizarro O, Johnson-Roberson M, Friedman A, Williams S and Henderson J. 2011. Reconstructing pavlopetri: mapping the world's oldest submerged town using stereo-vision. *Proceedings of the IEEE International Conference on Robotics and Automation.*

Mahony R, Kumar V and Corke P. 2012. Multirotor aerial vehicles—modeling, estimation, and control of quadrotor. *IEEE Robotics and Automation Magazine* **19**, 20–32.

Mallios A, Ridao P, Ribas D and Hernández E. 2014. Scan matching SLAM in underwater environments. *Autonomous Robots* **36**, 181–198.

Manson J, Petrova G and Schaefer S. 2008. Streaming surface reconstruction using wavelets. *Computer Graphics Forum (Proceedings of the Symposium on Geometry Processing)* **27**, 1411–1420.

Marchal P, Dehesa M, Gavrila D, Meinecke M, Skellern N and Viciguerra R. 2005. SAVE–U. Final Report. Technical report, Information Society Technology Programme of the EU.

Marcos M, Soriano M and Saloma C. 2005. Classification of coral reef images from underwater video using neural networks. *Optics Express* **13**, 8766–8771.

Marín J, Vázquez D, Gerónimo D and López AM. 2010. Learning appearance in virtual scenarios for pedestrian detection. *Proceedings of the Conference on Computer Vision and Pattern Recognition.*

Marin J, Vazquez D, Lopez A, Amores J and Leibe B. 2013. Random forests of local experts for pedestrian detection. *Proceedings of the International Conference on Computer Vision*, Sydney, Australia.

Marr D and Hildreth E. 1980. Theory of edge detection. *Proceedings of the Royal Society London, Series B: Biological Sciences* **207**, 187–217.

Martinelli A. 2012. Vision and IMU data fusion: closed-form solutions for attitude, speed, absolute scale, and bias determination. *IEEE Transactions on Robotics* **28**, 44–60.

Marzotto R, Fusiello A and Murino V. 2004. High resolution video mosaicing with global alignment. *Proceedings of the conference on Computer Vision and Pattern Recognition.*

Matthies L and Shafer S. 1987. Error modelling in stereo navigation. *IEEE Journal of Robotics and Automation* **3**, 239–248.

Mayer N, Häusser P, Fischer P, Cremers D, Dosovitskiy A and Brox T. 2015. A large dataset to train convolutional networks for disparity, optical flow, and scene flow estimation, *arXiv:1512.02134.*

McCall J and Trivedi M. 2006. Video-based lane estimation and tracking for driver assistance: survey. *IEEE Transactions on Intelligent Transportation Systems* **7**, 20–37.

McLachlan GJ. 2004. *Discriminant Analysis and Statistical Pattern Recognition*. Wiley Interscience.

McLauchlan PF and Jaenicke A. 2002. Image mosaicing using sequential bundle adjustment. *Image and Vision Computing* **20**, 751–759.

Mefford M, Flannagan M and Bogard S. 2006. Real-world use of high-beam headlamps. Technical report UMTRI-2006-11, Transportation Research Institute, University of Michigan.

Mehta A, Ribeiro E, Gilner J and Woesik R. 2007. Coral reef texture classification using support vector machines. *Proceedings of the International Conference on Computer Vision Theory and Applications*, pp. 302–310.

Meier L, Tanskanen P, Heng L, Lee GH, Fraundorfer F and Pollefeys M. 2012. PIX-HAWK: a micro aerial vehicle design for autonomous flight using onboard computer vision. *Autonomous Robots* **33**, 21–39.

Mellinger D, Lindsey Q, Shomin M and Kumar V. 2011. Design, modeling, estimation and control for aerial grasping and manipulation. *Proceedings of the IEEE/RSJ International Conference on Intelligent Robots and Systems*, pp. 2668–2673.

Mellinger D, Michael N and Kumar V. 2010. Trajectory generation and control for precise aggressive maneuvers with quadrotors. *Proceedings of the International Symposium on Experimental Robotics*.

Meuter M, Muller-Schneiders S, Mika A, Hold S, Nunn C and Kummert A. 2009. A novel approach to lane detection and tracking. *Proceedings of the IEEE International Conference on Intelligent Transportation Systems*, St. Louis, MO, USA.

Michael N, Fink J and Kumar V. 2010a. Cooperative manipulation and transportation with aerial robots. *Autonomous Robots* **30**, 73–86.

Michael N, Mellinger D, Lindsey Q and Kumar V. 2010b. The GRASP multiple micro UAV testbed. *IEEE Robotics and Automation Magazine* **17**, 56–65.

Michael N, Scaramuzza D and Kumar V. 2012a. Special issue on micro-UAV perception and control. *Autonomous Robots* **33**, 1–3.

Michael N, Shen S, Mohta K, Mulgaonkar Y, Kumar V, Nagatani K, Okada Y, Kiribayashi S, Otake K, Yoshida K, Ohno K, Takeuchi E and Tadokoro S. 2012b. Collaborative mapping of an earthquake-damaged building via ground and aerial robots. *Journal of Field Robotics* **29**, 832–841.

Mika S, Ratsch G, Weston J, Scholkopf B and Muller K. 1999. Fisher discriminant analysis with kernels. *Proceedings of the Neural Networks for Signal Processing, Workshop on the Signal Processing Society*, pp. 41–48.

Milgram D. 1975. Computer methods for creating photomosaics. *IEEE Transactions on Computers* **24**, 1113–1119.

Mills A and Dudek G. 2009. Image stitching with dynamic elements. *Image and Vision Computing* **27**, 1593–1602.

Mitzel D, Horbert E, Ess A and Leibe B. 2010. Multi-person tracking with sparse detection and continuous segmentation. *Proceedings of the European Conference on Computer Vision*, Crete, Greece.

Mobley CR. 1994. *Light and Water: Radiative Transfer in Natural Waters*. Academic Press, San Diego, CA, USA.

Mogelmose A, Trivedi MM and Moeslund TB. 2012. Vision-based traffic sign detection and analysis for intelligent driver assistance systems: perspectives and survey. *IEEE Transactions on Intelligent Transportation Systems* **13**, 1484–1497.

Mohan R. 2014. Deep deconvolutional networks for scene parsing. *Proceedings of the conference on Computer Vision and Pattern Recognition*.

Mohan A, Papageorgiou C and Poggio T. 2001. Example-based object detection in images by components. *IEEE Transactions on Pattern Analysis and Machine Intelligence* **23**, 349–361.

Montemerlo M and Thrun S. 2007. *FastSLAM: A Scalable Method for the Simultaneous Localization and Mapping Problem in Robotics*, vol. **27** of Springer Tracts in Advanced Robotics, http://www.springer.com/us/book/9783540463993.

Montemerlo M, Thrun S, Koller D and Wegbreit B. 2003. FastSLAM 2.0: an improved particle filtering algorithm for simultaneous localization and mapping that provably converges. *Proceedings of the International Joint Conference on Artificial Intelligence*, pp. 1151–1156.

Moore KD and Jaffe JS. 2002. Time-evolution of high-resolution topographic measurements of the sea floor using a 3D laser line scan mapping system. *Journal of Oceanic Engineering* **27**, 525–545.

Moore KD, Jaffe JS and Ochoa BL. 2000. Development of a new underwater bathymetric laser imaging system: L-bath. *Journal of Atmospheric and Oceanic Technology* **17**, 1106–1117.

Morales S and Klette R. 2009. A third eye for performance evaluation in stereo sequence analysis. *Proceedings of the Conference on Computer Analysis of Images and Patterns*.

Moutarde F, Bargeton A, Herbin A and Chanussot L. 2007. Robust on-vehicle real-time visual detection of American and European speed limit signs, with a modular traffic signs recognition system. *Proceedings of the IEEE Intelligent Vehicles Symposium*, Istanbul, Turkey.

Mueller M, Lupashin S and D'Andrea R. 2011. Quadrocopter ball juggling. *Proceedings of the IEEE/RSJ International Conference on Intelligent Robots and Systems*.

Mullen P, Goes FD, Desbrun M, Cohen-Steiner D and Alliez P. 2010. Signing the unsigned: robust surface reconstruction from raw pointsets. *Computer Graphics Forum (Proceedings of the Symposium on Geometry Processing)* **29**, 1733–1741.

Munder S and Gavrila DM. 2006. An experimental study on pedestrian classification. *IEEE Transactions on Pattern Analysis and Machine Intelligence* **28**, 1863–1868.

Murphy R. 2014. *Disaster Robotics*. MIT.

Murphy-Chutorian E and Trivedi M. 2009. Head pose estimation in computer vision: a survey. *IEEE Transactions on Pattern Analysis and Machine Intelligence* **31**, 607–626.

Najm W, Stearns M, Howarth H, Koopmann J and Hitz J. 2006. Evaluation of an automotive rear-end collision avoidance system. Technical report, U.S. Department of Transportation, http://www.nhtsa.gov/DOT/NHTSA/NRD/Multimedia/PDFs/Crash%20Avoidance/2006/HS910569.pdf.

Narasimhan SG and Nayar SK. 2002. Vision and the atmosphere. *Journal of Oceanic Engineering* **48**, 233–254.

Narasimhan SG and Nayar SK. 2003. Contrast restoration of weather degraded images. *IEEE Transactions on Pattern Analysis and Machine Intelligence* **25**, 713–724.

Narasimhan S, Nayar K, Sun B and Koppal S. 2005. Structured light in scattering media. *Proceedings of the International Conference on Computer Vision*.

Nefian A and Bradski G. 2006. Detection of drivable corridors for off-road autonomous navigation. *Proceedings of the IEEE International Conference on Image Processing*, Atlanta, GA, USA.

Negahdaripour S. 1998. Revised definition of optical flow: integration of radiometric and geometric cues for dynamic scene analysis. *IEEE Transactions on Pattern Analysis and Machine Intelligence* **20**, 961–979.

Negahdaripour S. 2012a. On 3D scene interpretation from FS sonar imagery. *Proceedings of the IEEE/MTS OCEANS Conference*.

Negahdaripour S. 2012b. Visual motion ambiguities of a plane in 2D FS sonar motion sequences. *Computer Vision and Image Understanding* **116**, 754–764.

Negahdaripour S and Madjidi H. 2003a. Robust optical flow estimation using underwater color images. *Proceedings of the IEEE/MTS OCEANS Conference*.

Negahdaripour S and Madjidi H. 2003b. Stereovision imaging on submersible platforms for 3D mapping of benthic habitats and sea-floor structures. *IEEE Journal of Oceanic Engineering* **28**, 625–650.

Negahdaripour S, Aykin MD and Sinnarajah S. 2011. Dynamic scene analysis and mosaicing of benthic habitats by FS sonar imaging—issues and complexities. *Proceedings of the IEEE/MTS OCEANS Conference.*

Negahdaripour S, Prados R and Garcia R. 2005. Planar homography: accuracy analysis and applications. *Proceedings of the IEEE International Conference on Image Processing.*

Neumann L, Matkovic K and Purgathofer W. 1998. Automatic exposure in computer graphics based on the minimum information loss principle. *Proceedings of the Computer Graphics International.*

NHTSA. 2007. Traffic safety facts. Technical report, National Center for Statistics and Analysis, https://crashstats.nhtsa.dot.gov/Api/Public/ViewPublication/811002.

Nicosevici T and Garcia R. 2012. Automatic visual bag-of-words for online robot navigation and mapping. *IEEE Transactions on Robotics* **99**, 1–13.

Nicosevici T, Gracias N, Negahdaripour S and Garcia R. 2009. Efficient three-dimensional scene modeling and mosaicing. *Journal of Field Robotics* **26**, 759–788.

Nieuwenhuisen M, Droeschel D, Beul M and Behnke S. 2015. Autonomous navigation for micro aerial vehicles in complex GNSS-denied environments. *Journal of Intelligent Robotic Systems* pp. 1–18, http://link.springer.com/article/10.1007/s10846-015-0274-3.

Nister D and Stewenius H. 2006. Scalable recognition with a vocabulary tree. *Proceedings of the conference on Computer Vision and Pattern Recognition.*

No Hands Across America Webpage. 1995. www.cs.cmu.edu/afs/cs/usr/tjochem/www/nhaa/nhaa_home_page.html.

Noh H, Hong S and Han B. 2015. Learning deconvolution network for semantic segmentation. *Proceedings of the International Conference on Computer Vision.*

NVIDIA at CES. 2016. NVIDIA Drive PX2 Autonomous Car Processing Engine Demo - CES 2016.

Ohlich B, Rodner E and Denzler J. 2012. Semantic segmentation with millions of features: integrating multiple cues in a combined random forest approach. *Proceedings of the Asian Conference on Computer Vision.*

Ohtake Y, Belyaev A, Alexa M, Turk G and Seidel HP. 2003. Multi-level partition of unity implicits. *ACM Transactions on Graphics* **22**, 463–470.

Ohtake Y, Belyaev A and Seidel HP. 2004. 3D scattered data approximation with adaptive compactly supported radial basis functions. *Proceedings of the Shape Modeling International.*

Ojala T, Pietikainen M and Harwood D. 1996. A comparative study of texture measures with classification based on featured distributions. *Pattern Recognition* **29**, 51–59.

Olmeda D, de la Escalera A and Armingol J. 2011. Far infrared pedestrian detection and tracking for night driving. *Robotica* **29**, 495–505.

Opelt A, Fussenegger A and Auer P. 2004. Weak hypotheses and boosting for generic object detection and recognition. Computer Vision – ECCV 2004, *Lecture Notes in Computer Science* **3022**, 71–84.

Papageorgiou C and Poggio T. 2000. A trainable system for object detection. *International Journal of Computer Vision* **38**, 15–33.

Park K, Kima H, Baek M and Kee CD. 2003. Multi-range approach of stereo vision for mobile robot navigation in uncertain environments. *Journal of Mechanical Science and Technology* **17**, 1411–1422.

Paul R and Newman P. 2010. FAB-MAP 3D: topological mapping with spatial and visual appearance. *Proceedings of the IEEE International Conference on Robotics and Automation*.

Paulsen RR, Baerentzen JA and Larsen R. 2010. Markov random field surface reconstruction. *IEEE Transactions on Visualization and Computer Graphics* **16**, 636–646.

Paz LM, Pinies P, Tardos JD and Neira J. 2008. Large-scale 6-DOF SLAM with stereo-in-hand. *IEEE Transactions on Robotics* **24**, 946–957.

Pelaez GA, Romero M, Armingol J, de la Escalera A, Munoz J, van Bijsterveld W and Bolano J. 2012. Detection and classification of road signs for automatic inventory systems using computer vision. *Integrated Computer-Aided Engineering* **19**, 285–298.

Pfeiffer D and Franke U. 2011. Towards a global optimal multi-layer Stixel representation of dense 3D data. *Proceedings of the British Machine Vision Conference*, Dundee, Scotland.

Pfeiffer D, Gehrig S and Schneider N. 2013. Exploiting the power of stereo confidences. *Proceedings of the conference on Computer Vision and Pattern Recognition*.

Pican N, Trucco E, Ross M, Lane D, Petillot Y and Ruiz I. 1998. Texture analysis for seabed classification: co-occurrence matrices vs. self-organizing maps. *Proceedings of the IEEE/MTS OCEANS Conference*, vol. **1**, pp. 424–428.

Piccioli G, de Micheli E, Parodi P and Campani M. 1996. Robust method for road sign detection and recognition. *Image and Vision Computing* **14**, 209–223.

Pinggera P, Franke U and Mester R. 2013. Highly accurate depth estimation for objects at large distances. *Proceedings of the German Conference on Pattern Recognition*.

Pizarro O. 2004. *Large Scale Structure from Motion for Autonomous Underwater Vehicle Surveys*. PhD thesis, Massachusetts Institute of Technology.

Pizarro O, Eustice R and Singh H. 2004. Large area 3D reconstructions from underwater surveys. *Proceedings of the IEEE/MTS OCEANS Conference*.

Pizarro O, Rigby P, Johnson-Roberson M, Williams S and Colquhoun J. 2008. Towards image-based marine habitat classification. *Proceedings of the IEEE/MTS OCEANS Conference*.

Pizarro O and Singh H. 2003. Toward large-area mosaicing for underwater scientific applications. *IEEE Journal of Oceanic Engineering* **28**, 651–672.

Pomerleau D. 1995. RALPH: rapidly adapting lateral position handler. *Proceedings of the IEEE Intelligent Vehicles Symposium*, Detroit, MI, USA.

Porter T and Duff T. 1984. Compositing digital images. *Proceedings of the SIGGRAPH*.

Prados R, Garcia R, Gracias N, Escartin J and Neumann L. 2012. A novel blending technique for underwater giga-mosaicing. *Journal of Oceanic Engineering* **37**, 626–644.

Prados R, Garcia R and Neumann L. 2014. *Image Blending Techniques and their Application in Underwate Mosaicing*. Springer International Publishing.

Rabe C, Müller T, Wedel A and Franke U. 2010. Dense, robust, and accurate motion field estimation from stereo image sequences in real-time. *Proceedings of the European Conference on Computer Vision*.

Ramos FT, Upcroft B, Kumar S and Durrant-Whyte HF. 2005. A probabilistic model for appearance-based robot localization. *Proceedings of the IJCAI Workshop on Reasoning with Uncertainty in Robotics*.

Ranney T, Mazzai E, Garrott R and Goodman M. 2001. NHTSA driver distraction research: past, present, and future. Technical report, National Highway Traffic Safety Administration, Washington, DC, http://www-nrd.nhtsa.dot.gov/departments/Human%20Factors/driver-distraction/PDF/233.PDF.

Rao M, Vazquez D and Lopez A. 2011. Color contribution to part-based person detection in different types of scenarios. *Proceedings of the International Conference on Computer Analysis of Images and Patterns*, Berlin Heidelberg.

Raphael E, Kiefer R, Reisman P and Hayon G. 2011. Development of a camera-based forward collision alert system. *SAE International Journal of Passengers Cars—Mechanical Systems* **4**, 467–478.

Rezaei M and Klette R. 2011. 3D cascade of classifiers for open and closed eye detection in driver distraction monitoring. *Proceedings of the Conference on Computer Analysis of Images and Patterns*.

Rezaei M and Klette R. 2012. Novel adaptive eye detection and tracking for challenging lighting conditions. *Proceedings of the Asian Conference on Computer Vision, Workshops*.

Ribas D, Ridao P, Tardós J and Neira J. 2008. Underwater SLAM in man made structured environments. *Journal of Field Robotics* **25**, 898–921.

Richmond K and Rock SM. 2006. An operational real-time large-scale visual mosaicking and navigation system. *Proceedings of the IEEE/MTS OCEANS Conference*.

Roman C and Singh H. 2005. Improved vehicle based multibeam bathymetry using sub-maps and SLAM. *Proceedings of the IEEE/RSJ International Conference on Intelligent Robots and Systems*, Edmonton, Canada.

Roman C and Singh H. 2007. A self-consistent bathymetric mapping algorithm. *Journal of Field Robotics* **24**, 23–50.

Roman C, Inglis G and Rutter J. 2010. Application of structured light imaging for high resolution mapping of underwater archaeological sites. *Proceedings of the IEEE/MTS OCEANS Conference*.

Romdhane N, Hammami M and Ben-Abdallah H. 2011. A comparative study of vision-based lane detection methods. *Proceedings of the Conference on Advanced Concepts for Intelligent Vision Systems*, Ghent, Belgium.

Ros G, Ramos S, Granados M, Bakhtiary A, Vazquez D and Lopez A. 2015. Vision-based offline—online perception paradigm for autonomous driving. *Proceedings of the Winter Conference on Applications of Computer Vision*.

Ros G, Sellart L, Materzynska J, Vázquez D and López AM. 2016. The SYNTHIA dataset: a large collection of synthetic images for semantic segmentation of urban scenes. *Proceedings of the conference on Computer Vision and Pattern Recognition*.

Rosenfeld A. 1969. *Picture Processing by Computer*. Academic Press, New York, NY, USA.

Rosten E and Drummond T. 2006. Machine learning for high-speed corner detection. *Proceedings of the European Conference on Computer Vision*.

Rothermel M, Wenzel K, Fritsch D and Haala N. 2012. SURE: photogrammetric surface reconstruction from imagery. *LC3D Workshop*.

Rousseeuw PJ. 1984. Least median of squares regression. *Journal of the American Statistical Association* **79**, 871–880.

Rousseeuw P and Leroy A. 1987. *Robust Regression and Outlier Detection*. John Wiley & Sons, Inc., New York, NY, USA.

Rubio J, Serrat J, López A and Ponsa D. 2012. Multiple-target tracking for intelligent headlights control. *IEEE Transactions on Intelligent Transportation Systems* **13**, 594–605.

Rublee E, Rabaud V, Konolige K and Bradski G. 2011. ORB: an efficient alternative to SIFT or SURF. *Proceedings of the International Conference on Computer Vision*.

Ruffier F and Franceschini N. 2004. Visually guided micro-aerial vehicle: automatic take off, terrain following, landing and wind reaction. *Proceedings of the IEEE International Conference on Robotics and Automation.*

Russell BC, Efros AA, Sivic J, Freeman WT and Zisserman A. 2006. Using multiple segmentations to discover objects and their extent in image collection. *Proceedings of the conference on Computer Vision and Pattern Recognition.*

Ruta A, Li Y and Liu X. 2010. Real-time traffic sign recognition from video by class-specific discriminative features. *Pattern Recognition* **43**, 416–430.

Sanberg WP, Dubbelman G and de With PH. 2014. Extending the stixel world with online self-supervised color modeling for road-versus-obstacle segmentation. *Proceedings of the IEEE International Conference on Intelligent Transportation Systems.*

Sappa A, Dornaika F, Ponsa D, Gerónimo D and López A. 2008. An efficient approach to onboard stereo vision system pose estimation. *IEEE Transactions on Intelligent Transportation Systems* **9**, 476–490.

Saripalli S, Montgomery JF and Sukhatme GS. 2002. Vision–based autonomous landing of an unmanned aerial vehicle. *Proceedings of the IEEE International Conference on Robotics and Automation.*

Sartori A, Tecchiolli G, Crespi B, Tarrago J, Daura F and Bande D. 2005. Object presence detection method and device. https://www.google.com/patents/US6911642.

Sawhney HS, Hsu SC and Kumar R. 1998. Robust video mosaicing through topology inference and local to global alignment. *Proceedings of the European Conference on Computer Vision,* Freiburg, Germany.

Scaramuzza D and Fraundorfer F. 2011. Visual odometry [tutorial] part1: the first 30 years and fundamentals. *IEEE Robotics and Automation Magazine* **18**, 80–92.

Scaramuzza D, Achtelik M, Doitsidis L, Fraundorfer F, Kosmatopoulos EB, Martinelli A, Achtelik MW, Chli M, Chatzichristofis S, Kneip L, Gurdan D, Heng L, Lee G, Lynen S, Meier L, Pollefeys M, Renzaglia A, Siegwart R, Stumpf JC, Tanskanen P, Troiani C and Weiss S. 2014. Vision-controlled micro flying robots: from system design to autonomous navigation and mapping in GPS-denied environments. *IEEE Robotics and Automation Magazine* **21**, 26–40.

Scharstein D and Szeliski R. 2002. Middlebury online stereo evaluation, http://vision.middlebury.edu/stereo.

Scharwächter T, Enzweiler M, Roth S and Franke U. 2013. Efficient multi-cue scene segmentation. *Proceedings of the German Conference on Pattern Recognition,* Saarbrücken, Germany.

Schaudel C and Falb D. 2007. Smartbeam—a high-beam assist. *Proceedings of the International Symposium on Automotive Lighting,* Darmstadt, Germany.

Schechner YY and Karpel N. 2004. Clear underwater vision. *Proceedings of the Conference on Computer Vision and Pattern Recognition.*

Schechner YY and Karpel N. 2005. Recovery of underwater visibility and structure by polarization analysis. *Journal of Oceanic Engineering* **30**, 570–587.

Schechner Y, Narashiman SG and Nayar SK. 2001. Instant dehazing of images using polarization. *Proceedings of the conference on Computer Vision and Pattern Recognition.*

Schindler G, Brown M and Szeliski R. 2007. City-scale location recognition. *Proceedings of the conference on Computer Vision and Pattern Recognition.*

Schmid C, Mohr R and Bauckhage C. 1998. Comparing and evaluating interest points. *Proceedings of the International Conference on Computer Vision*.

Schmid K, Lutz P, Tomic T, Mair E and Hirschmuller H. 2014. Autonomous vision-based micro air vehicle for indoor and outdoor navigation. *Journal of Field Robotics* **31**, 537–570.

Schmidt S and Färber B. 2009. Pedestrians at the kerb—recognising the action intentions of humans. *Transportation Research Part F* **12**, 300–310.

Schoellig A, Augugliaro F and D'Andrea R. 2010. A platform for dance performances with multiple quadrocopters. *Proceedings of the IEEE/RSJ International Conference on Intelligent Robots and Systems, Workshop on Robots and Musical Expressions*.

Schoening T. 2015. *Automated Detection in Benthic Images for Megafauna Classification and Marine Resource Exploration: Supervised and Unsupervised Methods for Classification and Regression Tasks in Benthic Images with Efficient Integration of Expert Knowledge*. PhD thesis, Bielefeld University.

Schönberger JL, Fraundorfer F and Frahm JM. 2014. Structure-from-motion for MAV image sequence analysis with photogrammetric applications. *International Archives of the Photogrammetry, Remote Sensing and Spatial Information Sciences* **XL-3**, 305–312.

Schreiber M, Knöppel C and Franke U. 2013. Laneloc: lane marking based localization using highly accurate maps. *Proceedings of the IEEE Intelligent Vehicles Symposium*, Gold Coast, Australia.

Seet G and He D. 2005. Optical image sensing through turbid water. *Proceedings of SPIE*, **5852**, 74–75.

Serikawa S and Lu H. 2013. Underwater image dehazing using joint trilateral filter. *Computers and Electrical Engineering* **40**, 41–50.

Sermanet P, Eigen D, Zhang X, Mathieu M, Fergus R and LeCun Y. 2014. OverFeat: integrated recognition, localization and detection using convolutional networks. *Proceedings of the International Conference on Learning Representations*.

Shen S. 2014. *Autonomous Navigation in Complex Indoor and Outdoor Environments with Micro Aerial Vehicles*. PhD thesis, University of Pennsylvania, Philadelphia, PA, USA.

Shen S, Michael N and Kumar V. 2011. Autonomous multi-floor indoor navigation with a computationally constrained MAV. *Proceedings of the IEEE International Conference on Robotics and Automation*.

Shen S, Michael N and Kumar V. 2012. Autonomous indoor 3D exploration with a micro-aerial vehicle. *Proceedings of the IEEE International Conference on Robotics and Automation*.

Shen S, Mulgaonkar Y, Michael N and Kumar V. 2013a. Vision-based state estimation and trajectory control towards aggressive flight with a quadrotor. *Proceedings of Robotics Science and Systems*.

Shen S, Mulgaonkar Y, Michael N and Kumar V. 2013b. Vision-based state estimation and trajectory control towards aggressive flight with a quadrotor. *Robotics: Science and Systems*.

Shi J and Tomasi C. 1994. Good features to track. *Proceedings of the Conference on Computer Vision and Pattern Recognition*.

Shiela M, David L, Peñaflor E, Ticzon V and Soriano M. 2008. Automated benthic counting of living and non-living components in Ngedarrak Reef, Palau via subsurface underwater video. *Environmental Monitoring and Assessment* **145**, 177–184.

Shihavuddin A, Gracias N and Garcia R. 2012. Online sunflicker removal using dynamic texture prediction. *Proceedings of the International Conference on Computer Vision Theory and Applications*.

Shihavuddin A, Gracias N, Garcia R, Campos R, Gleason AC and Gintert B. 2014. Automated detection of underwater military munitions using fusion of 2D and 2.5D features from optical imagery. *Marine Technology Society Journal* **48**, 61–71.

Shihavuddin A, Gracias N, Garcia R, Gleason A and Gintert B. 2013. Image-based coral reef classification and thematic mapping. *Remote Sensing* **5**, 1809–1841.

Shimizu M and Okutomi M. 2001. Precise sub-pixel estimation on area-based matching. *Proceedings of the International Conference on Computer Vision*, Anchorage, AK, USA.

Shin B, Xu Z and Klette R. 2014. Visual lane analysis and higher-order tasks: a concise review. *Machine Vision and Applications* **25**, 1519–1547.

Shum HY and Szeliski R. 1998. Construction and refinement of panoramic mosaics with global and local alignment. *Proceedings of the International Conference on Computer Vision*, Washington, DC, USA.

Singh H, Howland J and Pizarro O. 2004. Advances in large-area photomosaicking underwater. *IEEE Journal of Oceanic Engineering* **29**, 872–886.

Singh H, Roman C, Pizarro O, Eustice RM and Can A. 2007. Towards high-resolution imaging from underwater vehicles. *International Journal of Robotics Research* **26**, 55–74.

Singh R and Agrawal A. 2011. Intelligent suspensions. *Proceedings of the International Conference on Interdisciplinary Research and Development*, Thailand.

Sivaraman S and Trivedi MM. 2013. Looking at vehicles on the road: a survey of vision-based vehicle detection, tracking, and behavior analysis. *IEEE Transactions on Intelligent Transportation Systems* **14**, 1773–1795.

Sivic J. 2006. *Efficient Visual Search of Images and Videos*. PhD thesis, University of Oxford.

Skipper J and Wierwille W. 1986. Drowsy driver detection using discriminant analysis. *Human Factors* **28**, 527–540.

Smith RC and Baker KS. 1981. Optical properties of the clearest natural waters (200–800 nm). *Applied Optics* **20**, 177–184.

Sobel I. 1970. *Camera Models and Machine Perception*. Stanford University Press.

Socarras Y, Ramos S, Vazquez D, Lopez A and Gevers T. 2013. Adapting pedestrian detection from synthetic to far infrared images. *Proceedings of the International Conference on Computer Vision, Workshop on Visual Domain Adaptation and Dataset Bias*, Sydney, Australia.

Soriano M, Marcos S, Saloma C, Quibilan M and Alino P. 2001. Image classification of coral reef components from underwater color video. *Proceedings of the IEEE/MTS OCEANS Conference*.

Sou. 2015. Retrieved February 26, 2015, from www.soundmetrics.com/Products/DIDSON-Sonars.

Stallkamp J, Schlipsing M, Salmen J and Igel C. 2011. The German traffic sign recognition benchmark: a multi-class classification competition. *Proceedings of the conference on Computer Vision and Pattern Recognition*, San Jose, CA, USA.

Stokes M and Deane G. 2009. Automated processing of coral reef benthic images. *Limnology and Oceanography: Methods* **7**, 157–168.

Suaste V, Caudillo D, Shin B and Klette R. 2013. Third-eye stereo analysis evaluation enhanced by data measures. *Proceedings of the Mexican Conference on Pattern Recognition.*

Sun J, Zheng N and Shum H. 2003. Stereo matching using belief propagation. *IEEE Transactions on Pattern Analysis and Machine Intelligence* **25**, 1–14.

Sunderhauf N, Shirazi S, Dayoub F, Upcroft B and Milford M. 2015. On the performance of ConvNet features for place recognition. *Proceedings of the IEEE/RSJ International Conference on Intelligent Robots and Systems.*

Szegedy C, Toshev A and Erhan D. 2013. Deep neural networks for object detection, In *Advances in Neural Information Processing Systems 26* (ed. Burges CJC, Bottou L, Welling M, Ghahramani Z and Weinberger KQ), Curran Associates Inc., pp. 2553–2561.

Szeliski R. 1994. Image mosaicing for tele-reality applications. *Proceedings of the Winter Conference on Applications of Computer Vision.*

Szeliski R. 1999. Prediction error as a quality metric for motion and stereo. *Proceedings of the International Conference on Computer Vision.*

Szeliski R. 2006. Image alignment and stitching: a tutorial. *Foundations and Trends in Computer Graphics and Vision* **2**, 1–104.

Szeliski R and Shum HY. 1997. Creating full view panoramic image mosaics and environment maps. *Proceedings of the SIGGRAPH.*

Szeliski R, Uyttendaele M and Steedly D. 2008. Fast Poisson blending using multi-splines. Technical report, Interactive Visual Media, https://www.microsoft.com/en-us/research/wp-content/uploads/2008/04/tr-2008-58.pdf.

Tan RT. 2009. Visibility in bad weather from a single image. *Proceedings of the Conference on Computer Vision and Pattern Recognition.*

Tang S, Andriluka M and Schiele B. 2009. Detection and tracking of occluded people. *Proceedings of the British Machine Vision Conference*, London, UK.

Tango F, Botta M, Minin L and Montanari R. 2010. Non-intrusive detection of driver distraction using machine learning algorithms. *Proceedings of the European Conference on Artificial Intelligence*, Lisbon, Portugal.

Tao S, Feng H, Xu Z and Li Q. 2012. Image degradation and re-covery based on multiple scattering in remote sensing and bad weather condition. *Optics Express* **20**, 16584–16595.

Tarel JP and Hautiere N. 2009. Fast visibility restoration from a single color or gray level image. *Proceedings of the International Conference on Computer Vision.*

Tena I, Reed S, Petillot Y, Bell J and Lane DM. 2003. Concurrent mapping and localisation using side-scan sonar for autonomous navigation. *Proceedings of the International Symposium on Unmanned Untethered Submersible Technology.*

Tetlow S and Spours J. 1999. Three-dimensional measurement of underwater work sites using structured laser light. *Measurement Science and Technology* **10**, 1162–1169.

vCharge Project n.d. www.v-charge.eu.

VisLab. 2013. PROUD-Car Test 2013, vislab.it/proud/.

Thrun S, Montemerlo M, Dahlkamp H, Stavens D, Aron A, Diebel J, Fong P, Gale J, Halpenny M, Hoffmann G, Lau K, Oakley C, Palatucci M, Pratt V, Stang P, Strohband S, Dupont C, Jendrossek L, Koelen C, Markey C, Rummel C, van Niekerk J, Jensen E, Alessandrini P, Bradski G, Davies B, Ettinger S, Kaehler A, Nefian A and Mahoney P. 2007. Stanley: the robot that won the DARPA grand challenge, In *The 2005 DARPA Grand Challenge* (ed. Buehler M, Iagnemma K and Singh S) vol. **36** of *Springer Tracts in Advanced Robotics*. Springer-Verlag, Berlin / Heidelberg, pp. 1–43.

Timofte R, Zimmermann K and Gool LV. 2009. Multi-view traffic sign detection, recognition, and 3D localisation. *Proceedings of the Workshop on Applications on Computer Vision*, Snowbird, UT, USA.

Torralba A, Murphy KP, Freeman WT and Rubin MA. 2003. Context-based vision system for place and object recognition. *Proceedings of the International Conference on Computer Vision*.

Treat J, Tumbas N, McDonald S, Shinar D, Hume R, Mayer R, Stansifer R and Castellan N. 1979. Tri-level study of the causes of traffic accidents. Technical report, Federal Highway Administration, US DOT, http://ntl.bts.gov/lib/47000/47200/47286/Tri-level_study_of_the_causes_of_traffic_accidents_vol__II.pdf.

Tri. 2015. Retrieved February 26, 2015, from www.tritech.co.uk/product/gemini-720i-300m-multibeam-imaging-sonar.

Triggs B, McLauchlan PF, Hartley RI and Fitzgibbon AW. 1999. Bundle adjustment—a modern synthesis. *Proceedings of the International Conference on Computer Vision*, Corfu, Greece.

Troiani C, Martinelli A, Laugier C and Scaramuzza D. 2013. 1-point-based monocular motion estimation for computationally-limited micro aerial vehicles. *Proceedings of the European Conference on Mobile Robots*.

UNECE. 2005. Statistics of road traffic accidents in Europe and North America. Technical report, Geneva, Switzerland, http://www.unece.org/fileadmin/DAM/trans/main/wp6/pdfdocs/ABTS2005.pdf.

Uyttendaele M, Eden A and Szeliski R. 2001. Eliminating ghosting and exposure artifacts in image mosaics. *Proceedings of the Conference on Computer Vision and Pattern Recognition*.

Vaganay J, Elkins M, Willcox S, Hover F, Damus R, Desset S, Morash J and Polidoro V. 2005. Ship hull inspection by hull-relative navigation and control. *Proceedings of the IEEE/MTS OCEANS Conference*.

Valgren C and Lilienthal AJ. 2010. SIFT, SURF & seasons: appearance-based long-term localization in outdoor environments. *Robotics and Autonomous Systems* **58**, 149–156.

Van Woensel L, Archer G, Panades-estruch L and Vrscaj D. 2015. Ten technologies which could change our lives: potential impacts and policy implications. Technical report, European Parliamentary Research Service, http://www.europarl.europa.eu/EPRS/EPRS_IDAN_527417_ten_trends_to_change_your_life.pdf.

Varma M and Zisserman A. 2005. A statistical approach to texture classification from single images. *International Journal of Computer Vision* **62**, 61–81.

Vazquez D, López A, Marín J, Ponsa D and Gerónimo D. 2014. Virtual and real world adaptation for pedestrian detection. *IEEE Transactions on Pattern Analysis and Machine Intelligence* **36**, 797–809.

Viola P and Jones M. 2001a. Rapid object detection using a boosted cascade of simple features. *Proceedings of the conference on Computer Vision and Pattern Recognition*, Kauai, HI, USA.

Viola P and Jones M. 2001b. Robust real-time object detection. *International Journal of Computer Vision* **57**, 137–154.

Vogel C, Schindler K and Roth S. 2013. Piecewise rigid scene flow. *Proceedings of the International Conference on Computer Vision*.

Volow M and Erwin C. 1973. The heart rate variability correlates of spontaneous drowsiness onset. *Proceedings of the International Automotive Engineering Congress*, Detroit, MI, USA.

Wahlgren C and Duckett T. 2005. Topological mapping for mobile robots using omnidirectional vision. *Swedish Workshop on Autonomous Robotics*.

Walk S, Schindler K and Schiele B. 2010. Disparity statistics for pedestrian detection: combining appearance, motion and stereo. *Proceedings of the European Conference on Computer Vision*.

Wang J, Cipolla R and Zha H. 2005. Vision-based global localization using a visual vocabulary. *Proceedings of the IEEE International Conference on Robotics and Automation*.

Wang Y, Teoh E and Shen D. 2003. Lane detection and tracking using B-snake. *Image and Vision Computing* **22**, 269–280.

Wei J, Snider J, Kim J, Dolan J, Rajkumar R and Litkouhi B. 2013. Towards a viable autonomous driving research platform. *Proceedings of the IEEE Intelligent Vehicles Symposium*.

Weidemann A, Fournier G, Forand L and Mathieu P. 2005. Optical image sensing through turbid water. *Proceedings of SPIE*, **5780**, 59–70.

Weiss S, Achtelik M, Lynen S, Chli M and Siegwart R. 2012. Real-time onboard visual-inertial state estimation and self-calibration of MAVs in unknown environments. *Proceedings of the IEEE International Conference on Robotics and Automation*.

Weiss S, Achtelik MW, Lynen S, Achtelik MC, Kneip L, Chli M and Siegwart R. 2013. Monocular vision for long-term micro aerial vehicle state estimation: a compendium. *Journal of Field Robotics* **30**, 803–831.

Weiss S and Siegwart R. 2011. Real-time metric state estimation for modular vision-inertial systems. *Proceedings of the IEEE International Conference on Robotics and Automation*.

Weiss S, Brockers R, Albrektsen S and Matthies L. 2015. Inertial optical flow for throw-and-go micro air vehicles. *Proceedings of the Winter Conference on Applications of Computer Vision*.

WHO. 2013. Global status chapter on road safety.

Wikipedia n.d. Autonomous car, en.wikipedia.org/wiki/Autonomous_car.

Wöhler C and Anlauf JK. 1999. An adaptable time-delay neural-network algorithm for image sequence analysis. *IEEE Transactions on Neural Networks* **10**, 1531–1536.

Wojek C, Walk S, Roth S, Schindler K and Schiele B. 2014. Monocular visual scene understanding: understanding multi-object traffic scenes. *IEEE Transactions on Pattern Analysis and Machine Intelligence* **35**, 882–897.

Wozniak B and Dera J. 2007. *Light Absorption in Sea Water*, vol. **33** of *Atmospheric and Oceanographic Sciences Library*. Springer.

Wu S, Chiang H, Perng J, Chen C, Wu B and Lee T. 2008. The heterogeneous systems integration design and implementation for lane keeping on a vehicle. *IEEE Transactions on Intelligent Transportation Systems* **9**, 246–263.

Xiao J, Fang T, Zhao P, Lhuilier M and Quan L. 2009. Image-based street-side city modeling. *Proceedings of the SIGGRAPH*.

Xie Y, Liu LF, Li CH, and Qu YY. 2009. Unifying visual saliency with hog feature learning for traffic sign detection. *Proceedings of the IEEE Intelligent Vehicles Symposium*, Xi'an, China.

Xiong Y and Pulli K. 2009. Color correction based image blending for creating high resolution panoramic images on mobile devices. *Proceedings of the SIGGRAPH Asia*, Yokohama, Japan.

Xu J, Ramos S, Vazquez D and Lopez A. 2014a. Domain adaptation of deformable part-based models. *IEEE Transactions on Pattern Analysis and Machine Intelligence* **36**, 2367–2380.

Xu J, Vázquez D, López A, Marín J and Ponsa D. 2014b. Learning a part-based pedestrian detector in a virtual world. *IEEE Transactions on Intelligent Transportation Systems* **15**, 2121–2131.

Xu J, Ramos S, Vázquez D and López A. 2016. Hierarchical adaptive structural SVM for domain adaptation. *International Journal of Computer Vision*, DOI: 10.1007/s11263-016-0885-6.

Xu Z and Shin BS. 2013. Accurate line segment detection with hough transform based on minimum entropy. *Proceedings of the Pacific-Rim Symposium Image Video Technology*, Guanajuato, Mexico.

Yamaguchi K, McAllester D and Urtasun R. 2014. Efficient joint segmentation, occlusion labeling, stereo and flow estimation. *Proceedings of the European Conference on Computer Vision*.

Yang R and Pollefeys M. 2003. Multi-resolution real-time stereo on commodity graphics hardware. *Proceedings of the Conference on Computer Vision and Pattern Recognition*.

Yang S, Scherer SA and Zell A. 2014. Visual SLAM for autonomous MAVs with dual cameras. *Proceedings of the IEEE International Conference on Robotics and Automation*, Hongkong, China.

Yeh T, Lee J and Darrell T. 2007. Adaptive vocabulary forests for dynamic indexing and category learning. *Proceedings of the International Conference on Computer Vision*.

Yoerger DR, Kelley DS and Delaney JR. 2000. Fine-scale three-dimensional mapping of a deep-sea hydrothermal vent site using the jason ROV system. *International Journal of Robotics Research* **19**, 1000–1014.

Zeng Y and Klette R. 2013. Multi-run 3D streetside reconstruction from a vehicle. *Proceedings of the Conference on Computer Analysis of Images and Patterns*.

Zhang H. 2011. BoRF: loop-closure detection with scale invariant visual features. *Proceedings of the IEEE International Conference on Robotics and Automation*.

Zhang H and Negahdaripour S. 2003. On reconstruction of 3D volumetric models of reefs and benthic structures from image sequences of a stereo rig. *Proceedings of the IEEE/MTS OCEANS Conference*, San Diego, CA, USA.

Zhang H, Geiger A and Urtasun R. 2013. Understanding high-level semantics by modeling traffic patterns. *Proceedings of the International Conference on Computer Vision*, Sydney, Australia.

Zhang J, Marszalek M, Lazebnik S and Schmid C. 2006. Local features and kernels for classification of texture and object categories: a comprehensive study. *International Journal of Computer Vision* **73**, 213–238.

Zhao HK, Osher S and Fedkiw R. 2001. Fast surface reconstruction using the level set method. *Proceedings of the IEEE Workshop on Variational and Level Set Methods*.

Zhao W. 2006. Flexible image blending for image mosaicing with reduced artifacts. *International Journal of Pattern Recognition and Artificial Intelligence* **20**, 609–628.

Zhou D, Wang J and Wang S. 2012. Contour based hog deer detection in thermal images for traffic safety. *Proceedings of the International Conference on Image Processing, Computer Vision, and Pattern Recognition*, Las Vegas, NV, USA.

Zhou S, Jiang Y, Xi J, Gong J, Xiong G and Chen H. 2010. A novel lane detection based on geometrical model and Gabor filter. *Proceedings of the IEEE Intelligent Vehicles Symposium*, San Diego, CA, USA.

Zhu Z, Riseman E, Hanson A and Schultz H. 2005. An efficient method for geo-referenced video mosaicing for environmental monitoring. *Machine Vision and Applications* **16**, 203–216.

Ziegler J et al. 2014a. Making Bertha drive—an autonomous journey on a historic route. *IEEE Intelligent Transportation Systems Magazine*. http://ieeexplore.ieee.org/document/6803933/.

Ziegler J et al. 2014b. Video based localization for bertha. *Proceedings of the IEEE Intelligent Vehicles Symposium*, Dearborn, MI, USA.

Zingg S, Scaramuzza D, Weiss S and Siegwart R. 2010. MAV navigation through indoor corridors using optical flow. *Proceedings of the IEEE International Conference on Robotics and Automation*.

Zitova B and Flusser J. 2003. Image registration methods: a survey. *Image and Vision Computing* **21**, 977–1000.

Zufferey J. 2009. *Bio-inspired Flying Robots*. Taylor and Francis Group, LLC, EPFL Press.

Zufferey J and Floreano D. 2006. Fly-inspired visual steering of an ultralight indoor aircraft. *IEEE Transactions on Robotics* **22**, 137–146.

Index

Computer Vision in Vehicle Technology: Land, Sea, and Air, First Edition.
Edited by Antonio M. López, Atsushi Imiya, Tomas Pajdla and Jose M. Álvarez.
© 2017 John Wiley & Sons Ltd. Published 2017 by John Wiley & Sons Ltd.